Forensic Computer Crime Investigation

FORENSIC SCIENCE SERIES

Series Editor

Robert Gaensslen, Ph.D.

Professor and Director
Graduate Studies in Forensic Science
University of Illinois at Chicago
Chicago, Illinois, U.S.A.

Bitemark Evidence, edited by Robert B. J. Dorion
Forensic Computer Crime Investigation, edited by Thomas A. Johnson

Additional Volumes in Preparation

Forensic Computer Crime Investigation

Edited by

Thomas A. Johnson

Taylor & Francis
Taylor & Francis Group

Boca Raton   London   New York

A CRC title, part of the Taylor & Francis imprint, a member of the
Taylor & Francis Group, the academic division of T&F Informa plc.

Published in 2006 by
CRC Press
Taylor & Francis Group
6000 Broken Sound Parkway NW, Suite 300
Boca Raton, FL 33487-2742

International Standard Book Number-10: 0-8247-2435-6 (Hardcover)
International Standard Book Number-13: 978-0-8247-2435-1 (Hardcover)
Library of Congress Card Number 2005045482

Library of Congress Cataloging-in-Publication Data

Johnson, Thomas Alfred.
   Forensic computer crime investigation / Thomas A. Johnson.
      p. cm.
   Includes bibliographical references and index.
   ISBN 0-8247-2435-6
   1. Computer crimes--Investigation. 2. Criminal investigation. 3. Forensic sciences. I. Title.

HV8079.C65J64 2005
363.25--dc22
2005045482

Taylor & Francis Group
is the Academic Division of T&F Informa plc.

Visit the Taylor & Francis Web site at
http://www.taylorandfrancis.com

and the CRC Press Web site at
http://www.crcpress.com

Contents

Series Preface

The **Forensic Science Series** was conceived, and the first few volumes planned, several years ago under the Marcel Dekker imprint. Not long ago, Dekker and CRC Press both became part of the Taylor and Francis publishing company. CRC Press has had an extensive list of forensic science and investigative offerings for a long time. Accordingly, the series has now become a part of the CRC group of books in this field. Susan Lee, the editor at Dekker, and Rebecca McEldowney, the editor at CRC with whom I have worked on other projects, both deserve credit for making the transition an easy one.

For this series, we were thinking about specialized, comprehensive, reference books, especially in under-represented specialty areas. The first book in the series had to do with forensic odontology.

This book, edited by Dr. Thomas A. Johnson, covers forensic computer science and digital evidence, one of the newest and most rapidly emerging areas of investigations and forensic science.

If we can judge by the number of news reports on the subject, computer-based crime is a growing problem. Identity theft and associated mischief, financial fraud of other kinds, predators trolling the web for gullible and/or unsupervised children or adolescents, are all regularly seen now as new stories. Beyond that are the potential uses of computers, e-mail, web sites, and so on, for terrorist activities, including cyber-terrorism.

It is nearly impossible not to think of some aspect of computers or digital information now when mounting an investigation. E-mail has become a routine source of investigative information. The chips in telephone voice answering machines, cellular phones, pagers, and so forth can also provide investigators with crucial information, just as might handheld devices, or the hard drives from laptop or desktop computers. Recently, a couple of well-publicized break-ins at large databases containing personal information has made everyone think about how to secure the mountain of private data that is now in both private and government agency hands.

Thus, a book that focuses on the forensic computer science and digital information aspects of criminal and civil investigations, and terrorism, provides a welcome addition to the series. Prof. Johnson and his collaborators take us on this informative journey in this volume.

R.E. Gaensslen
University of Illinois at Chicago
April 2005

Preface

The expanding availability of computers within society coupled with their ease of use and the unregulated Internet, which provides any number of hacking and attack tools for free download, has introduced into our society new challenges and threats at the same time. Our nation's commercial, economic, and financial systems are now totally dependent on the rapid exchange of information, which requires a safe and secure exchange of data through our country's vast computer networks. In fact, it is our nation's entire infrastructure of our power grid, transportation systems, hospital and health systems, water systems, food production and distribution systems, and governmental agencies that are operated by our computers and require that they continue to operate with both assurance and authenticity. Our reliance on this infrastructure that has made our nation one of the richest and most dependable in the entire world is also our Achilles' heel, and these computer-based infrastructure systems are vulnerable to human error, natural disaster, and exploitative attacks. The rapid pace of scientific and technological advancement has provided additional benefits to society; nevertheless, we must also be aware of the unintended and latent dysfunctional consequences that occasionally accompany such rapid growth and change. How we mitigate and manage these risks will in some cases be effective and, in other situations, require risk avoidance strategies.

Now that personal computing is so ubiquitous within our society, we face not only the challenges of correctly using this computational power, but we must now guard our nation, our citizens, and our children from those who would use this computing power to exploit others. The opportunities to use this new digital environment that science has bestowed on us has ushered in a new paradigm in crime that has challenged and continues to challenge our law enforcement, prosecutors, and judiciary system to come to terms with successfully responding to the new ways in which criminal acts are perpetrated. The use of computers as an instrumentality to commit criminal activity, or those situations in which the computer becomes a target of a criminal act, all require the response of our criminal justice system to protect the interests of our society, while also assuring the rights of the accused and the general respect of privacy that are so venerated within our democracy.

The distribution of video streaming hard-core pornography that exploits our nation's children is now readily available within society. The use of encryption and steganography tools to conceal illegal materials continues to challenge our police and our legal system. The use of viruses in extortion schemes also shows evidence of how criminals are using technology to commit criminal acts in a more sophisticated and effective manner than in past years. Even more troubling is the global nature of these offenses occurring thousands of miles away and overlapping judicial systems that are ill-prepared for the appropriate statutory law to prohibit some of this behavior. Also, the requirement of obtaining search warrants in other jurisdictions and in other nations has mandated additional training and educational programs to be fully prepared for this new forum of criminal activity.

It is for these reasons that we have set forth some of the ways in which we have prepared our federal, state, and local authorities to address these challenges. This text is, therefore, illustrative of the manner in which over 3,000 law enforcement officers have been trained and countless university students from the disciplines of law, computer science, and forensic investigation have been introduced to this emerging body of knowledge.

Each of the contributing authors has provided insights into an area in which they have been responsible for assuming a leadership role. For example, Chris Malinowski served with distinction as the commanding officer of the New York City Police Department's Computer Crime Unit and knows the intricacies of staffing a Digital Investigative Unit with highly trained personnel.

Dr. William Tafoya's illustrious career with the FBI provides the background for his chapter on the characteristics and analysis of computer criminals. Ross Mayfield's insightful and creative use of software utilities and developing investigative strategies has enabled him to provide the Los Angeles Police Department with most effective case-solving techniques. Fred Cotton's detailing of training strategies for law enforcement officers is an important contribution, because Fred Cotton is regarded as one of our nations most effective and creative law enforcement trainers. Monique Ferraro and Joseph Sudol underscore the full range of challenges in preparing an Internet Crimes Against Children unit (ICAC); they are well-respected for their efforts in developing an ICAC unit for the Connecticut State Department of Public Safety that is regarded as one of the model ICAC units in our nation. Dr. Fred Cohen's contribution on digital forensic evidence is a critical and important part of this text. Dr. Cohen's reputation as one of our nation's premier forensic computer scientists is well-established for initiating some of the very first research in computer viruses. Finally, Dario Forte has contributed an international perspective that not only enriches this text but is genuinely reflective of the many contributions he has made to Interpol and numerous law enforcement agencies throughout the world.

Finally, the outstanding editorial work and perspective of Colleen R. Johnson who worked with each of the contributing authors and provided excellent guidance to each of us, merits our sincere appreciation, respect, and praise for her dedicated professionalism.

Acknowledgments

It is with a deep sense of appreciation that I thank each of my colleague contributing authors for their many years of service to improving our Forensic Computer Crime Investigation units and for their important contributions to this text. Their individual and collective service to our police departments and our universities has touched the lives of so many excellent individuals in law enforcement as well as those who are preparing for such careers. It has been my great honor and privilege to work with each of them.

To my wife, Colleen R. Johnson, for her patience, knowledge, encouragement, support, and understanding, I am truly grateful.

Editor

Dr. Thomas A. Johnson presently serves as Dean of the School of Public Safety and Professional Studies and also Dean and Director of the University of New Haven–California Campus. Dr. Johnson received his undergraduate education at Michigan State University and his graduate education at the University of California–Berkeley.

Dean Johnson founded the Center for Cybercrime and Forensic Computer Investigation and serves as Director of the Forensic Computer Investigation Graduate program. Additionally, Dean Johnson was responsible for developing the online program in Information Protection and Security at the University of New Haven. Dean Johnson also designed and developed the National Security and Public Safety Graduate Degree Program, which is being offered both at the Connecticut Campus and at Sandia National Laboratory in Livermore, California.

Currently, Dean Johnson serves as a member of the FBI Infraguard program and also is a member of the Electronic Crime Task Force, New York Field Office, U.S. Secret Service. The United States Attorney General appointed Dean Johnson a member of the Information Technology Working Group, and he served as Chair of the Task Force Group on Combating High Technology Crime for the National Institute of Justice. Dean Johnson was also appointed an advisor to the Judicial Council of California on the Court Technology Task Force by the California Supreme Court.

Dean Johnson has published two books and 13 referred articles; he holds copyrights on four software programs; and, in October 2000, his chapter "Infrastructure Warriors: A Threat to the U.S. Homeland by Organized Crime" was published by the Strategic Studies Institute of the U.S. Army War College. In addition to lecturing at the U.S. Army War College, Carlisle Barracks, he has also lectured at the Federal Law Enforcement Training Center and numerous universities.

Dean Johnson has appeared in both state and U.S. federal courts as an expert witness and was a member of the Select Ad Hoc Presidential Investigative Committee and consultant to the American Academy of Forensic Sciences in the case of Sirhan B. Sirhan, regarding evaluation of ballistics and physical evidence concerning the assassination of United States Senator, Robert F. Kennedy.

Computer Crime and the Electronic Crime Scene

1

THOMAS A. JOHNSON

In the mid-1960s our nation experienced its first series of criminal activity in which a computer was used as an instrument to perpetrate an economic crime. In his book, *Fighting Computer Crime*, Donn B. Parker reports that in 1966 the first federally prosecuted case of a computer crime involved a consultant working under contract with a Minneapolis bank to program and maintain its computer system. This case was unique: The individual was prosecuted for embezzlement of bank funds because he changed the checking account program in the bank's computer so that it would not identify and automatically notify bank officials of overdraft charges in his personal checking account (Parker 1997, 8).

By 1973, the largest recorded and prosecuted computer crime had occurred in Los Angeles and resulted in the destruction of the Equity Funding Insurance Company, with a loss of $2 billion. Twenty-two executives and two auditors were convicted for creating 64,000 fake people, insuring them and then selling those policies to re-insurers (Parker 1997, 65). Law enforcement agencies were not prepared for the use of sophisticated computers in these economic criminal acts. In fact, the first federal agencies to participate in these criminal investigations were the Internal Revenue Service (IRS) Criminal Investigation Division, the U.S. Secret Service, and the Federal Bureau of Investigation (FBI). When one examined the training provided by those agencies to their personnel, there was little or no instruction offered in terms of computers and their use in criminal acts. Agents who were assigned to these cases had to develop and refine their individual skills to address the challenges they were encountering in the field.

I.   Introduction and Historical Developments

The IRS Criminal Investigation Division (IRS-CID) was the first federal investigative agency to contract with a university to develop and refine the skills of
an elite group of special agents to confront this new and emerging trend in
criminal activity. Michael Anderson and Robert Kelso were among the first
group of IRS-CID agents to receive this training in computers and to play a
leadership role within their agency. Another pioneer in this newly emerging
field was Howard Schmidt, who would eventually be called on to serve as vice
chairman of the President's Critical Infrastructure Group. Howard's career
began in a small municipal police agency in Arizona, and he eventually served
in several important federal agencies where, through his vision and encouragement, he created programs to train other law enforcement personnel at the
local, state, and federal levels of government. Howard Schmidt's skills did not
go unnoticed by the corporate community, and, as computer crime was
increasing, the corporate community turned to him and a select few others for
assistance in combating these new developments in corporate criminal activity.

Universities also were not prepared for how computers might be used in
the commission of criminal activity. As a result, law enforcement had to rely on
the insights of such leaders as Howard Schmidt and Michael Anderson, who
were both instrumental in developing training seminars for their colleagues.
Indeed, the very beginning efforts of organizations such as the International
Association of Crime Investigative Specialists (IACIS), and the High Technology Criminal Investigation Association (HTCIA) were specifically developed to offer training, instruction, and sharing of information in this
important area. Eventually the HTCIA began developing chapters in various
states and regions and, to this day, is one of the most respected organizations
for professional, in-service training of law enforcement officials interested in
computers and their role in criminal activity.

If law enforcement agencies were ill-prepared for the challenges they
would confront in computer crime and economic crime cases, our prosecutorial agencies were even less prepared for this growing criminal activity. One
only has to examine the absolute dearth of statutory law in each of our states
to realize that we were not prepared to prosecute these cases. Once again,
our nation had to rely on a small cadre of people who saw these challenges
and played a most formidable role in providing their colleagues with the
training in this area. Leaders such as Kevin Manson, Tony Whitledge, Ken
Rosenblatt, Gail Thackeray, and Abigail Abraham provided enormous assistance not only to their colleagues but also to state legislators in the framing
of new statutory law to address this new criminal activity.

In the early 1980s the SEARCH Group, Inc., under the leadership of Steve
Kolodney (and afterwards, Gary Cooper), perceived a need for training law

enforcement managers in Information Management Systems. Fortunately, the SEARCH Group also had two outstanding pioneers in the field of training police officers in computers — Fred Cotton and Bill Spernow, who began one of our nation's first outreach efforts in training municipal and state police in this important area. The contributions that both Fred Cotton and Bill Spernow have made in this field are measured by the esteem in which their professional colleagues held them. The contribution of SEARCH Group is also evident in that during the entire decade of 1980 to 1990 they provided the only Peace Officer Standards and Training (POST) instruction to law enforcement officers in the state of California. Indeed, another major deficit of our nation's ability to address computer crime centered on the fact that virtually every one of our states' training agencies provided no training at all to their law enforcement agencies in computer crime. In fact, until the early 1990s, state POST agencies were not offering even occasional training courses or instruction in this area.

In the mid-1990s our nation experienced a greater collaboration between federal, state, and local law enforcement agencies in addressing mutual training strategies. The Information Technology Working Group was an important step forward, as then–U.S. Attorney General Janet Reno appointed a small group of approximately 40 people from agencies within the federal, state, and local communities to join together in developing a cooperative blueprint for how our nation might best confront the growing problem of individuals using computers as an instrument for committing crime. After a series of meetings, they decided on a strategy of "Training the Trainers" so that a new and larger population of officers could reach out to their colleagues and provide instruction in this new area of criminal activity. Accordingly, a training curriculum had to be developed, and the U.S. Department of Justice funded several meetings of the nation's leading experts in an effort to develop a series of courses that would be provided for state, federal, and local law enforcement personnel. After two years of course development, the National White Collar Crime Center was allocated the responsibility for delivering these courses to law enforcement personnel at the local and state levels. The federal effort of training new agents and in-service agents was allocated to the FBI, U.S. Secret Service, IRS-CID, U.S. Customs Agency, U.S. Postal Inspectors Division, and Federal Law Enforcement Training Center.

Having had the privilege of serving as a member of the Information Technology Working Group, as well as having been active in our higher-education community, I saw a critical need to begin to mobilize our university community to address the unique needs of our law enforcement and prosecutorial agencies in addressing this growing problem of computer crime. Ironically, our nation's universities had numerous computer science departments and over 1,000 criminal justice programs, but there existed no coherent educational strategy to provide the theoretical and pragmatic skill sets that were required if our justice community was to seriously make inroads into this growing problem. Computer science departments were focused on educating their students in programming languages, database skills, and a number of other areas that provided assistance only to a small subset of our justice communities need. At the same time, most, if not all but a few, educational institutions with criminal justice departments simply were not equipped with the faculty to address the problem of computer crime.

As a result of working in the area of computer crime since 1980, coupled with the knowledge of universities' computer science and criminal justice departments, in 1996 the University of New Haven formulated both a graduate and undergraduate certificate in forensic computer investigation. This certificate program includes a sequence of courses that address three target discipline areas: computer science, law, and forensic investigation. These course offerings were initiated in 1997 at both the main campus in Connecticut and the branch campus in Sacramento, California. Since we have had the privilege of working with our nation's leaders in this field, we have utilized over 21 outstanding experts who have joined us in the capacity of practitioners-in-residence; or distinguished special lecturers to offer this program. In 1998 we responded to the need for providing online educational courses and began offering both a graduate and undergraduate certificate in Information Protection and Security at both campus locations. In 2001 we began offering a Master's of Science in criminal justice with a concentration in forensic computer investigation at our main campus. Finally, in 2002, we began offering the nation's first Master's of Science degree in National Security with a concentration in Information Protection and Security. This graduate degree is offered both at the main Connecticut campus and the California campus at Sandia National Laboratory in Livermore, California. These programs developed at the University of New Haven serve as a model in our attempt for universities to play a larger role in providing both the training and educational courses to the men and women of our justice community.

Several of our nation's universities, aside from the efforts of the University of New Haven have made notable contributions in this area. Among these are Carnegie-Mellon Institute, with its formidable efforts in computer emergency response teams (CERT); Purdue University, led by the pioneering efforts of Eugene Spafford; the University of California at Davis, led by Matt Bishop's work in computer security; the Naval Postgraduate School Campus at Monterey, with its outstanding computer science department; and Dartmouth University's new program in research led by Michael Vattis. These are only a small section of the outstanding contributions being made by our academic community today.

II.   Crime Scenes with Digital and Electronic Evidence

The electronic crime scene that possesses digital and electronic evidence creates new challenges for the investigator. There exists uniqueness to this new environment not only because the evidence may be difficult to detect but also because of how its evidentiary value may be hidden through steganography and/or encryption. Furthermore, there is a degree of anonymity in which perpetrators can hide their true identity in the forging of certain criminal acts and endeavors. Therefore, the rapid technological advancements occurring in our society through the digitalization of data and information are presenting new challenges to investigators. This electronic evidence is both difficult to detect and quite fragile; therefore, the latent nature of electronic evidence requires very skilled investigators.

Additional challenges that continue to confront the investigator encountering an electronic crime scene center on the global nature of the evidence. In many criminal cases involving computers and electronic technology, we encounter multijurisdictional issues that challenge the very legal structure of all nations' legal and statutory codes. For example, today we find criminal enterprises being initiated from different nations throughout the world, and to effectively investigate, apprehend, prosecute, and convict these individuals we must utilize appropriate judicial search warrants. It is also necessary that the penal codes of the respective nations have statutory authority for legal action to be pursued.

The "I love you" virus in 2000, which caused an estimated $10 billion in damages, was released by an individual in the Philippines and created havoc to computer systems throughout the world. Despite the extensive damage, this case was not prosecutable because the Philippines did not have legal restrictions against behavior of this type when this virus was released.

Also, the attack on Citibank in New York by Vladimir Levin and members of a mafia group in St. Petersburg, Russia, created an enormous legal problem for the FBI because their investigator had to examine banking systems in over seven different nations where the electronic transfer of money was deposited. The application for search warrants and the timely tracking of this event was a challenge to even the most skilled set of investigators. Levin was arrested and sentenced to 3 years in prison and ordered to repay Citibank $240,000.

An additional problem with this new-age criminal activity that relies on technology and electronics is the ease with which one person can impersonate another through rather elaborate spoofing schemes. A related activity that has cost our nation's businesses an enormous financial loss is identity theft. This crime of identity theft generally takes the victim approximately 6 to

9 months of work with credit agencies, bill collectors, and other credit entities before they can have any semblance of restoring their good name and credit standing.

Since personal computers can store the equivalent of several million pages of information, and networks can store many times more than this amount of data, the location and recovery of evidence by a trained computer forensic specialist working in a forensic laboratory may take several days or weeks. As mentioned earlier, searching computer files is an extraordinarily difficult process, because files can be moved from one computer to another throughout the world in a matter of milliseconds. Files can also be hidden in slack space of the computer hard drive or stored on a remote server located in other geographic jurisdictions. Files can also be encrypted, misleadingly titled, or commingled with thousands of unrelated, innocuous, or statutorily protected files. It is to address these challenges that the FBI has developed a Computer Analysis Response Team (CART Team); the IRS has a Seized Computer Evidence Recovery Team (SCER Team); and the Secret Service has an Electronic Crime Special Agent Program (ECSAP) (U.S. Department of Justice 2002, 35).

It is evident that these new technologies are requiring more skills for our investigators, prosecutors, and judges. Accordingly, the role of our educational institutions in preparing current and next-generation criminal justice personnel to address these challenges is becoming more critical as each new technology is developed and introduced to our society.

III.   Computers, Electronic Equipment, Devices, and Information Repositories

In July 2001 the U.S. Department of Justice, through the Office of Justice Programs in the National Institute of Justice, released the Technical Working Group for Electronic Crime Scene Investigation's (TWGECSI) report, *Electronic Crime Scene Investigation: A Guide for First Responders*. The gathering of our nation's experts to organize their advice to assist law enforcement personnel and agencies in preparing to address this new paradigm change in crime was one of our nation's first important efforts to address this problem. The identification of the types of electronic equipment and its purpose was to inform law enforcement personnel of the potential use and value of such equipment.

Both first responders to crime scenes and investigative personnel must appreciate the unique attributes of electronic equipment and be prepared to identify and assess its importance at a crime scene. This suggests the types and purposes of electronic equipment should be well understood as to their functionality and value to their owner. Also, from the viewpoint of assessing the potential impact on the victim, a thorough knowledge of this new environment will prove most useful and beneficial to law enforcement because the crime scene must be protected and processed consistent with forensic science principles. Because electronic evidence is so fragile, we must train officers in the preservation and collection of electronic evidentiary materials. Digital evidence can easily go unrecognized, or be lost, if not properly processed. We must also ensure the integrity of digital evidence, because it is easily alterable. Therefore, the importance of training first responding officers to what is now becoming an electronic crime scene is an extremely critical function, and one that must be addressed by state and local law enforcement agencies throughout our nation.

Today, given the ubiquitous presence of computers, answering machines, hand-held personal digital assistants, facsimile machines, and other electronic equipment, almost any crime scene may conceal information of value in a digital format. The acquisition of this information is totally dependent on the actions of the first responding officer, who must have the ability to visualize and perceive the presence of such evidentiary material.

A.   The Value of Equipment and Information

The type of computer system or electronic environment the investigator may encounter at a crime scene has a certain tangible and intangible value to the owner, victim, suspect, or witness. Because this value is measured not only in financial terms but also in terms of informational value, there are numerous perspectives that the investigator must be prepared to analyze. It is possible that the owner of a computer system may become a victim or a suspect in a case involving criminal activity. For example, the computer system can be the target of criminal activity, or it can be an instrument to use to commit criminal activity. Data residing on the hard drive will provide the answer and appropriate documentation as to each possibility. More often than not, the information that resides within these computer and electronic systems is of greater value than the systems themselves. The proliferation of new technologies at extremely economical prices will continue to make the investigator's job more difficult. We now are in an era where computer communications can occur by using RAM CACHE, thus avoiding writing to the hard drive, and this can occur in a networked environment from any point to any other point within our world. Also, the development of encrypted hard drives will make the investigator's job both more difficult and more expensive. As RAM CACHE communications become used by those seeking to commit criminal activity, the impact will be felt by law enforcement, homeland security, national security, and intelligence agencies.

B.   Information Repositories — Informational Value

Just as information residing within electronic systems has value to the owner, victim, or suspect; there also exists value to law enforcement, prosecution, defense, and the judiciary as they engage their respective roles in the full investigative and judicial process.

The valuable information residing within these computers and electronic systems will permit our judicial system to measure the accuracy of allegations, establish the circumstances and truth as to the purported criminal activity, and demonstrate with documented digital evidence the nature of the criminal activity or violation. This, of course, is totally dependent on the correct processing of the electronic crime scene, both technically and legally. The search and seizure of any electronic systems must withstand the scrutiny of the Fourth Amendment and all appropriate case and statutory law.

It is incumbent on our law enforcement agencies to provide the technical competence to evaluate this new form of criminal activity; while at the same time being fully compliant with all appropriate legal mandates.

C.   Information Collection

The investigator may enhance the collection of information on a suspect or criminal by searching for electronic data that may reside in four specific locations:

1.   Computer hard drive
2.   File servers (computer)
3.   Databases from governmental agencies, as well as private and corporate databases
4.   Electronic record systems from governmental to private and commercial sectors

The first responding officers to a crime scene in which electronic equipment is present must recognize the presence and potential value of this electronic equipment. They also must provide the necessary security to ensure protection of potential evidence located on hard drives and file servers as the case moves from a preliminary investigation to a full investigation.

The searching and seizure of computer hard drives for the collection of information must be done within the parameters of a lawful search either incident to arrest or with appropriate judicial search warrants, or both. The investigator performing the search of a computer hard drive must be sufficiently trained and educated in the use of appropriate software utilities used in scanning hard drives. Furthermore, the officer must use the department's approved protocol for conducting such a search. This includes creating a disk image on which to perform the search of the targeted hard drive while maintaining the integrity of the original hard drive and ensuring that none of the data residing on the hard drive is modified by the software utilized to search for appropriate information. The imaged hard drive should also be duplicated for eventual defense motions of discovery, in the event the defense counsel wishes their forensic computer experts to review or perform independent analysis of the hard drive.

The collection of information on individuals, whether they are suspects, victims, or individuals of particular interest, can be obtained through a wide array of governmental and private electronic record systems. Financial reports and credit histories contain a vast storehouse of data not only on the individual in question but also on spouses, relatives, and friends. Because law enforcement agencies also have the responsibility of protecting the privacy of individuals, great care must be exercised in searching the enormous range of databases that now exist within our society. This implies that legal rules must be vigorously adhered to through use of subpoenas and application for judicial review or search warrants.

D.   Management of the Electronic Crime Scene

Managing an electronic crime scene is quite similar to any other crime scene, with the exception that specific skill levels and training background will be required of the forensic computer investigator. In addition, the type of crime committed will invariably call for an exceptional team effort by the seasoned crime investigator in cooperating with the electronic crime scene investigator. Because most police organizations do not have adequate resources to fully staff their departments with individuals who possess such demanding skill attributes, it is not uncommon to find that regional task forces have been developed to address these issues. However, this can lead to complications regarding jurisdictional issues, command and control, collection of evidence, and sharing of information with other members of the crime scene team. Because most electronic crime scenes are photo-rich environments, all of the traditional crime scene mapping, photographing, and diagramming are essential to the proper investigation. The crime scene may contain computers that may need to be searched not only for information residing on their hard drive but also for fingerprints and DNA from the keyboard, diskettes, and other areas of the computer. Therefore, a protocol for addressing such issues must be preplanned and available to all personnel, should implementation of such requirements be necessary.

E.   Electronic Crime Scene Procedures

The value of the National Institute of Justice's *Electronic Crime Scene Investigation: A Guide for First Responders* centers on the awareness and assistance that the typical first responding officers will need in both identifying and protecting electronic instruments found at the crime scene. Their publication provides brief descriptions, photographs, primary use, and potential evidence for:

- Computer systems and their components
- Access control devices, such as smart cards, dongles, and biometric scanners
- Answering machines
- Digital cameras
- Hand-held devices, such as personal digital assistants (PDAs) and electronic organizers
- Hard drives, both external and removable hard drive trays
- Memory cards
- Modems
- Network components with local area network (LAN) cards, network interface cards (NICs), routers, hubs, and switches
- Servers
- Network cables and connectors
- Pagers
- Printers
- Removable storage devices and media
- Scanners
- Telephones, such as cordless and cell phones
- Miscellaneous electronic items, such as the following:
  - Copiers
  - Credit card skimmers
  - Digital watches
  - Facsimile machines
  - Global positioning systems (GPS)

This booklet for the first responding officer provides a rich orientation to the types of devices one might encounter at an electronic crime scene. It also highlights the idea that data can reside in unusual electronic places that may have informational value to the crime scene investigator. At the same time, the first responder should note that data can be lost by unplugging the power source to an electronic instrument, and great care must be taken to protect the crime scene (National Institute of Justice 2001, 9–22).

There are occasions when the first responding official to a call-for-services event may not be a police officer; that official may in fact represent either a medical emergency or fire assistance call. In the event that these respondents perceive the incident as a potential crime scene, they will have the responsibility to call for police services, in which case there may be a multiagency responsibility for securing the potential or real crime scene. A recent example of this situation occurred in the "Frankel Case" in Stamford, Connecticut, where the first responding personnel to a fire alarm notification were fire personnel. After observing computers throughout the estate, including even in bathroom areas, plus what appeared to be a deliberate effort to burn computer components within the kitchen area of the estate, the fire personnel notified the fire arson investigator, who not only notified the local police department but also encouraged the local department to notify the federal authorities. Fortunately, this arson investigator had received educational courses in the area of computer crime and quickly realized the nature of the electronic evidence and took appropriate action.

It is interesting to note in this case that although the local police department had personnel trained in many areas, they did not have any personnel trained in electronic crime scenes. The arson investigator prevailed on them to contact a federal agency, who initially declined involvement in the case. The arson investigator was familiar with a guest instructor who had lectured in a computer crime course, so he called on her and described the situation. This guest instructor, who was also a federal agent well-trained in the area of computer crime, realized the importance and significance of the situation and subsequently notified the original federal agency as to the seriousness of this case. The federal agency reevaluated the situation and joined in a multiagency investigation that resulted in the arrest of the subject by German police authorities. Thus, the perseverance of the first responding personnel, along with their training and education, resulted in an international investigation of a multimillion-dollar fraud and embezzlement case. The scope of the computer involvement in this case can be assessed by the fact that it required 16 federal agents over 3 months to process all of the computer evidence in this case.

In most cases, the first responding officer's initial duty is to provide aid or assistance to a victim or victims if present. Second, it is incumbent on the responding officer to take into custody any suspect at the crime scene and to identify witnesses or ask them to remain until crime scene investigators arrive at the scene. Finally, the first responding officer must secure the crime scene to prevent contamination of the scene or destruction of materials that may possess evidentiary value. As the preceding case revealed, many times it is the education, experience, and initiative of a first responder that can go beyond the traditional role expectations and requirements and play an important role in the successful resolution of a case. This suggests that we really need more than technicians who will respond to crime scenes; we need those who have the benefit of a rich education and broad training perspective.

It is generally accepted as good police practice that, when entering an electronic crime scene in which there are no injured parties or suspects in need of detention, the following guidelines be followed:

1. Secure the scene so as to minimize any contamination of the scene.
2. Protect the evidence, and, if people are at the scene, do not permit anyone to touch any computers or other electronic instruments. Have all electronic devices capable of infrared connectivity isolated, so as to control for data exchange. This will include cell phones, PDAs, and other similar instruments.
3. Evaluate the electronic and computer equipment at the scene and make a determination as to whether assistance will be required in the processing of the scene. Few officers can be expected to handle the more complex and sophisticated electronic environments. In some cases, the need for a consultant may be required. Also, personnel with appropriate skills may be located from a regional or federal task force.
4. Observe whether any computers are turned on, and, if so, take the following precautions so as not to inadvertently lose any data on the computers:
    a. Photograph the computer screen if it is left on and it appears useful.
    b. Document the scene through videotape, photography, and crime scene sketches.
    c. Label and photograph all cards and wires running to and from the computer to peripheral devices.
    d. Do not turn off computers in the conventional manner because the computer could be configured to overwrite data. Therefore, in stand-alone computers, it is best to remove the power plug from the wall. Also, if a telephone modem line is in use, disconnect the cable at the wall. It is important when authorities encounter a network as opposed to a stand-alone computer that no one removes the power cord from the server. If the agency does not have personnel who are trained to work within a network environment, other assistance should be requested, and the scene should remain secured until such assistance is available.
    e. Collect any material germane to the electronic or computer environment, including manuals, peripherals, diskettes, and any medium capable of storing data.
5. Inform the crime scene supervisor, in the event the crime scene will require the use of fingerprinting powders to develop potential latent

prints on the computers, that no aluminum-based powders should be used to dust for fingerprints on the computer, because it could create electrical interference. In fact, the forensic processing of the computer and its hard drive should occur prior to any dusting for fingerprints. However, the forensic computer investigator and/or the person who will actually process the computer should also take care as to not preclude a subsequent search for traces of DNA evidence and an examination for latent fingerprints.

6. Take care in disassembling and packaging items for transport to either the police evidence and property room or the crime laboratory for the processing of the equipment:

   a. Maintain the chain of custody on all evidence; therefore, follow and document the appropriate protocols.

   b. Package, transport, and store electronic instruments and computers with minimal to no exposure to situations that might compromise the data residing within their storage mechanisms. Electronic instruments and computers are very sensitive to environmental temperatures and conditions and other radio-wave frequencies.

   c. Place a seizure diskette in and evidence tape over drive bays of computers that will be seized prior to removal and transportation.

7. Transport computers and other electronic instruments and evidence with caution so as not to damage or lose the fragile electronic data. It is advisable not to transport this equipment in the trunk of a police car because this is the area where the police unit's two-way radio is located, and the signals may damage the data reposing in the computer and other electronic instruments.

8. Store and maintain computers and electronic equipment in an environment that is conducive to preserving the data contained in that equipment and is free from any nearby magnetic fields.

In those cases where the forensic computer investigator may participate as a member of a raiding team, there will obviously be time to prepare and plan for appropriate action, as opposed to being called to a crime scene as a result of the first responding officer's request for assistance. In the case of a preplanned raid, the forensic computer investigator will clearly be aware of the criminal activity and will have the opportunity to engage in presearch intelligence. This will permit the opportunity to engage skilled personnel who will be able to process the scene on arrival. The presence of a network may be determined, and appropriate plans can be developed for processing this environment. Also, it may be possible to gather useful information about the situation from the Internet Service Provider (ISP). In short, knowledge about the location, equipment, type of criminal activity, and other pertinent facts will enable the forensic computer investigator to assist the prosecuting attorneys in the preparation of search and seizure warrants. Also, the involvement as a member of the raiding team will permit a more tailored plan in which minimal loss of data to the computer and electronic environment will occur.

F.   Initiating the Forensic Computer Investigation

Once a forensic computer investigator is called on to initiate a formal assessment of a case involving a computer, either as an instrument of crime, a repository of data, information associated with a crime, or a target of a criminal act, it will be necessary for the forensic computer investigator to prepare an investigative protocol to correctly gather and preserve any appropriate evidentiary material.

In the collection of evidence from a computer hard drive it is important to make a bit-stream copy of the original storage medium and an exact duplicate copy of the original disk. After the evidence has been retrieved and copied, the bit-stream data copy of the original disk should be copied to a working copy of the disk so that the analysis of the data will not contaminate the evidence. In the analysis of the digital evidence, you may have to recover data, especially if the users have deleted files or overwritten them. Depending on the type of operating system being used by the suspect, the computer investigator will determine the nature of the forensic computer tools that will be applied. For example, in examining Windows, DOS systems, Macintosh, UNIX, or LINUX systems, one has to understand the file systems that determine how data is stored on the disk. When it is necessary to access a suspect's computer and inspect data, one will have to have an appreciation and working knowledge of the aspects of each operating system (Nelson, Phillips, Enfinger, and Steuart 2004, 50–51, 54). For example, in Windows and DOS Systems one must understand the following:

- Boot sequences and how to access and modify a PC's system (CMOS and BIOS)
- How to examine registry data for trace evidence in the user account information
- Disk drives and how data is organized, as well as the disk data structure of head, track, cylinder, and sectors
- Microsoft file structure, particularly clusters, file allocation tables (FATs) and the NTFS; because data can be hidden, as well as files, that may suggest a crime has occurred
- Disk partition in which hidden partitions can be created to hide data

An excellent and detailed explanation of the UNIX and LINUX operating systems can also be found in the *Guide to Computer Forensics and Investigations* (Nelson, Phillips, Enfinger, and Steuart 2004, 74–76, 80).

Additional information on initiating a forensic computer investigation will be provided in greater detail in subsequent chapters of this text. In the interim, a brief taxonomy of crimes impacting the forensic computer investigator may be useful to review.

The computer as an instrument in criminal activity
- Child pornography and solicitation
- Stalking and harassment
- Fraud
- Software piracy
- Gambling
- Drugs
- Unauthorized access into other computer systems
- Denial-of-service attacks
- Data modification
- Embezzlement
- Identity theft
- Credit card theft
- Theft of trade secrets and intellectual property
- Extortion
- Terrorism

The computer as a target of criminal activity
- Theft
- Virus attack
- Malicious code
- Unauthorized access
- Data modification
- Intellectual property and trade secrets
- Espionage to government computer systems

The computer as a repository of criminal evidence
- Child pornography and child exploitation materials
- Stalking
- Unauthorized access into other computer systems
- Fraud
- Software piracy
- Gambling
- Drugs
- Terrorism-attack plans
- Terrorist organizations' Web-site recruiting plans
- Credit card numbers in fraud cases
- Trade secrets
- Governmental classified documents as a result of espionage activities

A most informative and detailed taxonomy that examines 14 criminal activities and directs the forensic computer investigator to assess these criminal activities against 5 categories where general information may be located and 70 categories in which specific information can be considered is provided in the National Institute of Justice's guide, *Electronic Crime Scene Investigation: A Guide for First Responders* (National Institute of Justice 2001, 37–45).

G.   Investigative Tools and Electronic Crime Scene Investigation

Forensic computer investigators have a number of software tools and utilities available for their use in analyzing a suspect's computer. A list of some of the tools available is as follows:

- Safeback
- Maresware
- DIBs Mycroft, version 3
- Snap Back Dot Arrest
- Encase
- Ontrack
- Capture It
- DIBS Analyzer
- Data Lifter
- Smart
- Forensic X

Each agency will equip their forensic computer investigators with hardware tools appropriate to disassemble a computer system and remove necessary components. In many cases the tool kit will also include necessary materials for packaging, transporting, storing, and evidencing materials. Depending on the workload and caseload of each agency, the use of software and tool kits will vary depending on the agency's needs and policies.

IV.   Legal Issues in the Searching and Seizure of Computers

The Fourth Amendment to the United States Constitution limits the ability of law enforcement officers to search for evidence without a warrant. The Fourth Amendment specifically states:

> The right of the people to be secure in their persons, houses, papers, and effects against unreasonable searches and seizures, shall not be violated, and no warrants shall issue, but upon probable cause,

supported by oath or affirmation, and particularly describing the place to be searched, and the persons or things to be seized.

A.   Searching and Seizing Computers without a Warrant

The United States Supreme Court has held that a search does not violate the Fourth Amendment if it does not violate a person's reasonable expectation of privacy. The U.S. Department of Justice's Computer Crime and Intellectual Property Section suggests in their July 2002 revised manual that a reasonable expectation of privacy of information stored in a computer is determined by viewing the computer as a closed container such as a file cabinet. The Fourth Amendment generally prohibits law enforcement from accessing and viewing information stored in a computer without a search warrant. However, this reasonable expectation of privacy can be lost if a person relinquishes control to a third party by giving a floppy diskette or CD to a friend, or bringing the computer to a repair shop (U.S. Department of Justice 2002, 8–10).

The Fourth Amendment applies only to law enforcement officers and does not apply to private individuals as long as they are not acting as an agent of the government or with the participation or knowledge of any government official. Therefore, if a private individual acting on his or her own conducts a search of the computer and makes the results available to law enforcement, there is no violation. In *United States v. Hall*, 142 F. 3rd, 988, (7th Cir. 1998), the defendant took his computer to a computer repairman who, in the process of evaluating the computer, noticed computer files that on examination contained child pornography. The repairman notified the police, who obtained a warrant for the defendant's arrest. The court upheld the action and rejected the defendant's claim that the repairman's search violated his Fourth Amendment rights (U.S. Department of Justice 2002, 13).

There are exceptions to requiring a warrant in computer cases, and these situations involve consent, exigent circumstances, and the plain-view doctrine, incident to arrest. The issues that emerge in consent center around parents, roommates, and siblings, and whether they have the authority to consent to a search of another person's computer files. The courts have held that parents can consent to searches of their minor child's room, property, and living space. However, if the child is living with the parents and is a legal adult, pays rent, and has taken affirmative steps to deny access to his parents, the courts have held that parents may not give consent to a search without a warrant (*United States v. Whitfield*, 939 F. 2nd, 1071, 1075 [D.C. Cir. 1991]).

The exception to requiring a search warrant in exigent circumstances is permissible if it would cause a reasonable person to believe that entry was necessary to prevent physical harm to the officers or other persons or to prevent the destruction of evidence.

The exception for requiring a warrant under the plain-view doctrine permits evidence to be seized if, in the process of conducting a valid search of a computer hard drive, the officer finds evidence of an unrelated crime while conducting the search (*Horton v. California*, 496 U.S. 128 [1990]). However, the exception to a warrant under the plain-view doctrine does not authorize agents to open and view the contents of a computer file that they were not otherwise authorized to open and view. In *United States v. Carey*, 172, F. 3rd 1278, (10th Cir. 1999), a detective, while searching a computer hard drive for drug trafficking evidence, found a JPG file and discovered child pornography. The detective then spent 5 hours and downloaded several hundred JPG files in a search not for drug trafficking, which the original search warrant authorized, but for more child pornography. The defendant argued to exclude the child pornography files on the grounds that they were seized beyond the scope of the warrant. The government argued the detective seized the JPG files because they were in plain view. The Tenth Circuit rejected the government's argument, stating that the first JPG file was appropriate, but they could not rely on the plain-view doctrine to justify the search for additional JPG files containing child pornography evidence beyond the scope of the warrant (U.S. Department of Justice 2002, 21–22).

In the situations of searches incident to an arrest, the courts have permitted a search without a warrant as an exception for electronic pagers. However, the courts have not resolved this issue with reference to electronic storage devices, such as PDAs, cellular phones, laptop computers, or those devices that contain more electronic information than pagers.

B.   Searching and Seizing Computers with a Warrant

To obtain a search warrant from a judicial officer requires the preparation of two important documents. The law enforcement officer must prepare first an affidavit, which is a statement made under oath that describes the basis on which the officer believes the search is justified by probable cause. The second document is the actual search warrant, which must describe the place to be searched and the items or persons to be seized. In federal search warrants it is also recommended that the officer or agent include an explanation of the search plan or strategy.

In criminal investigations involving the use of computers, it is important to describe in the search warrant whether the property to be seized is the computer hardware or the information that the computer contains. If the computer is an instrument of a crime, then the search warrant would specify the computer hardware itself. On the other hand, if the officer's probable cause is based on the information stored in the computer, then the search warrant would focus on the content of the relevant files rather than the storage device (*United States v. Gawrysiak*, 972 F. Supp. 853, 860 [D. N.J. 1997],

Aff'd 178 F. 3d 1281 [3D Cir. 1999; also *Davis v. Gracey*, 111 F. 3D 1472, 1480 [10th Cir. 1997]; U.S. Department of Justice 2002, 50–51).

Although criminal investigations and the requirements for fulfilling search warrant requirements will vary from state to state, as well as from state to federal jurisdiction, under the federal rules of criminal procedure, Rule 41 would be the guiding force in the previously described search warrant preparation and application. Another important consideration in preparation of search warrants will be whether the target of the investigation is a business, because the economic aspect of seizing computers could have devastating consequences for a legitimate business.

In fact, search warrant requirements for business establishments have to address the issue of reasonable expectation of privacy that people have in their office space. The issue of consent by business managers, supervisors, co-workers, and whoever has common authority over an area can be an important aspect if the search were conducted without a warrant. Another aspect of searching workplace environments would be the public workplace as opposed to the private workplace. The reasonable expectation of privacy would be at variance in the public workplace as opposed to the private workplace.

The complexity of forensic computer investigations entails an appreciation and understanding of the legal requirements both in terms of the elements of an offense and the procedural requirements for effecting a search and seizure of evidentiary material. In addition, the forensic computer investigator is also required to understand the intricacies of the computer itself, and how it might be used either as an instrument to commit a criminal offense or as a repository of criminal information.

V. Summary

This chapter has provided an introduction into the paradigm change that is occurring with reference to crime: Today's criminals are using computers as their instruments to take advantage of new technological possibilities. The forensic computer investigator has to be prepared to investigate these criminal acts in which the computer may be a target of the criminal. This implies that individual, corporate, and government computers are at risk as targets of opportunity. The data that resides in these computers has value and is subject to loss, in some cases at enormous expense. Therefore, the forensic computer investigator must be cognizant of this environment and how to develop systematic plans for investigating those who use computers and sophisticated electronic equipment in the commission of criminal acts. The computer also serves as a repository of data in which the criminal has either stored the fruits of his or her criminal activity, or provides evidence as to the unlawful actions the criminal has utilized in using his or her computer to attack or harm another individual, corporation, or government.

The categorization of an electronic crime scene rich in new technologies that store data and information of potential evidentiary value suggests that we must educate our law enforcement officers to recognize characteristics of and function effectively in this new environment.

References

National Institute of Justice. July 2001. *Electronic Crime Scene Investigation: A Guide for First Responders.* Washington, D.C.: U.S. Department of Justice.

Nelson, Bill, Amelia Phillips, Frank Enfinger, and Chris Steuart. 2004. *Guide to Computer Forensics and Investigations.* Canada: Thomson Course Technology, 25 Thompson Place, Boston, MA 02210.

Parker, Donn B. 1997. Fighting Computer Crime: A New Framework for Protecting Information. New York: John Wiley and Sons.

U.S. Department of Justice, Computer Crime and Intellectual Property Section, Criminal Division. July 2002. CCIPS Manual.

The Digital Investigative Unit: Staffing, Training, and Issues

2

CHRIS MALINOWSKI

At first glance, the staffing of any unit appears to be quite elementary: Enumerate the tasks to be performed, and then find the appropriate personnel with the skills required to perform the tasks. Unfortunately, this process is not as simple as it seems.

The problem in staffing and training an investigative unit, whether it is called a computer crime unit, computer investigations squad, computer lab, computer forensics unit, or some other title, is not a trivial one. Even the choice of a name is important because it indicates purpose and functionality.

The traditional method of establishing any unit is made more complicated by the nature of the work to be performed. The rapidly changing technical environment, staffing pressures, and support (or lack thereof) of the administration make establishment and maintenance of a unit challenging, to say the least.

As part of this chapter, I present some of my experiences that might help the reader understand the need for certain skills that should be either recruited or developed; herein lies a great part of the challenge faced by the unit.

Typically, a police department recognizes the need to stay current with the latest trends in crime. It will mandate that the department establish a computer crimes unit. Organizational charts are amended, policies rewritten, and budget lines promulgated. However, once the department establishes the unit, it may fail to realize that the unit requires extensive and continual support in order to fulfill the intended mission.

Rather than simply discuss the theoretical and possible routes to the destination, I will mention some of the speed bumps and detours along the road to the destination that I, as well as others, encountered in the journey. The unit as described provides a backdrop against which to measure and compare other units.

I.   Unit Name

The NYPD's (New York Police Department's) Cybercrime squad was founded as the Computer Investigations and Technology Unit (CITU). Essentially, it was tasked to perform computer investigations and handle technology issues for the Detective Bureau. These basically devolved to any computer-based requests or problems generated within the Detective Bureau.

The calls received, even a year or two after the inception of the unit, often had little to do with the actual mission, or else in some minor instances duplicated tasks performed by the Department's MIS Division. At one point the unit became a clearing house for the dispersal of personal computers to the various Detective Bureau commands. In an instance of laptops and the "no good deed goes unpunished" philosophy, since the laptops were purchased using federal funding, they were subject to inspection upon demand. The laptops were distributed to various Detective Bureau commands and assigned to individuals, and when those individuals were transferred or promoted and left the CITU, the devices somehow went with them. When selecting a unit name, select a name that clearly advertises the mission and avoid performing functions that other units are already performing on an agencywide basis.

II.   Mission Statement

Defining the mission statement helps clarify the areas of responsibility and defines the role of the unit within the overall organization. The process of defining the mission will also help point out potential conflict areas within intraorganizational jurisdictional mandates. Organizational policy must be determined from the onset in order to avoid duplication of effort, parallel investigations that step on each other, wasteful expenditure of resources, and potential internecine battles. The mission statement should include the purpose of the unit as well as clearly outline those tasks to be performed by the unit. The agency then needs to ensure that everyone is made aware of the unit, its role in the overall agency, its functions, and the services it performs.

Failure to ensure this organizational awareness can result in mishandled investigations and squandered resources. If part of the mission is to provide field support, then make provisions to provide that support consistently by allocating the appropriate resources. If the mission includes supporting seizures pursuant to search warrants that are routinely conducted, you need to consistently ensure the means of providing that assistance in the proper time frame and in the response scale required. For example, responding to an expected seizure of computer equipment at various sites on Super-Bowl Sunday will stretch the resources of any unit; however, be prepared and make arrangements to properly staff that event. A provision can be built into the guidelines asking that any units requesting technical assistance provide a prior notification, perhaps of 2 business days.

The mission of the unit should be based on realistic expectations. By examining other cyber units and their experiences, you can provide guidelines as to whether or not your unit will meet these expectations.

A critical component in formulating the unit is the administration's support in providing the necessary resources in the creation, as well as continued operation, of the unit. Typically, the resources start and end with the *initial* financial considerations; monies are allocated for the initial outlay for equipment and training, as well as for continued purchases of equipment and supplies over time. Due to the nature of the industry and technologies involved, it is often difficult to foresee some needs in order to adequately fit them into an overall budget.

Administrators should understand that the needs of the unit will often conflict with established guidelines regarding allocation of resources. Units can fail when administrators attempt to fit the nature of the work to existing guidelines. Instead, thought should be given to altering or expanding the guidelines to match the new types of work to be performed. This can be defined as the difference between merely reacting and responding to changing conditions and technologies.

Problematic areas may be those dealing with resources: manpower allocation, overtime, purchasing of equipment, and outsourcing of services. I suspect that, as departments grow larger, they become more inflexible in dealing with issues, particularly in these areas. It is possible that a bureaucratic lethargy and inertia builds such that it is simpler to deal with problems by adhering to policy, despite the fact that operations may be severely impacted. Eventually a special overriding exception may appear in the policy, rather than the original guideline being altered.

I have provided some typical examples in the list that follows. In determining the scope of your unit's work, do you wish your unit to handle or be part of the incidents listed? If so, realize that oftentimes they may cross over into areas covered currently by other units.

1. *An allegation of ongoing online narcotics sales is investigated and found to be substantiated. Is the fieldwork to be pursued by the narcotics unit, or by the computer crime squad, which has substantiated the crime?*

   Negotiations and interactions often take place in the cyber world. Tracking the origin and presentation of such evidence may require special understanding and skills, both in order to determine the source as well as pass as Internet users.

2. *An online auction house is used to offer items for sale. Computers and other tech equipment are being sold for relatively low prices, indicating possible stolen merchandise.*

   Investigations of this nature involve tracking of e-mails, as well as potential online conversations. This requires ensuring admissibility of the evidence. During the course of the investigation, there will be an exchange of money for goods, at which point it is hoped that the suspect will physically be present and be arrested.

   These cases most often will be reactive in nature, because nobody wishes to devote resources to an investigation in which either the suspect or the victim (or both) do not fall within their jurisdiction.

3. *The special victims/sex crimes unit is currently investigating a case in which a minor is alleged to have met with an adult. It is known that the two have had online chats and e-mail communications.*
   - *Suspected, but unknown, if adult had sexual contact with the minor. Minor denies relationship.*
   - *Minor claims relationship.*

   In either event, the minor's computer should be examined. Obviously the regular detective squad is not equipped to perform such an examination. In the case in which the minor admits the incident, finding corroborative evidence on the computer may result in the sex crimes unit arresting the suspect.

   In the event in which the minor denies the incident, and in which we fail to discover the smoking gun on the computer, we are left with an option. In fact, this situation has occurred, and my unit eventually arrested and brought in the perpetrator when he met one of my detectives, whom he believed to be an underage boy. Subsequent investigation and interviews resulted in the discovery of other incidents and victims, including the original victim.

4. *Spam e-mail issued to 10,000 people worldwide offers a list of kiddie porn video titles for sale. Included is the address in order to send the money. The location is within your jurisdiction.*

This is one specific example of *why* responsibilities must be clearly defined. The vice squad rolled on this allegation and obtained a *no knock* warrant, allowing them entry without notification. This they promptly did at 6 a.m. When I arrived at 8 a.m. and was made aware of this complaint, I discovered that this unit had already executed the search warrant. Needless to say, had they looked into the matter they would have discovered that their message did not originate from that location, or with the people at that location.

5. *Special victims receives a complaint of a "he said–she said" nature. Complainant alleges a date rape, obviously denied by the suspect. The two met online, and there are communications that took place online.*

Because of the nature of the rape allegation, the special victims unit arrested the suspect. Pursuant to the arrest, I received a call to perform the computer-based side of the investigation. This involved seizing and searching the suspect's computer (both at home, as well as at the business). The suspect, an established businessman, was arrested on a Friday and wound up spending the weekend in lockup.

In examining the hard drive we located what seemed to be exculpatory evidence indicating that the alleged victim was more than willing to engage in the behavior that was the basis of the arrest. The businessman was suing the City of New York for several million dollars, and after 7 years had recently reached a settlement prior to jury deliberation after a trial.

When I was called on to provide a sworn affidavit, one issue that was raised by the (now) plaintiff's counsel was the level or training and experience of those performing the actual computer examination, as well as my personal expertise. This is one reason why training of personnel is extremely important.

6. *Special victims is investigating a date rape at a university in which online communications existed.*

Retrieving information from mail servers, as well as seizing and examining electronic evidence, requires expertise. This is a support function, and not the prime investigative function, both from an investigative viewpoint as well as from the fact that this is a special victims–type case that requires their special knowledge of such cases. For that reason, this case falls within *their* mandate and not within a local precinct's detective squad mission.

Notwithstanding, case law regarding handling of e-mails and other electronic communications are not part of the standard training in the academies, which underscores the need for training of any specialized unit that routinely deals with and provides advice in these matters.

Likewise, the support falls within a cybercrime unit's mission profile. Execution of a search warrant on the site of the university yielded a computer used by the suspect, as well as recording devices, such as Jazz drives. The special victims squad seized the recording equipment. Unfortunately, although they are experts in matters of sexual crimes and crimes against minors, they are not computer technicians and neglected to seize the Jazz disks (media containing the data). This is comparable to taking the telephone answering machine, and leaving behind the tapes.

The reason I mention this is not to disparage the special victims unit — they do excellent work. Rather, I wish to reinforce the point that even if your unit has a mission statement and the department has a defined policy for dealing with digital evidence, there will generally be instances of this nature in which others fail to call for the proper support.

The rationale for failing to secure another unit's assistance may be as simple as a desire not to share the glory, or merely simple ignorance of policy. As stated elsewhere, the "glory" or "notice" issue is not to be underrated. Often the allocation of resources depends on being noticed by those controlling the resources.

7. *A bias incident needs to be investigated.*

Investigations of this nature may be handled by a specialized unit. Whether or not the department decides to employ a bias unit to deal with minority or otherwise politically sensitive groups, it must make a decision regarding the scope of a cyber unit's participation. The depth on involvement should be in the identification of any source of electronic information.

Certainly, a bias unit has the training to understand the departmental need to deal directly with the groups of people classified under bias incidents. Conversely, the cyber unit also has the training to understand the evidentiary needs particular to this type of digital evidence.

A caveat is in order here, as well in other cases; although it might be desirable to gather information on a particular group by monitoring their presence on the Web, this is an *intelligence* function. Decide whether or not your mission is to include this and, if so, whether the proper resources will be available.

One example is a request we received pursuant to a homicide at a nightclub to look up all things pertaining to the Goth culture on the Internet.

8. *The mayor or other public official has received a threat online.*

    Unless there is a specialized unit handling these issues, the immediacy of the threat dictates that the cyber unit should have at least a supporting role, if not the lead role, in the investigation.

9. *An investigation of public official or agency has begun.*

    Once again, there may be a specialized unit, or an inspector general's office handling such matters. Unless the cyber unit belongs to the department being investigated, it may be appropriate to limit participation to a supporting role in the investigation.

10. *An online threat has been made to a school.*

    An immediate response is required in these cases. Successful investigation, as well as prosecution, relies on the cyber unit being involved early on in order to locate the source of the threat, if it was communicated electronically.

11. *A case of intellectual property theft is being investigated.*
    * *Duplication of software*
    * *Dissemination of copyrighted material via computer networks*
    * *Proprietary information stolen*

    The nature of these crimes involves locating the information that is stolen, along with uncovering the trail by which it was taken, in many cases. The stolen information may be confidential or may be a work product, such as software. The type of information may result in nontangible evidence, which may require the resources of the cyber unit.

    As a brief aside, it may be prudent to consider a notification to the cyber unit regarding the loss of a laptop, because laptops often contain confidential information (both personal, as well as corporate).

12. *An alleged computer trespass is being investigated.*

    Proving that someone has been on a particular computer host without authorization requires skills positively not taught in the academies or given during detective training; therefore, it should remain in the domain of the cyber unit.

13. *The case involves computer tampering.*

    Just as the skills to pursue a trespass investigation are not part and parcel of the typical detective's training, these crimes require network and forensic skills in order to develop the case.

In one instance we responded to a large corporation. The complaint centered on a trader who had altered a computer model to degrade the valuation of commodities being traded. This model was utilized in order to advise clients so that they might make better-informed decisions.

The typical tampering case is what we would normally consider to be hacking. Although the word is not properly used, most people understand hacking to be an illicit entry and alteration of a computer system and its data.

14. *Identity fraud allegations are being investigated.*
   • *Steal identity for criminal benefit*
   • *Assume identity to impersonate another without monetary benefit (stalking and harassment)*

Although many instances of identity theft are low-tech, those involving computers or digital evidence require support from a cyber unit. Evidence needs to be preserved, analyzed, and investigated.

15. *Online stalking is suspected.*

Expertise in putting the perpetrator at the keyboard is critical. The case will either present existing evidence or require that an investigator assume the victim's identity. Evidence requires expertise to place the suspect, whereas identity assumption to further the case will require someone versed not only in tracking of persons on networks but also in *netiquette*, that is, the online culture and the technology involved.

16. *Sting operations may be necessary.*
   • *Child exploitation*
      • *Child pornography*
      • *Child luring*
      • *Traveler cases*

It is paramount in these cases to find the child, if missing, and to place the perpetrator at the keyboard. Handling of evidence requires special expertise, and in the event of assuming an online persona, the *creation* of the evidence requires special attention and processing.

   • *Public moral offenses*
      • *Narcotics*
      • *Prostitution*

Along with the business world, these enterprises have also gone online. The sole rationale for involvement is to determine the source of the network traffic, because intelligence and special concerns (such as gangs or organized crime) may exist.

- *Stolen property*

Investigations involving the sale in which an online site is used in order to transact the sale may result in some level of involvement by a cybercrime unit; essentially, in those cases, investigators try to place the seller at the keyboard. The scope of involvement by the cybercrime unit may be limited unless this is a pattern or a proactive case.

17. *Sensational cases may require investigation of computer technology.*

A sensational case brings computer-based equipment that belongs to the suspect or victim to your attention. Although it is rhetorical that a cybercrime unit does not catch the case, the unit may very well be asked to examine the evidence. The evidence needs to be examined for information that might be of interest to the investigating detectives.

In one incident, a homicide prompted the investigating unit to ask our unit to scour the Internet for any references to the suspect's name. Using standard tools to search the Internet, I discovered approximately 6,000 hits on the suspect's name. Most of these references were of no value to the investigation, yet they still required perusal. I estimated that looking through the entire range of returned data would require about 200 man-hours.

Although these examples are but a few, they help to illustrate the range of possible investigations. In some cases, the investigations are initiated by other units, and in others they may be self-initiated.

A broad and general mandate of a computer crimes unit might resemble the following:

- Investigate cases in which computers are used either as instrumentality of a crime or are the target of a crime.
- Assist in cases in which the computer may contain "fruits of the crime," or electronic evidence.
- Assist in cases in which part of the case resides in the electronic domain (i.e., used the Internet in order to communicate).
- Seize and secure digital evidence.
- Examine (search) digital evidence for the unit's cases.
- Examine digital evidence for the entire department or for other agencies.
- Provide expert testimony.

Depending on the scope of functions to be incorporated within the unit's mandate, skill sets will vary. For example, if the unit responds to an incident within a corporate setting, it may very well result in a minimal-intrusion examination of volatile settings and information on a particular machine. The knowledge to do this and to guarantee the least intrusion as possible is not taught at academies, or even to officers who might be first responders in such incidents. Additionally, the skill required to testify as to the manner in which any evidence was obtained is critical in order to communicate to a judge or jury any investigative results.

Investigators who assume identities online for various purposes need to be familiar with the communications medium, as well as conversant with the nuances of that medium: knowledge of netiquette and acronyms and emoticons, or smileys, are not part of standard training. These investigations require that a sworn member act as the technician, because evidence gathered may escalate into probable cause that a crime has been (or is about to be) committed.

One unspoken mission mandate that functions across all levels of the bureaucracy and across organizations is to secure future resources. One sure method for doing this is to take on newsworthy investigations. The selection of self-initiated investigations may assist in this regard. Thanks to the relative newness of computer crime, many incidents afford the opportunity to showcase this aspect of law enforcement. In fact, many crimes committed are new variations on old themes; however, the technology is what makes them provocative and newsworthy. A caveat is that once brought to light, *all* aspects of the investigation are subject to closer scrutiny, both within the department and in the public eye. My point is that opportunities exist to develop public awareness (and subsequently departmental attention) of the unit.

A.   One Unit's History

The NYPD established the Computer Investigation and Technology Unit, or CITU, in 1995. The unit was set up within the Detective Bureau and, specifically, within the Central Investigation and Resource Division of the Bureau (CIRD). CIRD was housed in One Police Plaza (1 PP) and contained units such as Hostage Negotiations, Technical Assistance and Response Unit (TARU), Special Victims Liaison Unit, Crime Stoppers, and the Photographic Unit.

Initially, CITU was staffed with one lieutenant, two sergeants, and a handful of detectives and police officers. The commanding officer (lieutenant) had no computer experience to speak of and had been transferred from a detective squad in the field. The two sergeant supervisors had *personal computer* (PC) experience. The detectives and police officers had a mix of PC experience as well as investigative experience. The investigative background varied because the personnel were pulled from both administrative staff and field staff; one detective had served in the Transit Department's police department in a variety of investigative and enforcement capacities prior to the merging of the departments into the NYPD. Another detective came from a squad that had investigated traditional crimes, up to and including homicides. Two detectives had served in administrative technical positions and had been responsible for computer applications within their respective offices, and one police officer had been with the Housing Police and was knowledgeable in telecommunications and telephony.

In 1996, I replaced the lieutenant as the new commanding officer of CITU. My background had been computer operations prior to joining the NYPD, patrol duties in a precinct, and then over a dozen years in the Information Systems Division of the NYPD. My computer experience covered both IBM mainframe technology (systems programmer/manager) as well as PCs. I had received a master's in management engineering from the Computer Science Department in the CW Post Campus of Long Island University, where I have been instructing since my retirement from the NYPD in 2000. During my tenure with the unit, I was the only person who actually coded to any degree.

The unit, in theory, was and is responsible for meeting the cybercrime needs for the entire NYPD, and thereby the entire City of New York. The police department is a small army of approximately 35,000 to 40,000 members, and the city has upwards of 8 million daytime residents, any of whom can be a victim or a subject of an investigation. Businesses range from small operations all the way up to major industries, such as banking institutions, investment firms, and service organizations.

Although your situation is probably nowhere as large and diverse, hopefully the rationale for including the background of members in the unit will become apparent, because I believe the problems I encountered are typical of many departments looking to establish and maintain such units.

III.   Investigations

A.   Responsibility

The overall responsibility for the investigation will be delineated in the mission statement and should be promulgated as policy. As stated earlier, selection of the responsible investigatory unit depends on the nature of the investigation and is concerned primarily with agency participation level (interagency, or where the agency itself is the subject of the investigation); the ability to further the investigation; and the need to preserve and present the evidence. Other factors, such as special expertise with either the victim or the offender, may also shift primary responsibility of the investigation. This bears on the utilization of resources.

Based on my experiences and in speaking with others in the field, investigations that can be conducted by other units with expertise from the cybercrime unit should be handled by the other unit. Handling investigations uses up resources: If your resources are better utilized pursing other investigations that cannot be handled by other units, allow the other unit to handle the investigation. The argument can be made that the case is developed by the cyber unit's lab team, or by submission of a subpoena; however, this often is simply an assistance function.

Investigation referrals can be taken when your investigators are required to substantially devote time and effort in substantiating the crime, locating the perpetrator, obtaining the digital evidence, and presenting it to judge and jury. Referrals can also be taken when most of the case cannot be pursued or furthered by another unit.

The tendency, especially in fledgling units, might be to grab all the cases it can. Bear in mind that the unit's resources are expended on these cases and may be better applied in actively pursuing those crimes that others cannot.

B.   Proactive versus Reactive

Which type of investigation should a unit pursue? The answer lies in the needs of the agency, as well as in the philosophy of the unit's mission. Many units feel that they wish to have proactive investigations. One type of investigation is that of an online chat for luring pedophiles, resulting in a date or exchange of e-mails, possibly including child pornography. Aside from the immediate aspects of possibly preventing harm to minors, oftentimes the act of catching someone in the act of attempting to meet a minor (albeit a pretend minor) will clear many prior cases of actual meetings.

In determining the investigations to pursue despite their start, remember that, because of the technology involved, the subject of an investigation probably will not reside in your jurisdiction. In those cases, your unit must refer the investigation to the other jurisdiction. There is another possibility: engaging the target of the investigation to appear in your jurisdiction, or issuing a warrant with the prospect of a protracted legal battle to bring him back to your jurisdiction.

It is up to the unit's leader to determine the balance of resources in pursuing the investigation and the potential return on the investment of resources. Although a target might be located for an online harassment (misdemeanor), the likelihood of obtaining an arrest warrant and extradition are extremely slim.

Another aspect of the proactive case is the amount of *time* it consumes: both in total hours and in the time of day or day of week. For example, an investigator enters a chatroom pretending to be a minor. Eventually a conversation with an alleged adult occurs during which the investigator feels that this adult may try to entice the minor to perform sexual acts, either over the

Internet or to meet IRL (in real life). The amount of time devoted to this online relationship can vary from minutes to potentially weeks. During this period, either a crime has occurred or will occur, or no crime is likely to occur. Hopefully, it has been determined that the subject resides in, or will travel to, your jurisdiction.

In addition to the total man-hours spent, the scattering of these man-hours across the calendar may wreak havoc with personnel issues: a continuation of a conversation might occur when the investigator is normally on RDO (regular day off) or has not reported for duty (tour changes may be problematic according to contract rules).

The unit will also need to consider having someone available, either within or on loan, for those occasions in which the subject wants to speak on the phone with the minor or expects to see someone young at a meeting location, such as a mall.

Property and theft cases may involve resources. A controlled delivery requires a team of people to handle the delivery, the subsequent arrest, and the inventory of goods that may be present.

A shipment to a hub of a parcel service will require that surveillance be posted because pickup may only be done during business hours and not by appointment. Our unit had several instances in which the target claimed he was going to pick up a package and failed to show, as our team was on the set. Although this is not different from the noncyber investigation, consider the effect it might have on the work if your lab rats had to man the surveillance as well.

C.   Productivity and Metrics

Understand how the performance of the unit and the commander will be measured. Although the work performed is different, in all likelihood the simplest manner in which to measure productivity already exists within the organization. Often they devolve down to caseload, case clearance rate, and monetary overtime.

The bottom line is that unless you manage to persuade the administrative powers-that-be otherwise, your unit (the round peg) will have to fit into the typical unit's model (square hole). Most often, the peg is hammered until it fits the square hole.

Determine whether the metric model imposed is real: If not, convince the administration that the model is not feasible, possibly for some of the reasons listed in this chapter.

One unspoken measure of productivity is *press time*. This has to do with public perception and notice of the unit's efforts by the administration. For this reason many units' leaders might appear to be headline hungry. The truth of the matter is that resources might increase due to positive press.

D.   Resources

Dependent upon the nature of the investigations that the unit's mandate includes, resources need to be available. It is up to the manager to provide those resources. More importantly, it is the administration's responsibility to appreciate and support the need to supply the *proper* resources, such as the following:

- Staff
- Equipment and supplies
- Time
- Money
- Outsourced expertise

Unlike many other units, simple numbers do not equate to manpower. As stated, because of the various aspects of the technology involved, one staff member cannot simply replace another. Temporary assignments from other units may not alleviate many tasks otherwise performed by unit members. Conversely, do not hesitate to utilize personnel for the purposes of observations, stakeouts, canvassing, or administrative trivia such as filing or the processing of property and evidence.

Purchase of equipment is essential. What is unfortunately not so obvious is that the manner in which procurement occurs requires careful handling of budgetary issues.

If requested to submit a plan for purchase of equipment and supplies, realize that it may be difficult to project what equipment will be needed. Often the reason for this difficulty resides in the fact that the technology either currently does not exist, or is in development. Requesting funding for unknown quantities of nonexistent products is difficult, and increasingly so as the budget projection window extends into the future. Short-term concerns are even difficult to predict because Moore's law (predicting the lifespan of computer technology) has shrunk to about half a year.

If your agency allows for *discretionary* or *investigative* funds, this may allow for some leeway in case of emergency. For example, setting up a lineup may require nominal fees to participants in the lineup, or travel expenses, or other costs incurred during the investigation. As long as these costs are accounted for, hopefully you will be in accordance with policy.

In the event that the fund is based on a grant supplied by another agency (federal or state), the account will certainly have oversight. Emergency purchases of equipment or supplies in order to conduct an investigation will be red-flagged. Proof of expenditure will be required; this means that, should you require a new peripheral that just hit the market in order to process evidence, or even the recording medium for the device, you must account for it. The device should not make its way into someone else's office.

Another means of obtaining equipment is through forfeiture. Typically your organization might decide that, pursuant to an arrest, part of the adjudication and penalty will be forfeiture of the equipment owned or used in the commission of the crime (e.g., a pedophile using a computer to chat online with children).

Although this is certainly one way of obtaining equipment, I tend to advise against it for two major reasons: (1) you avoid the appearance of impropriety (arresting solely to get equipment); and (2) by the time the equipment goes through the forfeiture process, even if the equipment is what you can use currently, Moore's law kicks in, and you might have obsolete equipment, subjecting you to reason 1.

In terms of time, how much do you have? How much do you need to devote? Cases languish for the simple reason of time. Often we do not have the ability to devote enough resources to a particular investigation in order to accomplish all we need in a timely manner. Time constraints require that we devote more man-hours to ensure that all the tasks are done.

Conversely, you need to ensure that you have the man-hours to throw into the problem. As stated earlier, the interchangeability of personnel is no longer true once technology enters the equation. Specifically, the skills required mean that a *particular* member's hours be devoted to the problem at hand. Unfortunately, this may not always be possible because of overtime constraints. As stated earlier, overtime issues can be touchy, both from the union perspective as well as from the administration's point of view. Contractual agreement may entitle that the member incurring the overtime elect the method of payment in cash or time. Administration would prefer time because in normal cases 1 man-hour can be replaced by another man-hour. This is not necessarily true in technical cases. Justification can be made by comparing your replacement's value to those of similar cases. Administration could probably appreciate better the argument that replacing a lab examiner with a programmer from the other division is comparable to having the police lab fingerprint technician process DNA evidence.

Accrual of overtime is closely reviewed due to possible abuse (aside from exceeding budgeted projections). It is quite possible that the closer to retirement a person is, the closer the scrutiny will be, because the pension is likely based on monies earned in the last year or so.

One year I had two unit detectives exceed cash overtime earnings. One exceeded earnings as he was performing essential lab work that could not be deferred (on a sensational murder case, among others). The other detective had been called out on a prolonged detail because of his diplomat training (protective services, etc.) for United Nations duty. Despite my protests that the overtime accrued on the UN detail would count in overtime totals, I was told that, because the monies came from another budget line, they would not count. Cynic that I am, I was not convinced. Sad to say, I was proven correct.

The result was that I was called to task for allowing these members to accrue overtime (out of 40,000 members they made the top 50 list). Despite accounting for every minute of their time and relating it to required and time-constrained essential tasks that could not be performed by other members, both members were enjoined from performing cash overtime for the next 6 months. The inability to use their skills then required attempting to replace those hours with another member's hours (hopefully qualified). This had the unfortunate effect of pushing back tasks the other members had been working on. A secondary effect was that evaluations (and possibly allocation of resources) may be dependent upon the strict liability of violating policy.

The point is not any unfairness but rather that, due to bureaucratic inertia, consideration needs to be given to balancing work, time, and resources *capable* of doing that work. Rather than looking at incidents such as this as hammering the nail that sticks out, administration should consider this an indicator that additional resources (or less work performed) are required.

IV.   Staffing

Depending on the mission, staffing considerations can vary widely:

- Functions
  - Investigate, assist others, or both
    - Field investigations
    - Lab investigations (examinations)
    - Provide testimony
- Degree to which unit is committed to assisting other units or agencies
- Nonmission tasks and responsibilities
- Is the need for sworn personnel to perform lab functions critical?
- Can you recruit the appropriate personnel into the unit?
  - Identification of personnel
  - Civil service constraints
  - Motivators
- Longevity and retention
- Cost per member
- Interchangeability factor

Resource Name	Initials	CivSerTitle	Group	Max. Units	Std. Rate	Ovt. Rate
John Jones	JJ	DetInv3	Investigator	100%	$27.40/hr	$0.00/hr
Jane Doe	JD	DetInv3	Investigator	100%	$27.40/hr	$0.00/hr
Michael Brown	MB	DetInv3	Investigator	100%	$27.40/hr	$0.00/hr
Jennifer White	JW	DetInv3	Lab	100%	$27.40/hr	$0.00/hr
Donald Doque	DD	DetInv3	Investigator	100%	$27.40/hr	$0.00/hr
Aliysha Germaine	AG	PolOff	Lab	100%	$23.25/hr	$0.00/hr
Theodore Billings	**TB**	**DetInv3**	**Investigator**	**100%**	**$27.40/hr**	**$0.00/hr**
Peter Paul	PP	PolOff	Lab	100%	$23.25/hr	$0.00/hr
James Carpenter	JP	DetInv3	Investigator	100%	$27.40/hr	$0.00/hr
John Cooper	JC	Sgt	Supervisor	100%	$30.65/hr	$0.00/hr
Brian Wheeler	BW	Sgt	Supervisor	100%	$30.65/hr	$0.00/hr
Charles Wright	CW	Lt	Supervisor	100%	$35.50/hr	$0.00/hr
Martha Senta	MS	PAA	AdminAide	100%	$15.75/hr	$0.00/hr

Figure 2.1   Staffing list for a nonspecialized unit.

Field investigations *ideally* should be conducted separately from lab examinations. I am stating the ideal, but, unfortunately, reality sometimes dictates that the same personnel who perform the examinations of the digital evidence also conduct field investigations. As I will discuss, this approach is counterproductive in more that just one aspect.

Figure 2.1 lists the staffing for a nonspecialized unit. The staff includes a lieutenant (commanding officer principal administrative side), two sergeants (supervisors), detective investigators, police officers, and administrative assistant (PAA).

We will examine different scenarios that utilize this staffing arrangement and determine the pros and cons of the different schemes.

The assumptions we make are the following: Lieutenants, sergeants, detectives, and police officers are sworn or uniformed members of the service, and the forensic specialist and PAA are civilian members. The workweek is approximately 43.5 hours for the uniformed personnel and 40 hours for civilian members (FLSA notwithstanding). The reason for this imposition is that accrual of time in excess of the weekly limit results in paying of overtime. Within the NYPD, uniformed members (below the rank of captain) have the negotiated option of taking overtime in cash, or in time. The decision is *not* mandated by supervision but rather is at the discretion of the employee. Technically, if the employee is ordered to perform a duty and elects not to accept the time option, then cash overtime must be paid.

Tours of duty are weekdays and span the day and evening hours; personnel do not perform scheduled tours on the late tour (midnights) or weekends normally.

Consider the following scenarios in utilizing personnel:

- Uniformed members performing dual roles
    - Investigator
    - Lab technician
- Uniformed members specializing
    - Detectives investigate
    - Police officers function as technicians
- Specialization including civilian members
    - Detectives investigate
    - Police officers as technicians
        - Supplement investigative effort
    - Civilian technicians
- Outsourcing of technical assignments and duties

A Gantt chart quickly demonstrates the times and resources involved in a typical project. A precinct detective unit forwards a complaint of a minor being involved in an online chat. The parents obviously are concerned regarding the possibility of the child having met an adult online.

The receipt of the complaint occurs late on a Friday, leading to an interview of the minor and family on the following Monday. The reason for the delay is the Monday-through-Friday nature of the unit.

On Monday the *catching* detective (Ted Billings) and his partner interview the minor and the family regarding this complaint. They obtain consent for seizure and examination of the computer. Billings removes the computer along with other materials in preparation of the examination.

At this point in the investigation personnel assignments can proceed in a variety of ways. Possibilities include:

- The case investigator performing the investigation
- Another lab specialist, sworn member performing the examination (detective or police officer)
- A civilian specialist performing the examination

A.   Case Investigator

The investigator is familiar with the case and has the knowledge to recognize any pertinent information that might be contained in the digital evidence. This could be construed as an argument to allow the case investigator to examine the digital evidence. Whether or not this logic applies is at the heart of the question as to whether or not the unit should be specialized. Should the case investigator also conduct the lab exam of the digital evidence? That depends on contract and civil service regulations, available resources, as well as other human-resources-type matters. Case investigators may wish to perform lab functions for a variety of reasons, such as job enrichment, maintaining control of their investigation, or acquiring skills in order to increase their market value.

Although an argument can be made for the investigator searching the digital evidence for information germane to his case, each investigator carries a caseload of several, if not tens, of cases. Typically, we can assume that each investigator might be carrying a caseload of a dozen open cases. The reality is that in a typical detective squad the number is much higher; however, in a unit handling a *specific* subset of investigations, the number may be around a dozen, depending upon total manpower.

The prime purpose of the investigator is to investigate. If the fear of not finding relevant digital information is of concern, then the investigator must spend time conferring with the examiner and reprocess the evidence, if required.

If we draw a parallel to cases that require forensic accounting, the investigator *communicates* to the specialist what he is looking for and discusses the results with the specialist. In a similar fashion, the lab tech can search for the information and communicate the results to the detective. If one argues that the investigator is required to also search the digital evidence, then perhaps by extension it might apply to having the *prosecutor* search the digital evidence because it might contain something that only *he* will pick out.

What *is* the advantage then of having the investigator perform the analysis of the evidence? The possibility that the investigator will recognize pertinent information that might affect the case in a more timely fashion is probably the first consideration. By removing the turnaround time of communicating with the examiner, the timeline may be shortened.

The downside to the usage of the case investigator is that the investigator needs to be versed in the usage of the tools used in securing and analyzing the evidence. In order to remain current, the investigator now needs to be trained in new technologies. In short, he has less time to pursue the actual investigative side of a case.

B.   Lab Specialist

The lab specialist has the training and ability to safeguard and search the digital evidence for any information the case detective might require. In doing so, the lab specialist can free up the investigator in order that he or she might pursue another case. In Figure 2.1, I presented a staff composed of all sworn uniformed members (with the exception of the administrative aide). Some of these members are assigned to the Lab group. Ideally, members of this group will process evidence and prepare reports for the investigative staff. These technicians should ideally report to a different supervisor than the investigative staff; however, unless the agency is a large one, there may be only one supervisor. In that event, the supervisor should strive to keep the two groups separate as far as duties are concerned.

The benefits of allowing specialists to process the evidence are that fewer people need to be trained in certain disciplines. Investigators have more time to devote to the investigation and the "shoe leather" aspects of the case. Additionally, because these people specialize in processing evidence, it is easier to substantiate them as qualified subject-matter experts, (SMEs); partially, this is attributed to sheer volume of work product. The fact that the people in this group routinely process evidence and write lab reports means that the consistency of the work product should be better ensured, and the amount of supervision regarding their training and monitoring may decrease.

There might be practical issues in utilizing uniformed personnel as lab technicians; for example, you run the risk of having them removed for details (parades, riots, public events, etc.). The other possibility is that civil service regulations may rear up and preclude a noninvestigator from working on evidence, because this might be deemed an investigatory function. This needs to be determined in each individual agency.

By replacing the uniformed specialist with a civilian specialist, potentially, the uniform member is freed up to pursue other duties, either within the cyber unit, or outside. Different agencies may restrict the scope of civilian availability in terms of working hours. If this problem exists, realize that oftentimes evidence needs to be recovered and safeguarded (preferably by a uniformed member) and examined at odd hours or on civilian holidays.

Can we alleviate all our problems if we use civilian lab technicians? In all likelihood, you will probably still have some problems. In some respects, getting the proper civilian staff may be more difficult than recruiting and retaining a uniformed staff. In large part, this depends on civil service law.

Recovering evidence may require instances in which the recovery is at the scene of a homicide; most would agree that it is preferable to send in a uniformed person to handle this evidence. This does not preclude using civilian lab technicians but simply means that a procedure be developed to allow uniformed first responders to perform seizures in the field.

C.   Simple Case: Dual Role

In this scenario, a complaint arrives at the unit regarding a conversation alleged to have taken place between a 12-year-old and an adult. The conversation is suggestive in nature, and the parents are concerned that the child is being lured online. The child and parents need to be interviewed, and consent must be secured for examination of the computer and related materials. While interviewing, the case detective catches another case involving a

Task Name	Duration	Start	Finish	Predeces	Resource Names	h 29, '03 M T W T F S S	Jul 6, '03 M T
Case #3:Complaint Received	0.3 hrs	7/4/03	7/4/03		Martha Senta	7/4 ▮ 7/4	
Case #3 : Interview Victim & family	1.5 hrs	7/7/03	7/7/03	1	Theodore Billings,Donald Doque	7/7 ▮ 7/7	
Case #8: Complaint Referred	1 day	7/7/03	7/7/03		Martha Senta	7/7 ▮ 7/7	
Case #3:Seizure of computer equipm	0.3 hrs	7/7/03	7/7/03	2	Theodore Billings,Donald Doque	7/7 ▮ 7/7	
Case #3:Voucher and log evidence	0.25 hrs	7/7/03	7/7/03	4	Theodore Billings	7/7 ▮ 7/7	
Case #3:Make 'best evidence' copy	3 hrs	7/8/03	7/8/03	5	Theodore Billings	7/8 ▮ 7/8	
Case #8: Phone Interview Witness	0.3 hrs	7/8/03	7/8/03	3,6,8SS	Theodore Billings	7/8 ▮ 7/8	
Case #3: Examination of Harddrive	20 hrs	7/8/03	7/10/03	6	Theodore Billings	7/8 ▮ 7/10	
Case #8: Interview Systems Personr	3 hrs	7/10/03	7/11/03	7,8	Theodore Billings,Donald Doque	7/10 ▮ 7/11	

Figure 2.2   Gantt chart for Detective Billings's tasks.

corporation. The corporate case involves a computer trespass and may also involve loss of corporate data and breach of confidentiality (of clients and corporate information). The initial corporate case interview may be conducted via telephone. Detective Billings determines that he requires speaking with corporation personnel subsequent to the telephone interview, and he sets up an appointment.

The Gantt chart in Figure 2.2 focuses on Detective Billings's tasks only insofar as the two cases are involved.

Taking into account Figure 2.2, we can determine that the start times of the tasks performed by Detective Billings are delayed. The nature of the tasks can additionally be constrained by depending on a prior task's ending (finish-start dependency). Not all tasks are of this nature because there are some tasks that may run in parallel, or may even interrupt other tasks.

An example of a task that might run in parallel is a telephone interview with the hacked corporation while Detective Billings is processing the copy process and has some downtime.

A Gantt chart is useful to visually present resource usage and map it against a calendar. If properly formulated, the information can yield a critical path that indicates those tasks forming a chain; a delay in this path will push back a completion date. A delay in another task may alter the critical path, so that a different chain or set of tasks now is the critical path.

A chain would consist of the following tasks:

- Seizure and securing of evidence
- Purchase and installation of hardware or software to process evidence
- Analysis of evidence
- Report of results
- Investigator actions

All things being equal, if the acquisition of some critical component required to process the evidence is delayed, the entire project is delayed.

Should the lab examiner be incapable of processing the evidence (exigent case), the start of the analysis task is pushed back, thereby delaying the project. If the analysis needs to be performed by a particular member, and due to a temporary assignment he is not available, barring replacement, the entire project is delayed.

In this example, if Detective Billings is replaced by a lab technician at the Best Evidence Copy task, then he is freed up to pursue other leads or initiate new cases.

D.   Participation with Other Agencies

This is potentially one method in which to fast-start an operation. By joining part of a task force, you can leverage the existing structure of that team and develop personnel with expertise. If your agency is not large enough to sustain its own cyber unit, this is one method of proceeding.

This approach is recommended for many agencies; it allows the sharing of resources, intelligence data, and networking to other agencies with the appropriate resources, should the need arise.

One reason to consider setting up your own unit is the expected inability of the task force to adequately process the nature or the volume of the work your agency expects to handle.

The cost effectiveness of training your own personnel may also be prohibitive; task forces may provide training, because they may be funded precisely for this purpose.

The other aspect has to do with retention of personnel. Although I will not quote Herzberg et al. regarding job motivators, it can be expected that properly trained personnel may have a limited life expectancy, because of their marketability in the private sector. The task force participation can better (although not positively) assure individual agencies that there will be a cadre of trained personnel to handle work.

E.   Civil Service: Performing Out-of-Title

Assignment of personnel to tasks is complicated by the requirement to ensure that personnel function within the scope of their civil service title. Allowing an employee to perform duties on any regular basis lays the groundwork for that employee to sue for that title. Needless to say, the administration would take a rather dim view of this because it violates several administrative policies: budgeting, resource allocation, and force counts, to name a few.

F.   Recruitment, Hiring, and Retention

The ability to locate and then to hire the appropriate personnel can be challenging. Because the base pay of the member does not increase, different motivators must be found to bring proper personnel into the fold of the unit. If members stand to lose overtime pay, or shift differential pay, these may be *demotivators*.

Locate members who possess the skills appropriate to the mission, and determine the trainability of those potential candidates.

Uniformed members can be sought and recruited from other units; however, often the other unit will be opposed to the move.

There is a different set of issues involved in recruiting civilian personnel. If you cannot recruit from within your agency, there might be new hires from a standing civil service list. If you are assigned a civilian on a provisional basis, because there is no officially promulgated list, then be aware that this person may have his or her position relinquished pursuant to a publishing of the official list. If that person *would have been hired*, you *might* be able to keep him. On the other hand, if there are persons who should have been hired before your civilian, you may lose him or her and pick up an unknown person.

Unlike other jobs, in which pay can be tied to performance, civil service often fails in its ability to recognize and reward employees monetarily. This may have effects on retention as well as initial recruitment into the unit, whether the member is uniformed or civilian.

G.   Administrative Issues

Overtime pay and time limits may have a bearing on all aspects of staffing, from initially recruiting people to keeping them. Although studies conducted cite that pay is not a motivator, the same studies cite that *lack of pay* can be a demotivator. In essence, civil service pays the same base pay according to rank. If someone is assured of making more in a current assignment, he or she will be less inclined to accept an assignment in which the likelihood of reduced income exists. The perception is of losing pay rather than of going back to base pay. As will be related, pay issues also have a bearing on the operational aspects of the unit.

Regardless of the success or failure of the unit commander in recruitment and selection of the team, one inescapable fact remains: Longevity of the individuals as part of the team will remain a serious factor in maintaining the viability of the unit.

H.   Retirement

Despite any writings to the contrary, my belief is that the majority of the sworn personnel will probably leave at the first opportunity, if not sooner. For example, the NYPD retirement currently calls for a retirement with half-pay pension after 20 years of service. Vesting out allows the uniformed member to retire after only 15 years of service with a reduced pension. In both cases, the pension payments start on the twentieth anniversary of joining the department.

The reason for many uniformed members remaining over 20 years is that many might not match the pay on the outside, as well as the benefits enjoyed by the membership (unlimited sick time, 5 weeks annual vacation, and tax-free pensions in the case of serious line-of-duty injury). For others, the police culture is the reason to stay with the job.

In general, any person with a marketable skill may seek employment on the outside. The overwhelming reason for this is twofold: pension considerations as well as the immediacy of a higher paycheck in the private sector.

I.   Advancement and Rewarding

In the event that the workplace is dictated by civil service regulations, it is inevitable that the very system that helps avoid job inequities and abuses will tend to work against performing a particular job.

Because civil servants do not receive annual bonuses based on performance, the mechanism for people to advance in pay scale is either to recognize service time contractually, receive special-duty pay grade, obtain a designated rank, or seek a promotion in civil service rank.

Aging out refers to any pay increase accorded to those employees who have attained a certain level of years on the job. Generally, this is a nominal amount of money that most people would consider nice, but not a deciding factor by any means in remaining in that job.

Many agencies offer a skills pay increase if the skill is required as part of the job. One example would be the ability to pay someone a premium for fluency in a language if that person is called on to use that skill. Unfortunately, many unions will not pursue this avenue during negotiations.

Designated rank is awarded, and with it comes an increase in pay. The rank is not protected by civil service law: In essence, the member serves at the pleasure of the commissioner or chief of the department. The rank is *banded* within the range of a base civil service rank. In the NYPD, the base rank of police officer had various designated ranks associated with it: police officer special assignment (possibly defunct), detective specialist, detective 3rd, detective 2nd, and detective 1st. The grades for detective increase in pay from 3rd to 1st, and the specialist is a noninvestigative title. Likewise, there are designated ranks for sergeant as well as lieutenant. For the ranks of captain and above, the base civil service rank is captain, with all others being designated as ranks. Obviously, there are many more rules; for the sake of this chapter we will not explore them.

The limitation of awarding a designated rank will cap the amount of money that personnel may receive in salary. Other considerations, while allowing the employee to earn more over the year, will actually increase the number of tours of duty to be performed, as well as potentially impact the employee negatively in other ways.

1.   *Unavailability of Personnel and the Interchangeable Man*

The nature of any job may make personnel unavailable for prolonged periods of time. Unfortunately, it is a fact of life on the job, and managers must deal with it. Some of the reasons might be:

- Medical leave for being sick
- Transfer to another assignment
- Promotion
- Suspension or other limitation of duty
- Details or special services

In general, you may still be carrying the person on the roll call; however, as far as the administration is concerned, your manpower is based on the total roster count.

Part and parcel with the job is the attitude (both by the officer and administration) that the average officer, by and large, is capable of being productive across a wide and disparate range of work environments. My opinion is that administration perpetuates this myth — they grew through the same culture.

In fact, normally dropping an officer cold into a new environment can work out, and most officers perform well when assigned new tasks as long as they are given the parameters and expectations of that task.

Although it might seem obvious that a person lacking computer skills should not be in a unit in which these skills are required, from firsthand experience I can attest to the fact that many assignments are made simply because a department needed a body, and the administration had a body to give you. (The often unsaid reason might be "we have no other place to put him.")

The normal assignment for people of this category might be clerical in nature, because they are often on extended medical limitations or bounced from patrol or investigative duties.

The other problem is that for civil service reasons (and department policy) you may be prohibited from utilizing that person in an investigative capacity, either due to the limited nature of their current status or to problems with utilizing someone in tasks not within the scope of their civil service title.

If you are the administrator who has assigned this person to the unit, it might *not* be a favor from several perspectives: (a) The person may be incapable of handling mission-critical tasks; (b) the person may be unable to conduct routine tasks; and (c) the administrative decision to assign a possible problem child not only fails to alleviate the unit's everyday concerns but in fact exacerbates them.

If you are not privy to police culture and responsibility, here is a simple example: As a supervisor on a parade detail, you are issued 10 "bodies" for the duration of the parade. Each of these people has come to the parade on their own, in uniform, and the first time you have ever laid eyes on them is at the site. One of these people is not in the uniform of the day, or otherwise has decided to adorn his uniform. This renders him no longer uniform with the others. Someone higher than you in rank decides on a vicarious lesson, and issues a rip to the offender, and then one to *you* for failing to supervise. Although this is a stretch, unfortunately it does happen, and serves to illustrate the notion of strict liability vis-à-vis the responsibility of the police manager. If you extrapolate this scenario to assigning a person with diminished capabilities, although you might incur agency repercussions, the worth of that person is in question if you were to take a benefits-to-liability ratio.

The process of helping out the cybercrime unit with the addition of nontechnical, untrained, unusable bodies other than for menial work is not necessarily beneficial. Combined with the fact that such people might have been placed there because nobody else could use them, or that they've gotten into trouble elsewhere, their presence is detrimental.

Routinely the interchangeable-man factor rears its ugly head in the other direction. For example, each September the United Nations requires that many diplomat-trained officers (typically detectives or supervisors) are assigned to that temporary duty. That person is essentially lost to the unit for that duration of time. Any other work to be done by this person cannot be performed while this person is loaned out. This becomes an issue for the following reasons:

- Your manpower count remains the same, even though your manpower is reduced in reality.
  - These assignments are done on a fair basis (spread out over commands) in order not to impact any one command inordinately.
- This member may accrue overtime in the outside assignment.
- Any replacement body is not truly a replacement unless the member loaned only performs menial tasks and not mission-critical ones.
- Tasks assigned to this member may languish awaiting his or her return, or if time-sensitive in nature, may have to be assigned to other members who, in turn, have their own time-sensitive tasks piling up.

If you were to examine a Gantt chart based on these circumstances, you would quickly see the effects of detail assignments. The bodies-to-work ratio must be maintained so that overtime is allocated to those members having to pick up the slack. The payment of cash overtime results in administrative oversight headaches, in which the commander (as well as *his* commander, and *his* commander and so on up the chain of command) is required to justify the expenditure of *cash* overtime and then explain how this will not occur in the future. This is definitely a sticky topic because such overtime may be used as a productivity measure of both the unit and the leader.

J.   Misuse of Personnel

Perhaps the term instead of *misuse* should be *inappropriate utilization of human resources*. In any event, it covers the gamut from out-of-title assignments to favors.

To some degree, I have already mentioned utilizing people outside the scope of their title assignments. Specifically, a police officer is a noninvestigative member. Using this person in the capacity of an investigator for a prolonged period of time may result in an unintentional promotion, depending on civil service law and union contracts. For various reasons, this plays havoc immediately with the supervisor or commanding officer and subsequently the effect percolates upwards in the chain of command. The supervisor should be aware of the need to contain (without permission) the extent to which people conduct tasks outside their titles. The immediate issue is that this demonstrates to management a lack of control, and secondarily (perhaps more importantly) budget issues ensue as well as command strength and manpower issues.

The command strength deals with the assignment and distribution of personnel throughout the department. The assignment also brings into play the financial resources dedicated to any particular unit. In the NYPD, units are assigned to divisions, and divisions fall within bureaus. Each bureau is allocated a budget, and lines within that budget. Needless to say, once a budget is impacted, accountability for changes in that budget can reverberate throughout the command structure. The manager should be aware of the budgeting within his or her own command, and how it derives from the parent command and so on. Failure to contend with these issues results in the inability to plead for required resources.

The entire department's command strength is a count of members in ranks. Budgeting is predicated on the command strength; therefore, when these numbers are skewed inadvertently, someone *will* notice.

It is inevitable that at some time or another, resources of the unit will be requested to provide services for other units. These favors can range from setting up someone's desktop computer, to setting up a PowerPoint demonstration, to writing an application.

If your agency already has a unit tasked for these purposes, then why is your cyber unit being asked to provide this service? In all likelihood, the answer is confidentiality, control, and determination of the work. You need to determine whether the latitude of the mission statement covers such incidents. Just as elsewhere, refusal to perform these tasks is difficult because the work can be ordered. Inevitably, the decision to do these favors, whether ordered or not, is a political one; a favor delivered may be a future favor to be returned. Conversely, a favor denied, may be a future request denied.

K.   Interviewing

The supervisor of the unit, aside from having the "basic promoted upward through the ranks" managerial skills should also have knowledge of project management skills. The issues involved in staffing and maintaining such a unit requires a working knowledge and understanding of the underlying technologies.

A major obstacle in staffing a unit is in the initial determination of a person's suitability to the task. The pool from which a manager draws available personnel is very shallow, and not very wide. Unfortunately, this often leads to settling for a candidate who might not be a good fit.

Having reviewed the potential areas that members might be working in, consider evaluating the current skill set as well as the *trainability* of that person. As stated earlier, all or some of these skills may be required in a unit, and all or some of these skills may be embodied in the same individual:

- Programming
    - Examination of target machine (scripts, code)
    - Ad hoc queries using standard office suite tools
    - Homegrown solutions requiring coding
- Forensic specialist
    - Operating system and hardware familiarity
        - Mechanic functions (backing up, evidence copy, acquisition of data)
    - Ad hoc queries using standard office suite tools
    - Patterning (recognition of the unusual)
    - Versed in forensic tool kit(s)
    - Network skills
    - Digital evidence
- Investigator
    - Technology overview
    - Network basics
    - Digital evidence first responder skills
- Supervisor
    - Working knowledge of law pertinent to cybercrime issues
    - Investigation supervision skills
    - Technology supervision skills
        - Project management skills

If you are in need of programmers either to write original code, or merely to interpret code on target systems, the first obvious choice is to solicit from within the organization for members currently functioning in that capacity. If your organization is not large enough to support a staff of information systems or MIS personnel, then other avenues must be explored. If your department does have such staff, the ability to draw from that staff may be impeded by ongoing projects that require a particular person to remain within their unit. Managers are extremely loath to release resources from their grasp; any resources that are easily obtained should be reevaluated. It is possible that members released with little fuss have been labeled problem children or have been of little value to the other manager. In other words, sometimes a donated employee should be subjected to closer scrutiny.

If your department or agency is small and does not have a standing force from which to draw, and you require a programmer type or a member having some programming background, then you have other options: (a) examine the benefits of utilizing another agency's personnel (task force, or loaner) and if this is not feasible then (b) search for an internal resource.

As stated earlier, joining forces with another agency is feasible and has the additional benefit of not costing your department training dollars. The downside is that, although you might require the work to be processed in a very short time frame, you are now subject to the other unit's workflow. Any task relying on completion of this initiative will be deferred as an external process becomes part of your critical path.

The other unspoken argument is that a quid pro quo might exist, and that cost may be prohibitive. Sharing work with another agency can result in sharing any benefits. These benefits may extend to resources, sharing a headline, or even not being *in* the headline when the news breaks. For various reasons, public notice is actively sought by many agencies. One reason may be personal gain in building up a curriculum vitae for advancement or retirement. Other reasons might be to ensure that an elected or appointed public official is perceived favorably. If resources are required, then attempting to obtain a grant or share of budgeting may be another reason for pursuing headlines. The other reason is simply to fulfill one of the police functions, to provide a sense of public security.

Looking for an existing resource can be easily done if a database of skills is available. For example, simply search for those with college backgrounds in either information systems or computer science. Additional means involve issuing bulletins for personnel who have those skills and have decided not to notify the department or update their personnel folder. A decade ago, finding such people was difficult, but as time passes more members of your department might have gone through a curriculum involving information technology courses.

If possible, determine whether the person has the appropriate skills. For example, if the person is required to code on a routine basis, consider administering an actual coding test.

Failing to find an existing programmer requires that you identify someone who is trainable. It has been suggested by numerous studies, and empirical evidence leads many to believe, that math skills are one predictor of coding capability (due to the level of abstract thinking required). Because there are few math or physics majors around police departments today, you can refer to the SAT or ACT math score as the best available source.

A lab technician used to be the person who was locked away in a cubicle, and once a week a pizza was slid under the door. Realize that the lab technician, as well as the investigator, will author reports and be called on to testify. If offered a choice between equally (technically) competent people, consider those possessing strong verbal and written skills.

L.   Training

1. Determine basic skill set of investigator and lab examiner
2. Identify target skill set
   - Quantify member count possessing skills required by unit
3. Training regimen
   - Time
   - Budget
4. Training coverage
   - Geographic
   - Temporal
   - Personnel
5. Identification of immediate and future training
   - Scheduled
   - Attrition
   - Other nonavailability of personnel

I am not a believer of leaving the obvious unstated. Training of personnel is *critical*. Depending on the philosophy of whether or not accreditation or certification is required, accordingly the training curriculum must match that desire and monies allocated toward that end.

A common failure is often seen in an agency providing initial training and subsequently failing to provide additional training. The need for ongoing training is essential due to the ever-changing nature of the technologies involved.

Many people feel the need for certification, such as a Cisco-certified examiner. The opinions on this aspect of certification vary. Although it might be desirable to have a person certified on Cisco equipment (or other vendor), it may not be essential. Certification assumes that a person has completed a course of study and indicates that a person has passed a test and is deemed as certified by that organization. This can be a nice shortcut when providing testimony. Establishing someone as an expert witness, however, does not require that he or she be certified.

The additional aspect is that certification applies to the technology existing at the time of the certification. As indicated earlier, time and technology wait for no man. If certification is a goal, then constant training and certification is required. The alternative is justifying to defense counsel how the examiner is an SME on equipment or technology developed *after* his certification.

Another method of obtaining certification is to get assistance during the course of the investigation. Alternatively, it is permissible to write SMEs into a search warrant.

Substantiation of expertise is the aim of the prosecution. Your aim should be to ensure that you can provide that substantiation, either through formal training, accreditation, participating in investigations, prior experience, or other avenues proving knowledge to the level of SME in the field. Bear in mind that defense counsel will attempt to attack the SME status of the investigator or examiner.

Training opportunities *do* exist for law enforcement personnel. The High Technology Crime Investigation Association (HTCIA) has local chapters that sponsor meetings. HTCIA meetings attract law enforcement as well as their public sector counterparts and academia. Generally, topics of current interest are presented, allowing members to obtain valuable knowledge. The other aspect that cannot be downplayed is the networking aspect. Attendance will allow investigators to meet other investigators in the field. The ability to contact others who have faced the same problems is invaluable. Some of these organizations sponsor annual conferences, during which time presenters offer information or demonstrations normally not seen by investigators. Often the attendance is at a reduced rate for those in government, or they offer sessions open only to those in law enforcement.

The National White Collar Crime Center provides training for law enforcement, and the cost to the agency is simply the transportation and the feeding of the members attending. Housed in Morgantown, West Virginia, this organization started by providing training such as basic data recovery in their facilities and has since expanded their operations both in terms of curricula as well as venues where they offer the courses. Much of the training is the result of a group that met several times a year and was composed of representatives from many law enforcement agencies from federal to local levels as well as corporate and academic representatives.

The Federal Law Enforcement Training Center (FLETC) also provides training opportunities. Their center in Georgia provides training sessions for law enforcement.

Universities are starting to offer courses in computer forensics and network security issues. One of these is the University of New Haven in Connecticut and its branch in California. One problem an administration may have is sending a member for training to a class in a university setting that offers credits for attendance. My suggestion is that administrations balance the possible perception of any impropriety in getting college credits.

Oftentimes, the private sector is willing to make available seats at in-house classes for their own personnel. Finding out about them is the problem, but joining organizations such at the HTCIA or others may allow contacts to be made whereby your organization is made aware of such training, or such training is created specifically for the public sector by the private sector.

The training paradigm offered by many of the federally sponsored training seminars and classes often has been at odds with the ability of the units in the state and local police agencies. Generally, the sessions offered were of 1 week's duration, if not 2 weeks. In speaking with representatives from the agencies' local law enforcement, I was given the impression that their administration would probably not entertain many such training sessions.

Be sure to budget time and money for seats at these sessions. I once budgeted and reserved seats for five members of my staff to travel to an adjoining state for a weeklong training session on securing and analyzing digital evidence. The personnel could all afford to be away for the week; they had no pressing tasks that could not be deferred or performed by other members; and the monies were already allocated to my budget line. However, the request was denied for all five members, and ultimately only two were allowed to travel for the training. The reason given by a gatekeeper in the organization was essentially based on the fact that another unit (the Bomb Squad) was only allowed to send two members for their training. Whether or not you encounter situations such as this depends upon your organization.

What effect did this have? Subsequent budgets must be based on needs and prior budgets. Mandates may slash a budget automatically by 10%, or your budget may be based on the expenditures (not the allocations) of the prior year's budget. Lastly, if the budget lines are different for training, supplies, capital equipment, and such, transferal of unused funding from one budget line (training) to another (equipment purchase) may be problematic.

Although the surface has been barely scratched, consider carefully the purpose and mission of the unit, and the level of support required to create it, maintain it, and administer it.

Consider also the risks along the way. Attrition of personnel as well as budgeting issues can cripple the unit. Failure to obtain proper training can have deleterious effects. In relating some of my experiences, perhaps you can avoid circumstances that would place you in that situation.

Understand the nature of the agency that controls the unit, as well as those agencies contributing to the unit and their needs. Even in the event that your agency is supplying your personnel to a task force, ensure that your agency's administration understands the conditions and constraints of these units.

V. Summary

The reader must remember that any consideration for planning and staffing a cyber unit begins with the definition. A clear and concise mission statement will guide and support plans. Failure to provide such a statement can result in duplication of effort, detrimental sharing of resources, or failure to obtain necessary resources in order to fulfill the mission.

Staffing issues such as recruiting and retention differ in many respects from those in the private sector. Not all motivators or demotivators applicable to the private sector necessarily have the same impact in the public sector. Motivators, such as rewarding for performance, do not exist in many public sector agencies or certainly not in the same form if they exist at all. Civil servants are restricted, by law or union regulations, from monetary benefits as seen in the private sector; for example, if the unit had a good year and closed more cases, there is no bonus.

Careful consideration must be given to the selection of and retention of personnel. The recruitment and selection process is constrained by the available candidate pool; furthermore, eligible candidates may not be lured away from their current assignments.

Retention motivators need to be identified. As noted, pay is probably not a viable motivator for retention. Other avenues must be explored and implemented; my suggestion is to ensure that staff has adequate training opportunities. Participation in technical seminars provides motivational opportunity for personal enrichment and growth. Affording the chance to work with current technology is another motivator.

The problem in providing these opportunities is that many managers may view it as hastening the day in which the staff will take leave. The counterargument is twofold: (1) Civil servants are bound by time constraints in terms of retirement and, more importantly, as far as the mission is concerned; and (2) failure to provide adequate training will hamper the unit's ability to meet the mission, or in fact cause the unit to fail miserably.

Perhaps the most difficult task is for the manager to overcome the reticence or even resistance of the administration in providing funding for training and technology. Every effort should be taken to rationalize the need for training, despite the possibility of staff departure due to training. In many instances, training of the administration is required in order to alert them to the very different nature of a cyber unit, both in staffing and their resource needs.

In essence, we need to remember that the cyber *investigative* unit falls somewhere between the paradigms of public sector law enforcement and private sector information technology teams. Management must draw from lessons learned in the private sector and apply those rules, where appropriate, and manage to find methods to overcome the encumbering regulations of the public sector world. In those instances in which we cannot overcome the limitations, management and administration need to realize that oftentimes the only solution is to hope for the best and plan for the worst. This risk analysis identifies the possibilities of retention failure (*one* specific example) and weighs it against the effects of failing to provide that training (which may very well lead to a staff member leaving), causing the mission to fail.

Criminal Investigation Analysis and Behavior: Characteristics of Computer Criminals

3

WILLIAM L. TAFOYA

In the 1982 sci-fi movie *Blade Runner*, Rick Deckard (Harrison Ford) is responsible for locating humanoids that escape from an off-world mining colony and, as stowaways, return — illegally — to Earth. Set in the year 2019 in Los Angeles, Blade Runners (detectives) are answerable for tracking down and "retiring" these so-called Replicants. Early in the movie there is a scene wherein technology and clever interviewing are combined in the investigative process to determine whether the suspect is indeed a replicant. As the person is questioned, use is made of a device reminiscent of a twentieth-century ophthalmology instrument employed to measure glaucoma. The suspect's eyes are examined as emotionally charged questions are posed. This proactive technique is undertaken to provoke a psychological response (rage) calculated to generate the physiological reaction of dramatic and sudden pupil enlargement (Roy). The hard sciences have already been integrated with the social sciences to successfully assess the behavior of violent offenders. At the leading edge of the twenty-first century, how long will it take to actually, and consistently, reproduce valid results of the kind depicted in this movie as it concerns computer criminals?

To the already controversial debate that surrounds the investigative technique popularly known as profiling, fuel will here be added to the fire by posing two questions: (1) Can the behavior of computer criminals be dependably, reliably, and accurately assessed? (2) Can such an evaluation be undertaken remotely and successfully? Based on accounts spanning more than

30 years, wherein violent offenders have been successfully profiled, I believe the answer is "yes" on both counts. However, there are important distinctions between those whose crimes have, heretofore, been profiled — serial killers, rapists, and bombers — and serial computer criminals (*crackers*). Five are noted here.

First is the important issue of operationally defining one's terms. The label *serial* offender has traditionally been applied to a criminal believed to have committed three or more of the same crimes (e.g., murder), in the same way (e.g., evidence of excessive brutality, referred to as *over-kill*). Ted Bundy was convicted of murdering three women. But he is believed to have taken the lives of more than 25 other women in five states in a 4-year time frame (Douglas and Olshaker 1995). Gilbert Escobedo confessed to raping 48 women. Authorities believe he violently assaulted twice that many victims in the Dallas area between 1985 and 1990 (Hazelwood and Burgess 1989). Theodore Kaczynski, the infamous Unabomber was responsible for the murder of 3 and serious injury of 23 others in his 17-year reign of terror (Graysmith 1997).

But it is not hyperbole to assert that in a single event, a lone computer criminal, or cracker, can victimize hundreds of thousands of individuals and thousands of systems worldwide in a matter of nanoseconds. How then shall the term *serial* be applied to such an offender? Does one virus that infects thousands unleashed by an individual, such as the recent MyDoom Virus (Lemos 2004), warrant being labeled *serial*? How do authorities know — if the cracker does not take credit — when a subsequent cyber attack is perpetrated, who is responsible? And even if someone does take credit, can we be certain that the person contending they are responsible is actually to blame for either incident? These are not idle or irrelevant questions. They are substantive both from a pragmatic (criminal investigative), as well as an academic (research) perspective.

I will contend that for computer criminals, like most rapists, the act for which they are apprehended is rarely the first offense (Hazelwood and Burgess 2004). Of the original cohort of FBI agent profilers, Roy Hazelwood, now retired, is one of the most prolific authors and consistent contributors to the scholarly literature on the subject. He advises that his research is consistent with the findings of Hunter (2001), Abel and Rouleau (1990), et al. In these studies rapists admitted to having sexually assaulted an average of between 7 and 20 women before they were apprehended the first time (Hazelwood 2004). I will contend that there is a parallel of predation with crackers. They likely have perpetrated many more than the standard three criminal acts or unauthorized intrusions before they are caught the first time. The estimate — 7 to 10 offenses — is also probably excessively conservative with respect to crackers. Some (too many) cyber predators have yet to be apprehended for their illegal transgressions. What then are the consequences of adjudication?

With conventional violent offenders, the track record for rehabilitation is not stellar. I suspect the same will be the case with many crackers. But the cybercrime phenomenon is too recent and the data too sparse to be able to make any credible assertions, let alone inferential statements about an unknown population, with regard to recidivism rates. Anecdotally, some who have been apprehended (*black hats*) have subsequently turned their skills to information security. Throughout the field such individuals are referred to as *gray hats* (Interpol 2002).

Second, violent serial offenders are always physically present at the crime scene. Computer criminals are almost never at the same location as their victims. The latter group routinely attacks victim systems far removed from their own physical location. Whereas a killer, rapist, or bomber is almost always vulnerable to detection during the commission of each crime, the computer criminal's actions are almost never detected until well after the attack has occurred and the attacker is safely distant from the literal crime scene.

Third, reviewing a murder crime scene involves the examination of tangible elements such as fluids, hair, and fibers. Evidence of a computer crime requires the assessment of invisible electronic zeroes and ones. Such evidence must be extracted from firewall logs, Intrusion Detection System (IDS) alerts, file servers, and so forth. The basic methodology involves what some authorities have referred to as *the three A's*: (1) acquiring the evidence without altering or damaging the original, (2) authenticating that the recovered evidence is the same as the originally seized data, and (3) analyzing the data without modifying it (Kruse and Heiser 2002, 3).

Fourth, the span of influence is different. Whereas the serial killer's actions impact three or more victims (as well as their families, friends, and neighbors), the reach of the serial computer criminal may damage thousands of systems and endanger the lives of literally millions of people. For example, a cyber attack directed at a nuclear power plant could result in the release of radioactive material into the atmosphere that could cause the death or debilitation of countless victims.

Finally, the more adept the killer, rapist, bomber, or computer criminal, the better able they are to cover their tracks, that is, destroy or delete evidence, physical or digital, from the crime scene. However, with physical crimes, it is nearly impossible to remove all evidence, particularly so-called trace or microscopic evidence that is invisible to the naked eye and therefore overlooked. But, in the case of computer crime, the greater the offender's skill set, the greater is the likelihood that they will be able to irrevocably eliminate all traces of the attack from the system assaulted, and to do so in a matter of seconds. This last is one of the most ignominious aspects of computer crime investigations.

One other distinction is important to highlight before proceeding: The media has dubbed those who commit computer crime as *hackers*. This is unfortunate. The term *hacker* has a venerable and reputable origin. In the 1960s, when computer memory was precious, it was desirable as well as seen as evidence of a high level of skill and egalitarianism to reduce the lines of source code to the absolute minimum while retaining the application's full operability. The procedure, referred to as *hacking*, was regarded as an indication of the competence of the programmer, called a hacker (Levy 1984). The discussion here focuses on individuals who will be referred to as crackers. *Crackers* are here defined as those who repeatedly use their technical skills and knowledge in violation(s) of the law and/or whose unauthorized intrusion into systems damages those systems or the data therein.

Before building a case for the proposition that crackers can be profiled, I will endeavor to clarify and expand the foundation of this arcane discipline. The purpose is to expose the myths about profiling in order to enable the reader to consider what from this knowledge base may be applicable to the assessment of the unique mannerisms, quirks, and characteristics of serial computer criminals (crackers).

I.   Annals of Profiling

The FBI popularized offender profiling in the mid-1970s. Since the early 1990s, the FBI has referred to what they do as criminal investigative analysis. But the old phraseology endures; for the popular press and law enforcement itself, even within the FBI, the term *profiling* continues to be used. Applied to serial computer crime investigation, a more apt descriptor, even if not as pithy, is proposed: cyber investigative behavioral assessment (CIBA). This phrase will be operationally defined. Described here too will be the history: premodern, its heyday — the FBI era — as well as contemporary times, of profiling. Various definitions will be presented. CIBA will then be operationally defined, and the rationale for doing so will be suggested. The literature on the topic will, of course, be reviewed. The discussion will include various mitigating, often conflicting, factors surrounding the use of profiling. Philosophical considerations, investigative and administrative issues, as well as related and scholarly concerns will be reviewed.

The primary use of profiling continues to be applied to the kinds of crimes for which it was honed: murder, rape, and, comparatively speaking, the less frequently occurring bombing and other terrorist acts (Hudson 1999). Although there is a nexus between such crimes and human sexuality, as well as behavioral and mental disorders, these topics will not be addressed.

There simply is insufficient data available to venture down this uncharted path. The phases of serial murder and rape will be outlined to determine what if any parallels exist with computer crimes. Offender typologies, victimology, and the behavioral assessment of the crime scene for both of these specific crimes will be alluded to, again, to consider what similarities might exist in the case of serial computer crimes. Finally, the expectation for the future of profiling generally and computer crime profiling specifically will conclude this discussion.

II. History

The individuals who have contributed to the annals of profiling are colorful in their own right. But there is insufficient canvas here to paint a portrait of any of them. Instead a few brushstrokes will be applied to help put into perspective a sketch of a topic that both fascinates and frustrates policing practitioners, the public, and pundits alike. By and large, the popularity of profiling can be laid at the doorstep of the FBI facilitated in large measure by the media's fascination with the technique. There are precursors and contemporary adherents whose contributions will be briefly noted as well.

A.   Premodern Antecedents

The first documented use of psychological profiling dates to the mid-1940s. Toward the end of World War II, psychiatrist Walter C. Langer and three of his colleagues were tasked with an unusual and groundbreaking assignment. The Office of Strategic Services (OSS), precursor to the Central Intelligence Agency (CIA), asked them to scrutinize the behavior of Nazi Germany's fuehrer, Adolf Hitler. By studying his every move, the OSS hoped Hitler's actions could be predicted. The report, which numbers more than 250 pages, concludes with a section entitled "Hitler's Probable Behavior in the Future" (Langer 1943).

To their credit and remarkable acumen, these physicians assigned probabilities and likely consequences for each possibility they outlined. Eight contingencies were set forth in their report: The military might revolt and seize Hitler, or he may seek refuge in a neutral country, fall into allied hands, get killed in battle, die of natural causes, go insane, be assassinated, or commit suicide. Two of these prospects are striking: assassination and suicide. The former was in fact attempted. On July 20, 1944, Lieutenant Colonel Count Klaus von Stauffenberg is credited with orchestrating the failed effort to end Hitler's life with a bomb at his East Prussia headquarters. The latter appraisal is even more remarkably prophetic (Langer 1943, 247–248):

This is the most plausible outcome.... being an hysteric he could undoubtedly screw himself up into the super-man character and perform the deed. In all probability, however, it would not be a simple suicide. He has too much of the dramatic for that and since immortality is one of his dominant motives we can imagine that he would stage the most dramatic and effective death scene he could possibly think of.... He might even engage some other fanatic to do the final killing at his orders.

On April 30, 1945, in his Reich Chancellery bunker in Berlin, Hitler and Eva Braun, his bride of 1 day, indeed took their own lives. Thereafter, someone removed the bodies from the bunker and set them ablaze. Who did so remains a mystery to this day. Although the precise date of the report is unclear, it seems reasonable to infer that it was issued well before the assassination attempt and clearly prior to the suicide. In an interesting coincidence, the charred bones of German cracker Karl Koch (Hagbard) were located in an isolated forest following the indictment of him and his associates: Hans Huebner (Pengo), Peter Carl, Dirk Bresinsky, and Markus Hess. This discovery followed the March 2, 1989, indictment by German authorities of the so-called Hannover Hackers for espionage. If Koch left one, the police did not find his suicide note (Stoll 1989).

The next verifiable use of profiling — the first in a criminal investigation — occurred in the mid-1950s. In this instance it was a grasping at straws that subsequently appeared to have been a stroke of genius. Beginning in 1940, over a period of more than a decade, 54 devices were placed in New York City, 37 of which exploded. These resulted in the maiming of 22 people. Amazingly, no one was killed in the perplexing bombings of public facilities. The first was detected November 16, 1940, a pipe bomb that had been placed on a West Sixty-fourth Street windowsill. This device was discovered, dismantled, and rendered harmless. Over the next 10 years several more bombs exploded at major New York City landmarks: Penn Station, Radio City Music Hall, the Empire State Building, Macy's Department Store, the Fifth Avenue Public Library, Grand Central Station, and others. Even when bombs failed to explode, however, the effect of their being detected nevertheless exacerbated public consternation.

Dubbed "The Mad Bomber" by the media, it was clear that the person responsible for the bombings held a grudge against Consolidated Edison (Con Ed) the city's power company, where the first device was discovered. This became evident because of the content of the letters sent to various newspapers in which Con Ed was castigated. The letters were always signed "F. P." When arrested the bomber said the initials stood for fair play — something sought, but not received from Con Ed. Through the mid-1950s, traditional investigation had turned up little in the case. But no one had been seriously injured nor complained loudly enough to generate more than perfunctory activity from the New York City Police Department (NYPD). Following the December 2, 1956, bombing of Brooklyn's Paramount Theater, however, six people were injured, three of them critically. Police Commissioner Stephen Kennedy felt compelled to make a public statement. A reassuring press release was issued. NYPD's crime lab director, Inspector Howard Finney, knew the commissioner's verbal balm would not soothe. Something more had to be done. In a second press release he announced that psychiatrist James A. Brussel had been retained to study the behavioral aspects of the Mad Bomber case.

The behavioral portrait Brussel constructed turned out to be amazingly accurate. After painstakingly reviewing all of the available data, Brussel concluded that the Mad Bomber was paranoid, fixated, obsessively meticulous, narcissistic, and sanctimonious. He worked for or had been employed by Con Ed. He was someone who saw himself both as victim and avenging angel. The detectives listened passively to this part of the assessment. They had already figured this much out by themselves. Finney then asked for a description. The psychiatrist hesitated but complied. Brussel said the bomber was symmetrically built. This raised the eyebrows, as well as the skepticism, of these conventionally minded and trained investigators. Even when explained point-by-point, the remainder of the profile seemed even more incomprehensible.

Brussel said that the bomber's ethnic origin was Eastern European, probably Slavic, and he was likely a Roman Catholic. English was not his first language. He had hidden Oedipal tendencies, no close friendships with men nor consequential relationships with a woman. Unmarried, he was probably still a virgin. He lived in Connecticut with a female relative, a spinster aunt or sister. He had or believed he suffered from a chronic ailment (heart disease, cancer, or tuberculosis) and that Con Ed was responsible for his malady. He was a polite, cooperative, fastidious, clean-shaven, middle-aged white male, neatly dressed. When located, he would be wearing a double-breasted suit, buttoned. This last was almost too much for the incredulous detectives to accept.

To their credit, the police did not dismiss the unbelievable assessment. Armed with Brussel's profile and under the command of Chief Inspector Edward Byrnes, the newly established Bomb Investigation Unit set about to track down the Mad Bomber. Comparing Workmen's Compensation Board claims with former employee personnel records, the file of a United Electric and Power (Con Ed's precursor) generator wiper was located. This person had filed a claim for permanent disability pay. He believed that he had contracted tuberculosis as the result of an on-the-job accident in which a backdraft of hot gases from a boiler had knocked him down. The company denied the claim. A 3-year letter campaign of complaints followed thereafter. The last entry in the file was dated 1937. Subsequently, nothing more was heard from the claimant. The first bomb was placed 3 years later. This information was discovered late Friday night, January 18, 1957.

The following Monday morning, January 21, 1957, detectives drove to the last known address of this person. To the amazement of the arresting officers, every point of Brussel's assessment was accurate. When he was taken into custody at the Waterbury, Connecticut, home of his two unmarried sisters where he lived, 53-year-old George Matesky was wearing a double-breasted suit, buttoned (Douglas and Olshaker 1996).

Part of Brussel's assessment (fixated, obsessive, meticulous, narcissistic, and sanctimonious), is very interesting. A significant number of accounts of interviews with and field observations of suspected crackers manifest these same characteristics. Although there is insufficient data to generalize to the entire population of serial computer criminals, it is reasonable to assume that these traits are parsimonious.

There are some striking and very interesting parallels between Matesky and a more recent infamous bomber, Theodore Kaczynski. Dubbed "The Unabomber" by the FBI, Kaczynski's 17-year odyssey has been chronicled in several books, including the very well balanced *Unabomber: A Desire to Kill* (Graysmith 1997). The Unabomber too was accurately profiled in 1993, but that assessment was not acted upon (Witkin 1997). Other events brought Theodore Kaczynski to justice (Scripps-Howard 1996).

B.   The FBI Era

In the late 1960s, FBI Supervisory Special Agent (SSA) Howard Teten began corresponding and consulting with Brussel about the concept of behavioral assessment. Teten and his partner, SSA Pat Mullany, were teaching applied criminal psychology at the FBI Academy. SSAs Richard Ault, Robert Ressler, and others became interested as well in this arcane subject and were mentored by Teeten and Mullany. Teeten began talking about the Mad Bomber case specifically, and profiling in general, in their National Academy (NA) classes. Many of their police officer students were intrigued. Upon returning to their agencies following their NA training, some began calling back to Quantico to ask for advice on open, unsolved murder cases.

In the mid-1970s, SSAs Ressler and John Douglas began conducting interviews of incarcerated known serial killers. This they accomplished on their own time while assigned to conduct so-called road schools, 3- to 5-day training that had been requested by law enforcement agencies. The interviews were conducted in prisons near these training sites.

The real breakthrough in the development of a knowledge base occurred, however, between 1979 and 1983. With input from the entire membership of the Behavioral Science Unit, a sophisticated protocol (interview questionnaire) was developed. Thereafter, this instrument was utilized to collect data for input into a not-yet-operational, specially designed, computerized analytical program. With the new protocol, data from 36 convicted sexual killer interviews were utilized. Actually, more than 36 interviews were conducted, but because of blatant obfuscation and verifiable fabrication, only 36 were included in the analysis.

In addition, data was compiled on 118 victims, most of whom were women. At this juncture, SSA Roy Hazelwood joined Douglas and Ressler. He took part in the majority of these latter interviews. A great deal was learned from and about the killers themselves. This data was independently corroborated with investigative and forensic documentation (Egger 1990; Jackson and Bekerian 1997). In this same time frame, police officers from around the nation increased requests for assistance from the Behavioral Science Unit, whose other faculty members by now were conversant with Teten's pioneering initiative.

In March 1984 the FBI received a $3.3 million grant from the National Institute of Justice (NIJ). The purpose of this grant was to fund the organizational development of the National Center for the Analysis of Violent Crime (NCAVC) and to implement the computer-aided Violent Criminal Apprehension Program (VICAP). The NCAVC was established at the FBI Academy, Quantico, Virginia, and became operational in May 1985; the Behavioral Science Unit was then merged with the NCAVC.

VICAP was the brain-child of the late Pierce Brooks. Retired from the Los Angeles Police Department, he was a renowned homicide detective and subsequently served as chief of police of Eugene, Oregon, and Lakewood, Colorado. Brooks had long believed in the sharing of resources and information, as well as consultation on complex investigations. Doing so, he reasoned, would add substantially to the solution of unsolved serial murder and rape cases, as well as missing person cases. As an NIJ consultant to the FBI on the 1984 grant, Brooks envisioned VICAP as the means to that end and the NCAVC as the national clearinghouse for such knowledge.

Initially, reports of solved and unsolved murders and rapes were entered into the VICAP database. Later, other crimes were added. It was expected that detectives from throughout the nation would eagerly complete VICAP reports and routinely submit them to the NCAVC. Data mirroring the volume of homicide and rape cases nationwide was anticipated to routinely, steadily, and immediately flow into VICAP. Each time a new unsolved case was received, the data was input and the elements compared with like factors previously entered in the database. If there were similarities that matched between characteristics of the new case and one (or more) already entered in the database, the system would register the correlations. When this happened, notice was sent to the respective law enforcement agencies. This would enable the agencies' detectives to compare notes and bring the cases to successful conclusions.

In principle the concept was elegant, the intent noble. But VICAP never achieved its potential. In large part this was due to factors beyond the control of the FBI. Simply and bluntly stated, it was a matter of indolence. Police detectives complained that the VICAP form was too long and took too much time to complete. Recognizing the necessity for cooperation in these voluntary submissions, the form was revised and streamlined down to 15 pages (189 items). But still the complaints continued; the submissions became a trickle not a torrent. Without a steady flow of data — the lifeblood of any system — the chances of successfully matching unsolved serial crimes diminished.

The heyday of the NCAVC was probably from 1985 to 1995. In that decade a number of significant undertakings were achieved. For example, several Behavioral Science Unit members authored a large number of journal articles and a handful of books on profiling and serial murder, rape, and arson. These publications added considerably to the previously meager body of knowledge in this domain. VICAP and its parent, NCAVC, serve, it seems, as perfect models as infrastructures to support the basis for profiling of computer criminals (Reboussin 1990).

Another innovation was an artificial intelligence (AI) computer program developed under the direction of a Ph.D. Electrical Engineer David J. Icove. In 1990, he and two other members of the Behavioral Science Unit completed a 5-year project to bring online a LISP-based Expert System built on a then state-of-the-art platform, a DEC VAX 11/785 minicomputer. The intent of this project was to have the system serve as an automated assistant for human profilers (Reboussin 1990). The system, dubbed "Profiler," never made it beyond prototype stage. This project too has been subsequently discontinued. But again it would appear to be a perfect vehicle for capturing the knowledge base of the unique mannerisms, quirks, and characteristics of computer criminals.

Perhaps the most visionary in this sequence of FBI accomplishments, however, was another since-cancelled undertaking. Roy Hazelwood oversaw the 10-month Police Fellows program that also began in 1985. The curriculum was designed to train seasoned homicide investigators in the skills of profiling. By January 1990 two dozen police profilers had been trained. In this group of 25 were investigators from 12 different police agencies, and eight detectives from major metropolitan agencies. Also trained were two secret service agents and two agents of the Bureau of Alcohol, Tobacco, and Firearms. In addition, one member of the Royal Canadian Mounted Police was so trained. Training a geographically diverse cadre of specialists that could provide assistance to agencies in surrounding jurisdictions in those cases that appeared to be the work of a serial offender was the FBI's goal.

FBI agents in the field also received training, but their training was of a shorter duration and for a different purpose. Once trained, these field agents, designated profile coordinators, were to serve as liaisons between local law enforcement agencies and the Behavioral Science Unit at the FBI Academy in matters that related to the investigation of serial crimes. Of the many reasons for regretting the cancellation of this particular program, at the top of my list is that the NCAVC would have provided the perfect infrastructure for training a cadre of computer crime profilers. Although many may now contend that no one could have predicted the deluge of computer crime we face today, there were at the time some whose Cassandra-like forecasts fell on deaf ears. The NCAVC has also undergone organizational changes, and VICAP has been operationally modified.

C.   Successes and Failures

Comparable commentary cannot be offered with regard to the success or failures of profiling. That is so due to the confidential nature of the use of profiling. Its use does not lend itself to chronicling the events, places, and people involved until after the case is closed, if at all. That is, only until and unless someone has been charged with the crime(s) is such information made available for public consumption. If charges cannot be brought against the offender(s), it is unlikely that investigative techniques — such as profiling — will be revealed. The exceptions are few and far between. Some have been featured in the print and electronic media, usually to the consternation of the profilers, the chagrin of the law enforcement agency with jurisdiction, and the choleric indignation of the prosecutor.

A review of the literature on profiling in a later section will make note of the contributions that have been made recently in this field by practitioners, former practitioners, scholars, researchers, and journalists. Dramatists have contributed as well. Some have published lifelike fiction as well as recounted the escapades of certain true-life serial killers. The accounts of some serial computer criminals have also been chronicled by the Fourth Estate in recent years, most notably the notorious Kevin Mitnick (Shimomura and Markoff 1996).

III. Profiling Defined

A great deal of confusion still remains about profiling, despite the fact that the term *profiling* is readily recognizable and in wide public use. One reason has to do with the lack of a uniformly agreed upon definition. Plato (c427–347) said that if one is preparing to engage in a discussion of 4 hours duration, 2 of the 4 hours should first be spent defining one's terms. This important admonition has too often been overlooked to the detriment of many discussions, and specifically as it concerns the topic of profiling generally as well as computer crime profiling specifically. Another reason for the confusion has to do with the media attention (print and electronic) that has focused on profiling. Responsible television journalism, such as Bill Curtis's A&E *Justice Files*, PBS's *Nova*, and similar History Channel programming, have reported on the use of criminal profiling. Unfortunately, there are also wildly exaggerated fictional depictions of profiling. These, unfortunately, receive a larger share of the public audience than do the programs that are true to life. The current crop of exaggerated fictional shows includes the aptly titled *Profiler* and *Millennium*, both NBC television weekly shows. And there is, of course, Fox television's runaway sensation now in syndication, *The X-Files*.

There is no generally accepted definition of offender profiling. What it is and what is its purpose is widely debated. A number of terms have been used to characterize the same thing. In addition to the succinct *profiling*, the following appellations are also used synonymously: criminal profiling, offender profiling, criminal personality profiling, psychological profiling, profile analysis, and the FBI's criminal investigative analysis.

One definition depicts profiling as "a means of examining through forensics and the behavioral sciences possibilities derived from an incident that has already occurred." This author further states that "the best that can be hoped for is to better understand the crime, its perpetrator, and his motivation" (Kelleher 1997, 14). Another definition states that the purpose of profiling is "to identify and interpret certain items of evidence at the crime scene which would be indicative of the personality type of the individual or individuals committing the crime" (Swanson, Chamelin, and Territo 1984, 700–701). The FBI's Hazelwood and Douglas (1980, 5) defined profiling as the following:

> An educated attempt to provide ... specific information as to the type of individual who committed a certain crime.... A profile is based on characteristic patterns or factors of uniqueness that distinguishes certain individuals from the general population.

Five years later, the FBI further refined this definition as "the process of identifying the gross psychological characteristics of an individual based upon an analysis of crimes ... committed and providing a general description of the person, utilizing those traits" (Ressler, et al. 1985, 3). The distinguished

Diagnostic and Statistical Manual of Mental Disorders (DSM-IV) does not include a definition of profiling (APA 1998).

A.   CIBA Defined

Applied to the investigative niche of computer crime, a new, succinct definition for CIBA is offered that includes five criteria. First, it is a *process*, a procedure brought to bear in the evaluation of a crime scene. Second, it makes use of *forensic evaluation* (preservation, identification, extraction, documentation, interpretation, and statistical analysis of computer data). Third, it draws on the knowledge of certain *social sciences* (criminology, criminal justice, and sociology). Fourth, it draws upon a body of *clinical* knowledge from the medical and mental health professions (psychology, psychogenics, and psychiatry). Fifth, its purpose is to *narrow the focus* on the behavioral type or characteristics of an offender in a particular criminal investigation — computer crime. I have chosen to label this set of proposed criteria as CIBA. These propositions appear to be consistent and parsimonious with Kilger's MEECES conceptualization (Kilger 2003). Such compatibility will go a long way to further the scientific rigor of CIBA.

CIBA more aptly describes what is involved in the profiling of computer criminals. Several additional considerations are offered. First, the domain of its use, at least since the 1980s, has been and continues to be primarily criminal investigations. Second, use of the word *psychological* is rejected. The assessment rendered is not based on an interview of the subjects (suspects) themselves. The disciplines of psychiatry and psychology are steeped in the tradition of one-on-one interviews and consultation. The clinician's work with a patient often involves several sessions before a diagnosis is rendered. That is never the case in the use of the procedures under discussion. Thus, the qualification in the definition offered: the clinical *knowledge*, rather than their skills. Third, *psychological* is rejected on another count: The word excludes consideration of other factors or quirks that the digital crime scene may reveal. For example, file-naming conventions are frequently matters of convenience rather than specific, necessary technical necessities. But the use of certain phraseology may suggest a behaviorally relevant idiosyncrasy that may not be a simple anomaly but rather a telling marker.

IV.   Review of the Literature

The foundation in the profiling niche was clearly laid by the FBI. Articles and books have been authored by several members of the FBI Academy's Behavioral Science Unit (e.g., Ault and Reese 1980; Hazelwood and Douglas 1980; Hazelwood 1983; Ressler 1985; Lanning 1986; Icove 1986). Others are the writings of non-agent FBI personnel (e.g., Pinnizzotto 1984; Howlett et al. 1986; Reboussin 1990). Some are FBI agent collaborations with scholars (e.g., Ressler and Burgess 1985; Douglas, Ressler, and Burgess 1986; Douglas et al. 1986, 1992; Ressler et al. 1986; Hazelwood and Burgess 1987, 1989; Ressler et al. 1988; Hazelwood and Warren 1989, 1990; Dietz et al. 1990). Since retiring from the FBI, some of the Behavioral Science Unit personnel have contributed additional material to this body of knowledge (e.g., Douglas and Olshaker 1995, 1996, 1997, 1998; Ressler and Shachtman 1994, 1998; Vorpagel 1998; Icove et al. 1998; Hazelwood 2004).

Other law enforcement officers have also made important contributions (e.g., Keppel 1989, 2003; Geberth 1981, 1990; Kelsoe 1996). From outside the United States important contributions to the literature include thoughtful works (e.g., Copson 1995; Rossmo 1996; Canter and Alison 1997; Jackson and Bekerian 1997; Marshall et al. 1998). Journalists too have contributed to the literature in important ways, both in fictional accounts (e.g., Bruno 1995; Carr 1994, 1997) and nonfiction (e.g., Graysmith 1997; Bruno 1993; Cahill 1987).

Physicians and academicians have contributed to this genre (e.g., Samenow 1984; Egger 1984, 1998; Dietz P. E. et al. 1990; Hickey 1991; Turco 1998). Criminologist Eric Hickey has carefully articulated the present-day picture of profiling in the United States. Synopsizing novels and nonfictional tract, text, and treatise, he draws a comprehensive picture of modern profiling (Hickey 1991).

An excellent perspective of the European experience is provided by Dutch and British scholars, respectively, Jackson and Bekerian (1997). The contributors in this anthology succinctly describe the research that has been conducted in the past 15 years. Sociologist Lundgren (1997) critically examines the prevailing social/psychological model. He makes a case for the way in which this model has become dominant in serial murder cases. Experimental psychologists Zagrodzka and Fonberg, in Feshback and Zagordzka (1998), ask whether predatory behavior is a model of complex forms of human aggression. Myers and Burgess, in Van Hasselt and Harsen (1998), discuss the major theoretical perspectives of serial murder and sexual homicide. Psychiatrist Ross (1998) makes a compelling case for reassessing the way in which violent criminals are dealt with by society.

As it relates specifically to computer crime investigation publications, little about profiling has yet to appear with any consistency in this segment of the literature. Notable exceptions in texts include the work of Kilger et al. (2002), Gudaitis (2001), and Casey (1999, 2000). Standout journal articles include the contributions of Edmond and West (2003), Gudaitis (2000), and Greenfield (1999).

V.   Uncertainties

A number of problems must be dealt with in any criminal inquiry. This is generally so in a homicide investigation and especially in a known serial killer investigation. Four areas will be addressed here that relate to computer criminal profiling: conceptual considerations, investigative dilemmas, interagency obstacles, scholarly concerns, and related issues.

A.   Conceptual Considerations

Philosophically there are some important considerations associated with profiling. There are legitimate authorities, and there are charlatans who claim expertise as profilers. There are three categories of American investigators I regard as authentic profilers. FBI agents (active duty and retired) who have trained at the FBI Academy's Behavioral Science Unit are one category. (Of course, not all FBI agents receive this training.) Other law enforcement officers (active duty and retired) trained by the FBI, are also qualified profilers. The third group constitutes the handful of criminal investigators (active duty and retired) who were trained other than at the FBI Academy but who, nevertheless, are legitimate profilers. In my estimation, there are fewer qualified profilers in this latter category.

Outside of law enforcement there are also individuals qualified to construct a criminal profile — some physicians, for example. Psychiatrists specifically educated in dealing with abnormal human behavior and experienced at interviewing criminals could do so, as did James Brussel in the Mad Bomber investigation. Under the best of circumstances, however, it is difficult to assess human behavior. Some of the most talented of such psychiatrists have been duped by savvy criminals (Samenow 1984; Yochelson and Samenow 1976). Scholarly individuals with graduate degrees in a social science discipline such as psychology fall into a gray area. This is because it is a rare academic who has had hands-on experience. Few have interviewed a known or acknowledged serial offender. Fewer still have examined a crime scene. Reading about profiling does not make an expert profiler, and talking to a self-described hacker or cracker does not make an expert cyber profiler.

Lacking an appropriate background but having a gift for gab and familiarity with the jargon, empirics take advantage of the gullible and desperate. Amongst the unscrupulous are those who have no relevant education, training, nor experience. Unfortunately, some of these opportunists are former law enforcement officers; still others are lettered. As in any endeavor in life, the watchword for the prospective employer is *caveat emptor* (buyer beware). A useful rule of thumb is to check the bona fides of the prospective consultant (profiler). If they are legitimate, they will have an established reputation and a verifiable track record. NDAs (nondisclosure agreements) notwithstanding, profilers who offer their services should be willing to identify the law enforcement agencies and/or corporations where they have undertaken profiling consultations and their points of contact.

B.   Investigative Dilemmas

A major hurdle not easy to overcome is that the senior detectives, who typically investigate homicide or computer crime cases, frequently lack a background in the behavioral sciences. They may also dismiss outright the utility of the behavioral sciences generally and profiling specifically. Their examination of a crime scene may thus overlook important behaviorally relevant clues. Another problem is that the first responder may be an inexperienced patrol officer who also lacks relevant training. This lack of experience may result in the crime scene being compromised. As it concerns computer crime scenes, disturbing the crime scene may mean destroying the evidence. A third problem is that there seems to be a direct correlation between the spectacular nature of the crime and the number of unassigned personnel who show up at the crime scene. It has not happened yet in a computer crime case — but it will. Unless organizationally prohibited, some who have no need to be at the crime scene will nevertheless make an appearance. They want to look around and will sometimes push their way past the rookie protecting the crime scene. Executives, who ought to know better, are sometimes the worst offenders.

C.   Interagency Obstacles

It is not uncommon for serial offenders to commit their crimes in more than one jurisdiction. But agencies conduct investigations as they present themselves sequentially, usually singly. By the time a series of serial cases becomes evident, multiagency involvement frequently becomes obvious and inevitable. Each agency finds itself in a situation in which it must interact with one or more other agencies. Inevitably, each believes they should be in charge. Predictably, each believes their way of doing things is superior to the way the other(s) are handling the investigation. Insecurity turns to defensiveness that leads to obstructionism. Failure to share, cooperate, or coordinate information are the major ways in which displeasure is expressed over the undesirable situation.

This confounding circumstance is what Egger (1984) termed "Linkage Blindness," which is the unwillingness of the agency head (or some other authority figure) to admit that outside assistance is needed to solve a case in their jurisdiction. As it concerns computer crimes, bringing in a consultant does not yet seem to have been a widespread problem — but it will. Linkage blindness is most evident when agencies at different levels must interact. For example, when a suburban agency must work with a big city agency, when a municipal agency must work with a state agency, or when any of the former must work with a federal agency. This can occur intra-agency as well. The desire for glory, promotion, or even something as trivial as overtime pay has driven some detectives in one unit to hold back information from investigators in another unit within the same agency. This problem has surfaced in several high-profile serial murder investigations: David Berkowitz, Larry Eyler, and Ted Bundy, to name but three (Douglas and Olshaker 1998). This amounts to cutting off one's nose to spite one's face. But it happens consistently. I postulate that this is not solely an American phenomenon. Petty professional jealousy and insecurity has long existed in law enforcement. There is little indication that the problem will soon resolve itself or that computer crimes will be exempt.

D.   Scholarly Concerns

The FBI's profiling program too has its detractors. One highly qualified critic asserts that it "lacks ... validity and reliability ... and ... a proper theoretical basis" (Rossmo 1996, 71–72). Another skeptic contends that the inferences drawn from the data rest on too meager a baseline. That is, the original sample size was inadequate (Copson 1995). There are also those who question the utility of profiling altogether (Levin and Fox 1985). In spite of such controversy, to a large extent "many, if not all, of the psychological profiling units in other countries have been modeled on the FBI approach" (Jackson and Bekerian 1997, 6). It is also noted that renowned psychiatrist and adviser to the American Psychiatric Association Park Elliott Dietz applauds the work of the FBI. He says, "I think I know as much about criminal behavior as any mental-health professional and I don't know as much as the Bureau's profilers do" (Michaud 1986, 42). Although expertise in this investigative niche may not be easy to objectively evaluate, its mantle continues to be bestowed upon the FBI. For this reason, if no other, it is hoped that the FBI will be the vanguard for the development of the first wave of certified cybercrime profilers.

E.   Related Issues

Professional recognition of profiling as a legitimate technique, at least in the United States, lacks academic standing. Few institutions — I know of none — confer a degree in this esoteric field. Just over two dozen institutions have recently been identified that do offer coursework in this domain. Some schools in the United States that have been noted for the quality of their programs are the Illinois School of Professional Psychology, Fielding Institute (Santa Barbara, California), University of Virginia, and Northwestern University. The only cyber counterpart that has surfaced, thus far, is the CyberPsychology Institute at Brandeis University (Waxman 2003).

There is also a lack of published work or organizational reporting. Too little of it reports scholarly research with a sufficiently large baseline to be able to infer from a sample to its population of offenders or to assess the accuracy of the techniques utilized. Fortunately, an excellent source of material concerning conventional profiling is available at the FBI Academy Library, thanks largely to the efforts of Ms. Cynthia Lent. Quantico probably holds the single largest collection of profiling literature in the world. It is expected that the FBI Academy will also become the major repository for computer crime profiling literature. "Profiling," a chapter in the forthcoming second edition of *Know Your Enemy* by the Project Honeynet staff (Kilger, Arkin, and Stutzman 2002), will make a significant contribution to this embryonic niche of the profiling literature. Insofar as violent crime profiling practitioners are concerned, the most reputable and experienced of the consulting firms in this arcane domain is the Academy Group of Manassas, Virginia. Many of the profiling pioneers, the original FBI Academy Behavioral Science Unit faculty, constitute its primary staff. A cyber counterpart of such expertise has not yet emerged publicly.

VI. Education and Training

In the past, training, investigative consultation, and research were available almost exclusively from the FBI. This limitation virtually ensured that the majority of law enforcement investigators would never receive training in this esoteric topic. Increasing interest by individual scholars and researchers has changed this situation. Still, criminal justice and criminology curricula should be further expanded in this regard. So should the offerings in psychology and sociology departments. Most university and college courses in these domains that offer anything beyond a course or two in abnormal behavior are practically nonexistent. A notable recent exception is the School of Public Safety and Professional Studies at the University of New Haven, where one may earn a master's degree in criminal justice with a forensic-psychology concentration (Monahan 2003).

Some additional suggestions are offered that will enhance law enforcement's ability to identify the behavior of serial violent offenders, as well as computer criminals. For example, many law enforcement agencies today hire candidates who hold a bachelor's degree. At the federal level, a baccalaureate has long been an explicit entry-level requirement. For state, county, and municipal law enforcement, a college degree is today a de facto condition of employment in a high percentage of such agencies. At least annually, detectives assigned to investigate serial violent offenses and computer crimes should receive a minimum of 40 hours of instruction in advanced behavioral sciences.

The case study method could also easily be incorporated into such training. This undertaking simply requires that law enforcement chief executives authorize their directors of training to assign a staff member to orchestrate the instruction. Blocks of instruction in the behavioral sciences for all police officer basic training academies should be increased. In most law enforcement agencies the least amount of time is devoted to behavioral sciences as compared to any other topic in basic academy curricula. Heightening the awareness of recruits is important because it is often the least seasoned officers who are assigned to secure a crime scene of a violent crime or cybercrime. Knowledge of serial offender patterns would enable these officers to better protect the crime scene until the arrival of crime scene analysts and detectives. For criminal justice and criminology majors, a practicum or internship should be required. Virtually every police officer that, as a student, had such an experience has raved about the value of this experience. A number of academic institutions recognize the importance of such an experience for their students and align themselves with the law enforcement community to facilitate a more encompassing educational experience that will enable and enhance the process of profiling.

VII. Science or Art?

Some dismiss art as less important an exposition of reality than science. The elements of an oil painting are not quantifiable as in the case of chemistry, for example. There is great beauty in art. Sometimes without uttering a syllable, art can communicate excellence and precision, as in the familiar phrase, a picture is worth a thousand words. The artist is uniquely talented and, in their field, has capabilities far beyond those of most people, including the average scientist. Time is taken to address this distinction because of the kind of criticisms that have been leveled at profiling. Profiling has elements of both art and science. That it is not exclusively one or the other does not negate its utility. Nor is profiling any less valuable an investigative tool to aid in the type of criminal investigation for which it is intended than, say, blood typing is in determining that the dark viscous substance found at the crime scene is O-negative blood — probably human. Critical evaluation is an important feature of the scientific method. But denigrating profiling because it does not fit the status quo is adherence to dogma, not science.

A.   The Status Quo

Conventional wisdom is critical of that which does not fit the well-established order of experience. It questions the validity and utility of whatever is not a traditional precept or maxim of the tried and true. The topic of resistance to change, particularly in policing, is well-documented. Like all disciplines, law enforcement has conventions that are long-standing and seldom questioned. This has been the case in criminal investigations, especially amongst homicide detectives. Here too there are accepted practices and procedures (rituals and incantations) that are passed on by the seasoned detective (wise old shaman) to the newly promoted detective (acolyte) who learns primarily through on-the-job training. The novice is told that, if they are to succeed, they must do what they are told by their elder without question. And the pattern repeats itself generation after generation. This pattern has been described as a model or paradigm.

Much has been accomplished by the established order, the discipline's paradigm. However, from time to time the sacred tenets of the past fail to produce the expected outcome. Occasionally, those not tied to the old established order venture into new realms in search of ways to achieve desirable results. Those who do so, however, risk incurring the wrath of the defenders of the status quo. Thomas S. Kuhn (1996) set forth a grand theory of "paradigm shifts" in his 1962 landmark work, *The Structure of Scientific Revolutions*. This concept may already be applicable to profiling of serial violent criminal offenders. It could easily be the case for computer crime investigations if procedures are not established to thwart this malady.

B.   Profiling Process

Profiling is intended to assist the investigator by directing attention — narrowing the focus — on specific behavioral traits discovered at the crime scene that are indicative of a series of serial crimes. The procedure is premised on the conviction that certain types of offenses reflect the personality type of the offender(s). These predators exhibit quite unique patterns of behavior. The tangible evidence and intangible pointers help to evolve the offender's personality type. Indicators of the expression of rage, hatred, fear, and other emotions are difficult for the untrained to identify. The techniques used to help identify these characteristics were developed in the mid-1970s to 1980s at the FBI National Center for the Analysis of Violent Crime. The ability to recognize these traits is most helpful in highly atypical and bizarre sexually oriented crimes. These types of cases lack a typical motive or suspect. In serial cases, conventionally trained investigators frequently overlook important behavioral clues because what they see doesn't make sense and so is dismissed from further consideration. The more violent and abnormal the crime, the more beneficial profiling can be (Ault and Reese 1980).

Sufficient data has not yet demonstrated a parallel for serial computer criminals. Such findings may not be far in coming, however, because a long-term project is ongoing at the FBI Academy (Jarvis 2003). Profiling is not meant to substitute for a well-structured criminal investigation in a violent crime nor a computer crime.

A violent crime profile includes three basic components:

- Crime commission reconstruction
- Behavior exhibited during the attack
- Post-offense behavior

A violent crime profile may suggest the following information about the offender:

- Race, sex, and age range
- Marital status
- Sexual maturity level
- Interpersonal communication development
- General employment
- Mode of transportation
- Police record or lack thereof
- Reaction to questioning by police
- Probability of having committed similar offenses
- Likelihood of striking again

These factors are also relevant in computer crime profiling. The entire basis for an accurate profile relies on the exceptional examination of the crime scene, whether it be in the physical world or the digital realm. Also essential are detailed interviews of victims and witnesses. Cursory interviews can result in critical delays in acquiring crucial information or in losing that information altogether. Important elements of the predator's behavior and/or personality type can be surmised and assessed in hopes of properly directing the investigation. Several things may suggest themselves:

- Discernable pattern
- Linkages to other like crimes
- Suspect pool generated and prioritized
- Investigative direction
- Motive
- Containment strategy
- Proactive techniques
- Interview and interrogation tactics

Although I will contend that a profiler should be a behavioral scientist, detectives and police officers can and should be trained to recognize behavioral characteristics at the crime scene. The evidence may be indicative of the offender's emotions and personality traits (Ault and Reese 1980). Generally, police officers will be the first responders at a crime scene, including, perhaps, computer crime scenes. First responders can either protect and preserve the crime scene or inadvertently destroy valuable behavioral — as well as physical and digital — clues left at the crime scene.

C.   Risk Levels

Individuals and their home computers are certainly vulnerable to attack or victimization by many means, such as from stalkers, pedophiles, pornographers, identify theft crackers, and other cyber predators. A host of personal dynamics contributes or leads to vulnerability. Still, the risk levels described here will focus on systems' dynamics rather than individual activity per se. Certain dynamics related to the victim system bear great impact on the investigation and the ability of the detective to solve that crime. For example, when employees leave an organization, are their user names and passwords immediately revoked or is there lag time before such action is taken? Can employees access the organization's information systems remotely? If so, is this privilege revoked immediately after termination of employment? Risk levels are one such dynamic, and as important in computer crime cases as they are in conventional crimes.

1.   Low Risk

Low-risk systems are small and generally are those that are not connected to the Internet. Not that such systems cannot be victimized, but rather the risk is lower because there will be a smaller number of threats from a limited number of insiders than from those who gain access via the Internet.

2.   Moderate Risk

Moderate-risk systems are those that, regardless of size or function, permit their staff to access the Internet and whose information security measures are cursory and unenforced or nonexistent (Boni and Kovavich 2000; Icove et al. 1995).

3.   High Risk

High-risk systems, large or small, are those that are connected to the Internet. Cutting off access to the Internet, however, does not, in and of itself, reduce vulnerability to attack. Some authorities believe that the trusted insider is a bigger threat than are "script kiddies" who are believed to constitute the vast majority of computer crackers.

B.   Behavioral Assessment of the Crime Scene

An experienced investigator, while collecting the victim's background information, will also be alert for indicators that a crime scene can yield. Upon arrival at the scene, it is imperative that the investigator determines the scope of the scene and secures it. Serial killers have specific identifiable motives, although they may be hard to understand in the midst of an atypical crime scene. This is likely to be the case with regard to a serial cracker as well. Bizzare material is given great attention in the FBI profiling program.

If a pattern exists, even if not readily identifiable, a first responder should not be fooled by a change in expected modus operandi (MO). Some serial offenders will do this at the end of a spree to evade detection. It is likely that such behavior will become evident as cybercrimes become more pronounced. With violent offenses (murder, rape, bombings), many spree events cross several jurisdictional boundaries. This is almost always the case with serial computer crimes. Linkage blindness (Egger 1984) shouldn't be allowed to cripple a computer crime investigation.

Multiagency task forces have been established in notorious or otherwise high-profile serial killer investigations, as in the Green River Killer case in the Pacific Northwest, for example (Keppel and Birnes 2003). This most certainly is an option worth planning for in the case of a serial computer criminal investigation.

1.   *Victimology*

Rape is an act of violence in which the offender uses sex as a way to express hostility, anger, and a desire for power and control. A rape victim has survived a potentially life-threatening situation. Things such as freedom of choice and decisions that control both mind and body have been stripped away. This type of traumatic event affects the victim greatly both physically and, more importantly, psychologically. A study conducted by Burgess and Holestrom (1979) analyzed 1600 victims of rape and determined that these victims had similar characteristics that are associated with post-traumatic stress disorder. The results of these interviews lead the researchers to coin the term *rape trauma syndrome* (Burgess and Holmstrom 1979). Victims ranging from diverse ethnic and socioeconomic backgrounds consistently described similar physical and emotional symptoms during, immediately following, and over a prolonged period of time after the rape. In 1980, the American Psychological Association incorporated rape trauma syndrome into its DSM-IV. Rape trauma syndrome was to be classified as a form of post-traumatic stress disorder. Rape and serial computer crime appear to have many parallels. At this early date in the development of empirical evidence in computer crime cases, it would appear to be useful for computer crime investigators and corporate information security staff to draw upon the rape investigation literature for pointers.

2.   *Typology*

Criminal justice academics Taylor and Loper (2003) as well as Carter and Katz-Bannister (2000) have done some fine preliminary work developing typologies building on the earlier work of Parker (1998). Classifying the serial computer criminal is crucial in determining the underlying motivating causal factors. Classification is made by assessing and analyzing the written, physical, and digital behaviors that exist in each attack. Interpreting the intrusion from the cracker's point of view will greatly assist the investigator in understanding what motivates an offender. Four categories of rapists have been identified: power reassurance, power assertive, anger retaliatory, and sadistic (e.g., Lanning 1986; Hazelwood et al. 1987). Each category of rapist has a general group of prominent behavioral characteristics that enable the police to tailor the investigation to these specific actions. I believe this is possible with computer criminals as well. The investigator should be aware that just as the rapist's behavior may become dynamic, so too will be the case with the cracker. These changes in behavior may require a reclassification of typology. The offenders' MO may change over time with experience and egocentric thinking. *Modus operandi* is defined as the actions taken by an offender to perpetrate the offense successfully (Ressler, Burgess, and Douglas 1988). This behavior will evolve, and successful outcomes will remain; whereas unsuccessful outcomes will be modified or eliminated. Essentially, crackers learn from their actions, and these results teach them what does and does not work. The offenders' signature will be the common denominator that the police must identify for constructing an accurate profile. *Signature* is defined as a repetitive ritualistic behavior that the offender usually displays at every crime scene (Ressler et al. 1988). Signature is overtly expressed through actions taken at the crime scene; these stem directly from the offender's fantasies. This action will give the investigators a clearer understanding of the mechanisms that drive this offender to commit these crimes. While investigating these offenses, the investigator should first analyze the attack independent of all others that seem to be related. After this is completed, characteristics may then be cross-referenced, identifying any common denominators. These findings will direct the investigators and assist in the classification of the type of offender that is being sought.

VIII. Predictive Indicators

Both as individuals and as part of a research population, the behavioral traits of serial computer criminals will garner greater and greater interest from the research community. As these traits are studied, their importance in identifying serial computer criminals will become more and more important. A comprehensive index of traits of conventional serial offenders by Norris (1988) should be carefully evaluated for their applicability to serial computer criminals. In his offering Norris refers to such traits as *prediction indicators* and systematically defines the value of each. This formulation appears to be an important starting point for the construction of a system specifically applicable to serial computer criminals.

Space limitations preclude each item listed from being explained in depth here. However, this format may serve as a preliminary checklist. Knowledge of information like this can lead to the development of an instrument that will help professionals in identifying such traits in individuals, hopefully before they engage in intractable criminal activity. Practitioners in many areas of the criminal justice system should be made aware of these indicators, because an offender may come to the attention of different components of the criminal justice system at different times and, thus, to different practitioners in the system. I have modified the list of rapist indicators. This modified list includes most, but not all, of the indicators offered by Norris and others. It is believed the following apply to serial computer criminals in the making. The first professional to alert others in the system about an individual who displays an excessive number of these indicators could avert that person from becoming a full-blown serial computer criminal. A caveat is offered. Most teenagers go through a period of testing the limits of authority and harboring self-esteem concerns. Only in the extreme and chronic repetition of these traits are they viable indicators of a propensity toward serial criminal behavior. In priority order, I believe these indicators are as follows:

1. Compulsiveness
2. Feelings of powerlessness or inadequacy
3. Excessive preference for solitary activity
4. Focus on a task at hand to the exclusion of everything else
5. Inability to control one's temper
6. Inability to tell the truth
7. Inability to take responsibility for one's own actions
8. Avoidance of age-appropriate responsibilities
9. Poor performance at school
10. Ritualistic behavior
11. Preoccupation with deviant sexual behavior/hypersexuality
12. Alcohol- or drug-abusing parents
13. Victim of physical or psychological abuse
14. Experimentation or abuse of drugs or alcohol
15. Unhappy childhood
16. Cruelty to animals
17. Fire setting
18. Bed wetting
19. History of serious head trauma

20. Injuries incurred at birth
21. Symptoms of neurological impairment
22. Evidence of genetic disorders
23. Biochemical imbalance
24. Severe memory disorders
25. Suicidal tendencies

IX. Methodology

1. Modus Operandi
   - Signature
   - Style of technical attack
   - Victimology
   - Content-driven
   - Text of message
   - Technical data specifics
   - Pattern recognition
   - Case dependent
2. Creatures of Habit
   - Repeat what works (MO)
   - Repeat what feels good (Sig)
   - Operate to the level of their abilities
3. Technique
   - Cadence
   - Rhythm
   - Keystroking pattern
   - Antidote of sysadmin of child porn IRQ
   - File-naming quirks
   - Linguistic and cultural markers
   - Stimuli elicits behavioral responses
   - Scientific evidence

X. Indicators of Further Positive Developments

It is appropriate to ask, what scientific evidence supports the contention that profiling will evolve and that serial computer criminals can be profiled? Three of the most promising recent developments that suggest this contention is viable are neurolinguistic analysis, neurotechnology research, and the intrusion prevention system Checkmate (Psynapse 2003).

A.   Neurolinguistic Analysis

From his analysis of *Primary Colors*, published anonymously in 1996, English professor and the leading authority on attributional theory, Donald Foster (2000), concluded that this book was authored by *Newsweek* columnist and CBS commentator Joe Klein. Klein denied the assertion, holding up Foster to ridicule. But Foster's assessment was subsequently vindicated when Random House, the publisher of *Primary Colors*, acknowledged Klein's authorship. Computer scientist Peter Neumann has observed, "RISKS readers are by now accustomed to being suspicious of purported computer evidence. Here, the winnowing out of Joe Klein's identity by Professor Foster is in retrospect very impressive" (Neumann 1996). Also in the mid-1990s Dr. Foster was a consultant to the FBI on the Unabomber investigation. Foster's work and further contributions to the literature on attributional theory can almost certainly be expected to shed considerable light on the ability to validly and reliably identify behavioral characteristics of serial computer criminals.

B.   Neurotechnology Research

Since 1993 neuroscientists at the University of California at Los Angeles (UCLA) Brain Mapping Center have been using magnetic resonance imaging (MRI) technology to explore the landscape of the human brain. Its Director, John Mazziotta, believes that "the secrets of our thoughts and talents aren't just hidden in dead cells under a microscope but in our own buzzing, rushing minds" (Kahn 2001, 109). The 10-year research efforts are aimed at building an omnidimensional, computerized database that synthesizes all the subspecialties of neurological research. Mazziotta further believes that "tiny aberrations drag us from normalcy into schizophrenia." Brain mapping will surface the evidence (Kahn 2001, 108).

C.   Checkmate

Based on behavioral theory and methodology, Washington, D.C.–based Psynapse Technologies (2003) has developed a state-of-the-art intrusion prevention system called Checkmate. This assessment engine tracks behavior to determine whether *intent* to inflict harm is present. When Checkmate detects a threat, it either blocks access automatically or provides an alert before damage occurs. The system detects new forms of attack unlike signature detection technologies that identify only known attacks for which rules have been incorporated in their program. Checkmate also recognizes when nontypical network activity is a genuine threat, which is distinguished from anomaly detection systems that only flag perfectly legitimate but unusual behavior (Psynapse 2003).

XI. Insider Threat

A particularly thorny issue has to do with those instances in which a trusted insider is the offender. Insiders have unique knowledge that could forestall being identified or prosecuted even if identified. An outsider, no matter how carefully the cracker cases (i.e., surveillance prior to an attack) the target, there is always the opportunity to be detected. This threat is much less likely to result in exposure of the insider, who can more easily justify or explain away their activities.

XII. The Future of Cyberprofiling

Earlier it was noted that in the United States conventional profiling languishes under several disquieting issues. Four major and four lesser, but nevertheless important, credibility concerns are noted that should be addressed if CIBA is to avoid repeating history. These must be resolved if the profiling of cyber offenders is to develop professional recognition and respect. First, individuals (civilian or sworn, employees or contractors), who assert expertise should be required to submit evidence of their qualifications and expertise to agencies that retain their services as profilers. Second, authentication should be established and easily available for verification. A certificate of subject-matter mastery — not simply attendance at seminars or other training programs — should be mandatory. Third, an academically accredited institution of higher learning should issue this certificate. Fourth, state licensing should be established. In addition, (a) a professional association should be established. One of its first orders of business should be to set forth (b) a code of ethics. Next, (c) a certifying body, akin to the certified public accountant (CPA), professional engineer (PE), or the board certification of the American Medical Association (AMA) and the American Bar Association (ABA), should be established. Finally, (d) this association should establish a registry of its certified members.

Profiling is only one of several investigative tools. The average police officer and the typical detective may never encounter a serial offender — killer or cracker. Still, the use of profiling can assist in identifying, prioritizing, and even eliminating suspects in criminal cases committed by a serial computer criminal. The profiling technique attempts to paint a behavioral portrait of an offender in serial cases. This procedure is based on the premise that a digital crime scene reflects a pattern of behavior of a limited type of perpetrator who specializes in the commission of crime undertaken in a particular manner. Crime scene demeanor goes well beyond MO. This chapter is premised on the strong belief that a well-educated and properly trained computer crime investigator can develop the skills to recognize such patterns. Knowledge in the behavioral sciences (sociology, psychology, criminology, and criminal justice) will significantly aid in the investigation and identification of potential suspects that might otherwise be overlooked. Fusing the social sciences with the forensic sciences applied to the use of computer technology will be a tremendous asset to the future of what I have dubbed cyber investigative behavioral assessment (CIBA) — profiling.

Profiling will remain an important and increasingly used investigative tool throughout the Western world. It can reasonably be expected that the results of rigorous academic research will refine and sharpen the process. The findings from replication and longitudinal studies will surely reduce threats to internal validity and mitigate reliability concerns.

Perhaps this tract will encourage others to contribute their own research to the literature by offering assessments as to the validity, reliability, and viability of this variation of conventional profiling. There is currently but a sliver of the body of knowledge of criminal investigation that concerns itself with helping investigators to recognize behavioral traits left at the scene of a crime. There is even less in the literature as it concerns serial computer criminals.

At a recent FBI Academy workshop, "Confronting the Future Challenges of Cybercriminal Behavior Conference," social scientist Max Kilger (2003) discussed his augmentation of a long-standing intelligence community concept, the acronym of which is MICE (money, ideology, compromise, and ego). Kilger's variant is MEECES (money, entertainment, ego, cause or ideology, entrance to a social group, and status). The results of this undertaking by the FBI, as well as the important work of Kilger and his Project Honeynet colleagues are steps in the direction of a positive outcome.

References

Abel, G. G, and J. L. Rouleau. 1990. The Nature and Extent of Sexual Assault. In *Handbook of Sexual Assault: Issues, Theories, and Treatment of the Offender*, edited by D. R. Laws and H. E. Barbaree. New York: Plenum Press.

American Psychological Association (APA). 1998. *Diagnostic and Statistical Manual of Mental Disorders (DSM-IV)*, 4th ed. (7th printing). Washington, D.C.: American Psychiatric Association.

Ault, R. L., and J. T. Reese. 1980. A Psychological Assessment of Crime Profiling. *FBI Law Enforcement Bulletin* 49:3 (March): 22–25.

Boni, W., and G. L. Kovacich. 2000. *Netspionage: The Global Threat to Information*. Boston: Butterworth Heinemann.

Bruno, A. 1995. *Seven*. New York: St. Martin's.

Bruno, A. 1993. *The Iceman*. New York: Dell.

Burgess, A. W., and L. L. Holmstrom. 1979. *Rape: Crisis and Recovery*. Bowie, MD: Robert J. Brady Publisher.

Cahill, T. 1987. *Buried Dreams: Inside the Mind of a Serial Killer*. New York: Bantam Books.

Canter, D. V., and L. J. Alison, eds. 1997. *Criminal Detection and the Psychology of Crime*. Brookfield, VT: Ashgate.

Carr, C. 1997. *The Angel of Darkness*. New York: Random House.

Carr, C. 1994. *The Alienist*. New York: Random House.

Carter, D. L., and A. J. (Katz) Bannister. 2000. Computer Crime: A Forecast of Emerging Trends. An Independent Research Project Report, School of Criminal Justice, Michigan State University.

Casey, E. 2000. *Digital Evidence and Computer Crime*. San Diego: Academic Press. See esp. Using Digital Evidence and Behavioral Evidence Analysis in an Investigation, 161–170.

Casey, E. 1999. Cyberpatterns: Criminal Behavior on the Internet. In *Criminal Profiling: An Introduction to Behavioral Evidence Analysis*, by B. Turvey. London: Academic Press.

Copson, G. 1995. Coals to Newcastle? Part 1: A Study of Offender Profiling. Paper 7. London, England: Police Research Group Special Interest Series, Home Office.

Dietz, P. E., R. R. Hazelwood, and J. Warren. 1990. The Sexually Sadistic Criminal and His Offenses. *Bulletin of the American Academy of Psychiatry & Law* 18: 163–178.

Douglas, J. E. and M. Olshaker. 1998. *Obsession*. New York: Scribner.

Douglas, J. E., and M. Olshaker. 1997. *Journey into Darkness*. New York: Scribner.

Douglas, J. E. and M. Olshaker. 1996. *Unabomber*. New York: Pocket Books.

Douglas, J. E., and M. Olshaker. 1995. *Mind Hunter*. New York: Scribner.

Douglas, J. E., A. W. Burgess, A. G. Burgess, and R. K. Ressler. 1992. *Crime Classification Manual*. Lexington MA: Lexington Books.

Douglas, J. E., R. K. Ressler, A. W. Burgess, and C. R. Hartman. 1986. Criminal Profiling from Crime Scene Analysis. *Behavioral Sciences & the Law* 4: 401–421.

Edmond, B. and R. L. West. 2003. Cyberpsychology: A Human-Interaction Perspective Based on Cognitive Modeling. *Journal of Cyberpsychology and Behavior* 6:5 (October): 527–536.

Egger, S. A. 1990. *Serial Murder: An Elusive Phenomenon*. New York: Praeger.

Egger, S. A. 1998. *The Killers Among Us*. Saddle River, NJ: Prentice Hall.

Egger, S. A. 1984. A Working Definition of Serial Murder and the Reduction of Linkage Blindness. *Journal of Police Science and Administration*, 12: 348–357.

Feshbach, S., and J. Zagrodzka, eds. 1998. *Aggression: Biological, Developmental, and Social Perspectives*. New York: Plenum Publishing.

Foster, D. W. 2000. *Author Anonymous*. New York: Henry Holt and Co.

Geberth, V. J. 1990. *Practical Homicide Investigation*, 2nd ed. New York: Elsevier.

Geberth, V. J. 1981. Psychological Profiling. *Law and Order* 29(September): 46–52.

Graysmith, R. 1997. *Unabomber: A Desire to Kill*. Washington, D.C.: Regnery Publishing.

Greenfield, D. N. 1999. Psychological Characteristics of Compulsive Internet Use: A Preliminary Analysis. *Journal of Cyberpsychology and Behavior* 2:5 (September).

Gudaitis, T. 2001. The Human Side of Incident Response. In *Incident Response: A Strategic Guide to Handling System and Network Security Breaches*, by E. E. Schultz and R. Shumay. Upper Saddle River, NJ: Pearson, 207–246.

Gudaitis, T. 2000. Cybercrime and the Hidden Aspects of Incident Response. *Information Security Bulletin* 5: 3 (April): 15–24.

Hazelwood, R. R. 2004. Personal conversation with the author by telephone January 29th.

Hazelwood, R. R. 1986. NCAVC Training Program: A Commitment to Law Enforcement. *FBI Law Enforcement Bulletin* 55:12(December).

Hazelwood, R. R. 1983. The Behavior-Orientated Interview of Rape Victims: The Key to Profiling. *FBI Law Enforcement Bulletin* 52:9 (September): 8–15.

Hazelwood, R. R., and A. W. Burgess, eds. 2004. *Practical Aspects of Rape Investigation: A Multidisciplinary Approach*, 4th ed. New York: Elsevier.

Hazelwood, R. R., and A. W. Burgess. 1989. The Serial Rapist: His Characteristics and Victims. *FBI Law Enforcement Bulletin* 58:2 (February): 18–25.

Hazelwood, R. R., and A. W. Burgess. 1987. An Introduction to the Serial Rapist. *FBI Law Enforcement Bulletin* 56:9 (September): 16–24.

Hazelwood, R. R., and A. W. Burgess, eds. 1987. *Practical Aspects of Rape Investigation: A Multidisciplinary Approach*. New York: Elsevier.

Hazelwood, R. R., and J. E. Douglas. 1980. The Lust Murderer. *FBI Law Enforcement Bulletin* 49:4 (April): 18–22.

Hazelwood, R. R., and J. Warren. 1990. The Criminal Behavior of the Serial Rapist. *FBI Law Enforcement Bulletin* 60:2 (February): 11–16.

Hazelwood, R. R., and J. Warren. 1989. The Serial Rapist: Characteristics and Victims. *FBI Law Enforcement Bulletin* 58:1 (January): 10–17.

Hazelwood, R. R., P. E. Dietz, and A. W. Burgess. 1983. *Autoerotic Fatalities*. Lexington, MA: Lexington Books.

Hazelwood, R. R., R. K. Ressler, R. L. Depue, and J. E. Douglas. 1987. Criminal Personality Profiling: An Overview. In *Practical Aspects of Rape Investigation: A Multidisciplinary Approach*, edited by R. R. Hazelwood and A. W. Burgess. New York: Elsevier, 137–149.

Hazelwood, R. R., et al. 1982. Sexual Fatalities: Behavioral Reconstruction in Equivocal Deaths. *Journal of Forensic Science* 27:4 (October): 764–773.

Hickey, E. W. 1991. *Serial Murderers and Their Victims*. Belmont, CA: Wadsworth.

Hollinger, R. 1988. Computer Hackers Follow a Guttman-like Progression. *Social Science Review* 72:199–200.

Howlett, J. B., K. A. Hanfland, and R. K. Ressler. 1986. The Violent Criminal Apprehension Program — VICAP: A Progress Report. *FBI Law Enforcement Bulletin* 55:14–22.

Hudson, R. A. 1999. *Who Becomes a Terrorist and Why: The 1999 Government Report on Profiling Terrorists.* Guilford, CT: Lyons Press.

Hunter, J. A. 2001. The Sexual Crimes of Juveniles. In *Practical Aspects of Rape Investigation: A Multidisciplinary Approach*, 3rd ed., edited by R. R. Hazelwood and A. W. Burgess. New York: Elsevier, 409.

Icove, D. J. 1986. Automated Crime Profiling. *FBI Law Enforcement Bulletin* 55:12(December).

Icove, D. J., K. Seger, and W. VonStorch. 1995. *Computer Crime: A Crimefighter's Handbook.* Sebastopol, CA: O'Reilly and Associates.

Icove, D. J., V. B. Wherry, and J. D. Schroeder. 1998. *Combating Arson-for-Profit: Advanced Techniques for Investigators*, 2nd ed. Columbus, OH: Battelle. See esp. 51–55.

Jackson, J. L., and D. A. Bekerian, eds. 1997. *Offender Profiling: Theory, Research and Practice.* Chichester, UK: John Wiley and Sons.

Jarvis, J. P. 2003. Confronting the Future Challenges of Cybercriminal Behavior Conference, FBI Academy, Quantico, VA (August 18–22).

Kahn, Jennifer. 2001. Let's Make Your Head Interactive. *Wired* 9: 8 (August): 106–115.

Kelleher, M. D. 1997. *Flash Point: The American Mass Murderer.* Westport, CT: Praeger.

Kelsoe, P. L. 1996. *Criminal Investigative Analysis Quarterly Newsletter* 1:1(September) Corona, CA: Pique Publising.

Keppel, R. D. 1989. *Serial Murder: Future Implications for Police Investigators.* Cincinnati, OH: Anderson.

Keppel, R. D., and W. J. Birnes. 2003. *The Psychology of Serial Killer Investigations.* San Diego, CA: Academic Press.

Kilger, M. 2003. Exchange with the author at the workshop, Confronting the Future Challenges of Cybercriminal Behavior Conference, at the FBI Academy, Quantico, VA (August 21).

Kilger, M., O. Arkin, and J. Stutzman. 2002. Profiling. In *Know Your Enemy*, by Honeynet Project. Reading, MA: Addison-Wesley.

Kruse, W. G., II, and J. G. Heiser. 2002. *Computer Forensics: Incident Response Essentials.* Boston: Addison-Wesley.

Kuhn, T. S. 1996. *The Structure of Scientific Revolutions*, 3rd ed. Chicago: University of Chicago Press.

Lanning, K. V. 1986. Child Molesters: A Behavioral Analysis. Monograph, Washington, D.C.: National Center for Missing & Exploited Children.

Levin, J., and J. A. Fox. 1985. *Mass Murder.* New York: Plenum Publishing.

Levy, Steven. 1984. *Hackers: Heroes of the Computer Revolution.* New York: Doubleday.

Levy, S., 1984. *Hackers: Heroes of the Computer Revolution.* Garden City, NY: Anchor Press.

Lundgren, D. C. 1997. Conceptualizing Serial Murder: A Sociological Critique of the Psychological Paradigm. unpublished Paper, Board of Studies in Sociology, Stevenson College, University of California, Santa Cruz.

Marshall, W. L., et al, eds. 1998. *Sourcebook of Treatment Programs for Sexual Offenders.* New York: Plenum Publishing.

Michaud, S. C. 1986. The FBIs New Psyche Squad. *New York Times Magazine* (October 26):40, 42, 50, 74, and 76–77.

Monahan, L. 2003. Criminal Justice Faculty Meeting, University of New Haven, May 2.

Norris, J. 1988. *Serial Killers: The Growing Menace.* New York: Doubleday.

Osterburg, J. W., and R. H. Ward. 1997. *Criminal Investigation,* 2nd ed. Cincinnati, OH: Anderson. See esp. 150–153.

Parker, D. B. 1998. *Fighting Computer Crime.* New York: John Wiley & Sons.

PBS. 1992. Mind of a Serial Killer. Nova Television Public Broadcasting System, Program #1912 (October 18).

Pinnizzotto, A. J. 1984. Forensic Psychology: Criminal Personality Profiling. *Journal of Police Science and Administration* 12(1):32–36.

Project Honeynet. 2002. *Know Your Enemy.* Reading, MA: Addison-Wesley. See esp. Profiling Review, 260–26,1 and Psychological Review, 262–264.

Reboussin, R. 1990. An Expert System Designed to Profile Murderers. In *Computers in Criminal Justice; Issues & Applications,* edited by Schmalleger, F. Bristol, IN: Wyndham Hall Press, 237–243.

Ressler, R. K., ed. 1985. Violent Crimes. *FBI Law Enforcement Bulletin* 54:1–3.

Ressler, R. K., and A. W. Burgess. 1985. The Split Reality of Murder. *FBI Law Enforcement Bulletin* 54:7–11.

Ressler, R. K., and T. Shachtman. 1998. I Have Lived in the Monster: Inside the Minds of the World's Most Notorious Serial Killers. New York: St. Martin's.

Ressler, R. K., and T. Shachtman. 1994. Whoever Fights Monsters. New York: St. Martin's.

Ressler, R. K., A. W. Burgess, and J. E. Douglas. 1988. Sexual Homicide: Patterns and Motives. Lexington, MA: Lexington Books.

Ressler, R. K., A. W. Burgess, J. E. Douglas, and R. L. Depue. 1985. Criminal Profiling Research in Homicide. In Rape and Sexual Assault: A Research Handbook, edited by A. W. Burgess. New York: Garland, 343–349.

Ressler, R. K., A. W. Burgess, J. E. Douglas, and A. McCormack. 1986. Murderers Who Rape & Mutilate. Journal of Interpersonal Violence 1:3: 273–287.

Ressler, R. K., et al. 1980. Offender Profiles: A Multidisciplinary Approach. FBI Law Enforcement Bulletin 49:9 (September): 16–20.

Ross, D. 1998. *Looking into the Eyes of a Killer*. New York: Plenum Publishing.

Rossmo, D. K. 1998. Geographic Profiling. Presentation at the annual conference of the National Criminal Intelligence Service, the Henry Fielding Centre for Police Studies and Crime Risk Management, University of Manchester (March 18), Manchester, England.

Rossmo, D. K. 1996. Targeting Victims: Serial Killers and the Urban Enviroment. In *Serial and Mass Murder: Theory, Research, and Policy*, edited by T. O'Reily-Fleming. Toronto: Canadian Scholars Press.

Samenow, S. E. 1984. *Inside the Criminal Mind*. New York: Times Books.

Shimomura, T., with J. Markoff. 1996. *Take-Down*. New York: Hyperion.

Stoll, C. 1989. *The Cuckoo's Egg: Tracking a Spy through the Maze of Computer Espionage*. New York: Doubleday.

Strentz, T. 1988. A Terrorist Psychosocial Profile: Past and Present. FBI Law Enforcement Bulletin, 57: 4: 11–18.

Strentz, T. 1981. The Terrorist Organizational Profile: A Psychological Role Model. In *Behavioral and Quantitative Perspectives on Terrorism*, edited by Y. Alexander and J. M. Gleason. New York: Pergamon Press.

Swanson, C. R., N. C. Chamelin, and L. Territo. 1984. *Criminal Investigation*. New York: Random House.

Tafoya, W. L. 2003. The CyberPsychology of Serial Cyber Offenders. Colloquium, Cyberpsychology Institute, Brandeis University (November 18), Waltham, MA.

Tafoya, W. L. 2001. Wetware Whacking: Profiling the Computer Hacker. Keynote Address, Defcon 9 Conference (July 13) Las Vegas, NV.

Tafoya, W. L. 1998. Offender Profiling. National Criminal Intelligence Service Conference, the Henry Fielding Centre for Police Studies and Crime Risk Management, University of Manchester (March 18), Manchester, England.

Tafoya, W. L., and T. M. Gudaitis. 2003. Profiling the Computer Intruder. Computer Security Institute Conference (November 3) Washington, D.C.

Taylor, R. W., and D. K. Loper. 2003. Computer Crime. In *Criminal Investigation*, 8th ed., by C. R. Swanson, et al. Boson: McGraw Hill, 584–625. See esp. The Hacker Profile and The Computer Criminal Profile, 610–613.

Thieme, R. 2001. Profile of a Profiler. *Information Security* 4:4 (April): 90–96 (Interview of William L. Tafoya).

Thomas, D., and B. D. Loader. 2000. *Cybercrime: Law Enforcement, Security and Surveillance in the Information Age*. London: Routledge.

Turco, R. 1998. *Closely Watched Shadows: A Profile of the Hunted and the Hunter*. Bookpartners.

Van Hasselt, V. B., and M. Hersen, eds. 1998. *Handbook of Psychological Approaches with Violent Offenders*. New York: Plenum Publishing.

Vorpagel, R. 1998. *Profiles in Murder*. New York: Plenum Publishing.

Waxman, H. S. 2003. Interview, Cyberpsychology Institute, Brandeis University (November 18) Waltham, MA.

Yochelson, S., and S. E. Samenow. 1976. *The Criminal Personality*, 3 vol. New York: Jason Aronson.

Web Sources

CSC. 2002. How CSC's Bill Tafoya Applies Creative Thinking to IT Security. Office of Homeland Security, Computer Sciences Corporation, Falls Church, VA. Online at: http://www.csc.com/features/2002/17.shtml.

Golubev, V. 2003. Criminalistic Characteristics of Cybercrimes' Committees. Online at: http://www.crime-research.org/eng/library/Golubev.mar.html.

Hulme, George V. 2003. The Mind of a Hacker. *Information Week*. Online at: www.informationweek.com/story/showArticle.jhtml?articleID=16000606.

Interpol European Working Group on Information Technology Crime. 2002. White Hat v. Black Hat. SC Infosec Opinionwire. Online at: http://www.infosecnews.com/opinion/2002/12/11_01.htm.

Journal of Cyberpsychology and Behavior. Online at: http://www.liebertpub.com/pagedisplay/Toc.asp?id=10.

Karnov, C., R. Landels, and D. Landels. 1994. Recombinant Culture: Crime in the Digital Network. Online at: http://www.cpsr.org/privacy.

Kilger, M. 2000. Determining When Something Is NOT Random. The Smoo Group IDS (July 25). Online at: http://www.shmoo.com/mail/ids/jul00/msg00135.shtml.

Langer, W. C., et al. 1943. A Psychological Analysis of Adolph Hitler: His Life and Legend. Report Prepared for the Office of Strategic Services, Washington, D.C. Online at: http://www1.ca.nizkor.org/hweb/people/h/hitler-adolf/oss-papers/text/profile-index.html.

Lemos, R. 2004. MyDoom Variant Targets Microsoft. *New York Times* (January 28). Online at: http://www.nytimes.com/cnet/CNET_2100-7355_3-5149504.html.

LSU. 2003. Research on the Profiling Problem in Cybersecurity and Anti-Terrorism. Peter P. Chen, Principal Investigator, Louisiana State University. Online at: http://www.lsu.edu/ncsrt/ncsrt/ncsrt_cybersecurity.htm.

Neumann, P. G. 1996. The RISKS Digest. 18:26 (July 19). Online at: http://catless.ncl.ac.uk/Risks/18.26.html#subj1.

Neurotechnology Research, Brain Mapping Center, University of California at Los Angeles. Online at: http://www.neurology.ucla.edu/brainmap.htm.

Psynapse Technologies. 2003. Checkmate. Intrusion Prevention System. Online at: http://www.psynapse.com.

Rogers, M. 1999. Psychology of Hackers: Steps Toward a New Taxonomy. Online at: http://escape.ca/~mkr/.

Roy, G. nd. Plot Summary for Blade Runner (1982). Online at: http://www.imdb. com/title/tt0083658/plotsummary.

Saita, A. 2001. Hacker Psychology. Information Security (June). Online at: http://infosecuritymag.techtarget.com/articles/june01/features_hacker_ psychology.shtml.

Scripps-Howard. 1996. How David Kaczynski Came to Realize Brother Might Be Unabomber. Sacbee. Online at: http://www.unabombertrial.com/archive/ 1996/041096-4.html.

Thieme, R. 2001. Profile of a Profiler. *Information Security* 4:4(April): 90–96. Online at: http://infosecuritymag.techtarget.com/articles/april01/features_q&a.shtml.

Verton, D. 2001. Analysis: Insiders a Major Security Threat. CNN.com. Online at: http://www.cnn.com/2001/TECH/industry/07/11/insider.threat.idg/?related.

Witkin, G. 1997. Did the FBI Ignore the "Tafoya Profile"? *U. S. News & World Report* (November 17): 24. Online at: http://www.usnews.com/usnews/issue/97117/ 17unab.htp.

Acknowledgements

Appreciation is expressed for the invaluable contributions of Max Kilger, Terry Gudaitis, and David J. Icove for their ideas, suggestions, and inspiration with respect to the assessment of the behavior of computer abusers. Thanks are also owed to Mark Brenzinger and Wayne A. Johnson for their input in the collaboration of an earlier albeit unpublished effort, the focus of which was the articulation of noncomputer crime profiling.

Investigative Strategy and Utilities

4

DEPUTY ROSS E. MAYFIELD

I.   Introduction

The purpose of this chapter is to acquaint the reader with an investigative strategy that has evolved through the investigation of numerous cases at a number of police and sheriff's departments. This strategy is not the only one in use for computer crime investigations — it is simply one that has worked for me and many of my students. The strategy is focused on the minimum steps and effort required to successfully clear criminal cases where critical evidence is associated with computer usage or storage. Although this strategy evolved in the criminal investigation environment, I have successfully used elements of it in civil and corporate investigations. Utilities used by the computer crime investigator will be referred to in functional terms, because specific tools and utilities are in a period of rapid development and change. Part of the essence of this chapter is to demonstrate that a growing percentage of ordinary crimes have evidence in computer environments, and that computer crime presently involves policing in a rapidly changing technological environment. Case examples will be provided to illustrate these points. Mayfield's Paradox will be presented to establish that the determined computer crime investigator can make it unrealistically expensive for a criminal to deny the investigator access to a system.

The computer crime investigative strategy presented here can be summarized as follows:

1. Determine whether there is probable cause that a specific crime has been committed.
2. Determine what jurisdiction has authority to investigate the case.
3. Gather intelligence about the case.
4. Determine the critical success factors to close the case.
5. Gather critical evidence about the case.
6. Prepare exhibits, findings, and reports for prosecutors.
7. Provide expert testimony, if needed.

At the time of this publication, large backlogs of cases exist where critical evidence is associated with computers. For example, a large Southern California police department currently has a backlog of over 6,000 identity theft cases — most of which are likely to involve computer evidence and records. In a time of law enforcement triage, it is hoped that the strategy presented here may be of some use to investigators clearing cases.

II.   The Growing Importance of Computer Forensic Investigations

The North Hollywood shoot-out case is a textbook example of how computer forensic investigation is becoming an important factor in ordinary crime investigation. A television docudrama called "44 Minutes" has been produced about this case. In this case, two gunmen dressed in full body armor robbed a Bank of America branch in North Hollywood, California. The Los Angeles police department (LAPD) responded, eventually killing both suspects after a 44-minute gun battle. In short, this was a low-technology bank robbery case in which both suspects were already dead.

The LAPD robbery homicide division performed the follow-up investigation of this case. While serving as an LAPD reserve officer I was assigned to perform the computer forensic examination of computer equipment taken from the location where the suspects were believed to be living. The equipment consisted of a 286-based PC, a 386-based PC, a 486-based PC, and a laptop. During the examination of these computers for evidence, it was determined that one of the suspects was an avid computer user and programmed in C++. Spread across the different generations of computers was a large amount of information in a continuous pattern of file dates. However, this pattern of continuous usage stopped on the 486 PC on a certain date nearly a year earlier. This seemed inconsistent to me, so I asked my partner to find out whether there were any other events in the case associated with this abrupt stoppage of computer activity. My partner discovered that the day after the computer entries stopped, the suspects had committed a previous bank robbery and had gotten away with close to $1 million each.

I surmised that, based on the pattern discovered during the computer forensics, if this suspect had $1 million in cash, he would not be using the 486 PC. The suspect would be using a high-end Pentium PC, and the pattern of continued usage would be continued on that PC. Since no such PC was found at the search warrant site, I concluded that the suspects were not living at the site of the search warrant, contrary to what had been previously thought.

The commander of the Robbery Homicide Division later confirmed that this supposition was correct, and, because of this supposition, detectives were sent back to the site to talk to the neighbors. The neighbors reported that the suspects were only seen occasionally collecting the mail and then leaving. It was a safe house. The follow-up investigation was refocused on finding where the suspects actually lived. Not only was their primary residence discovered, but more safe house locations were found as well.

In conclusion, this case was a low-technology bank robbery in which both suspects were already dead; however, computer forensic investigation played a significant role in the follow-up investigation.

III. Computer Crime Investigations Viewed as a System

For the purposes of this chapter, a *system* is defined as a process consisting of inputs, to which operations or value-added activities are performed, and outputs. For computer crime investigations the inputs are cases that come from:

1. Internal investigations — Police internal-affairs investigations are one example of cases in the internal investigations input category. Most computer crime investigations conducted by corporate security are of this type.
2. Police reports from citizen and business criminal complaints — This category typically supplies the largest number of cases to process for a law enforcement computer crime investigation unit.
3. Case referrals from other agencies — These cases are typically from another law enforcement agency that has taken a police report criminal complaint and determined that another agency has jurisdiction.
4. Cases from department proactive investigations and stings — A typical example of this case input category type is one in which a department's detective division has one of its officer's pose as a 13-year-old in an Internet chat room to obtain violations from preferential offenders.

After the case is input for a department, it is assigned to a detective or computer crime investigator.

IV. Is There a Crime?

The first step of this strategy is for investigators to make their own determination of whether there is reasonable cause to believe that one or more specific crimes have been committed. In practice, it is usually very obvious from the case that a crime has occurred, but if a specific violation has not been identified, it is time to close the case and move on to the next one. For example, let's take a case where it is alleged that a suspect gained unauthorized access to a victim's computer account but did not commit fraud, theft, or vandalism. If the state's computer crime law reads that unauthorized access is not a crime unless fraud, theft, or vandalism occurred, then what the suspect has done is not a crime. Therefore, the investigator does not have probable cause to continue the case investigation.

V.   Who Has Jurisdiction?

Determining who has jurisdiction in interstate or international Internet cases is not always easy. This is also true in determining the lead agency for a multijurisdictional cooperative investigation. Prosecutors can be a valuable reference in case of doubt. If an investigator determines that their agency does not have jurisdiction for a case, then the case should be referred to the proper agency and the next case started.

VI.   Gathering Intelligence about the Case

Having established that a crime has been committed and that the investigator's agency has jurisdiction, the next step in this investigative strategy is to gather enough intelligence about the circumstances of the case for the investigator to decide what are the critical success factors of the case. The type of intelligence gathered in this step varies greatly depending on what category of crime is being investigated, but, regardless of the type of case, two tools are recommended: a chronological case log and a large case board.

The *chronological case log* is simply a record where each investigative action is listed according to date, time, action, and result. This log can be written on paper or maintained in an electronic file, and the categories of the entries can be tailored to the investigator's department needs or policies. This log is often helpful in discovering clues in a case, and can be useful in mentally refocusing on the case when the investigator is working multiple cases at the same time. The log also becomes a source for creating findings, of fact, summarizing investigative reports, analyzing evidence and using as a reference in testimony.

Figure 4.1   Example case board.

A large *case board* can be a chalkboard, white board, or large piece of paper on the wall where case intelligence information can be written, drawn, and posted to view. It can serve as an intelligence collection point when multiple investigators are working different leads on the same case. It is also helpful in demonstrating status and progress to supervisors. The case board serves as a tool in discovering associations between seemingly unrelated intelligence entries of the case. In my experience, the essence of most cases has come together on the case board during the intelligence phase of an investigation.

The type of intelligence gathered varies by the crime category being investigated. Examples might include the following:

- Closed-source information on suspects from the Department of Motor Vehicles (DMV), criminal history databases, military records, or similar source
- Open-source information about suspects obtained from Internet search engines and commercial databases
- Witness statements
- Suspect interview results

- Informant statements
- Addresses
- Internet domain registration
- Web site or file transfer protocol (FTP) site information
- Results from network scanning such as host IP addresses, open ports, DNS (domain name service) tables, operating systems in use, and network topology maps
- Internet satellite photos of the crime scene, suspect's business site, or site to be raided
- Employee phone extension lists
- Employment history
- Organizational charts

Typically, the more intelligence information the investigator can gather, log, and place on the case board, the better. Intelligence from making phone calls, using data terminals, and searching the Internet is surprisingly quick and easy to obtain. In many cases, I have been able to draw a complete topology map of a suspect's network from remote network scanning alone.

Three examples follow to show some material appropriate for a case board. For network intelligence I first focus on domain name registration with registers such as Network Solutions. There are a variety of Web page whois tools, but I usually use the Linux command whois. This is the result of a domain registration lookup on mayfield.org:

```
[Querying whois.publicinterestregistry.net]

[whois.publicinterestregistry.net]

NOTICE: Access to .ORG WHOIS information is provided
to assist persons in determining the contents of a
domain name registration record in the PIR registry
database. The data in this record is provided by
Public Interest Registry for informational purposes
only, and PIR does not guarantee its accuracy. This
service is intended only for query-based access. You
agree that you will use this data only for lawful
purposes and that, under no circumstances will you
use this data to: (a) allow, enable, or otherwise
support the transmission by e-mail, telephone, or
facsimile of mass unsolicited, commercial advertising
or solicitations to entities other than the data
recipient's own existing customers; or (b) enable high
volume, automated, electronic processes that send
queries or data to the systems of Registry Operator
or any ICANN-Accredited Registrar, except as reasonably
necessary to register domain names or modify existing
```

```
Domain ID:D61511-LROR
Domain Name:MAYFIELD.ORG
Created On:08-Feb-1996 05:00:00 UTC
Last Updated On:12-Dec-2003 21:29:16 UTC
Expiration Date:09-Feb-2009 05:00:00 UTC
Sponsoring Registrar:R42-LROR
Status:OK
Registrant ID:0-691272-Gandi
Registrant Name:Ross Mayfield
Registrant Organization:Ross Mayfield
Registrant Street1:270 N. Canon Dr.
Registrant City:Beverly Hills
Registrant Postal Code:90210
Registrant Country:US
Registrant Email:ross@espgroup.net
Admin ID:AR41-GANDI
Admin Name:CONTACT NOT AUTHORITATIVE see
http://www.gandi.net/whois
Admin Organization:GANDI SARL
Admin Street1:see also whois.gandi.net
Admin City:Paris
Admin Postal Code:75003
Admin Country:FR
Admin Phone:+33.1
Admin Email:support@gandi.net
Tech ID:AR41-GANDI
Tech Name:CONTACT NOT AUTHORITATIVE see
http://www.gandi.net/whois
Tech Organization:GANDI SARL
Tech Street1:see also whois.gandi.net
Tech City:Paris
Tech Postal Code:75003
Tech Country:FR
Tech Phone:+33.1
Tech Email:support@gandi.net
Name Server:FULL1.GANDI.NET
Name Server:FULL2.GANDI.NET
```

Although most suspects try to hide as much registration information as possible, they must provide an administrative contact, technical contact, and at least two name servers.

I then check to see whether the name servers will allow a zone transfer. There are many tools to do this, but I generally use dig or nslookup from a Linux system. For example, the DNS records retrieved remotely for search.org are as follows:

```
[search.org]
  search.org.          SOA    ns1.search.org
hostmaster.search.org. (55 86400 3600 604800 86400)
  search.org.          NS     ns1.search.org
  search.org.          NS     ns2.search.org
  search.org.          MX     10  mail.search.org
  search.org.          MX     15  sgisrv1.search.org
  search.org.          A      64.162.18.2
  mail                 A       64.162.18.2
  ns1                  A      64.162.18.2
  ns2                  A      64.162.18.20
  www                  A      64.162.18.35
  searchweb            A      64.162.18.12
  listserver           A      64.162.18.2
  sgiserver7           A      64.162.18.25
  www.icac             A      64.162.18.42
  sgisrv1              A      64.162.18.191
  webmail              A      64.162.18.191
  www.aindex           A      64.162.18.36
  www.jtrc             A      64.162.18.30
  www.it               A      64.162.18.37
  www.integration      A      64.162.18.38
  webreports           A      64.162.18.205
  www.nibrs            A      64.162.18.39
  www.infoexchange     A      64.162.18.40
  sgiserver1           A      64.162.18.10
  blackbox             A      64.162.18.5
  sgi2k1               A      64.162.18.20
  news                 A      64.162.18.21
  search.org.          SOA    ns1.search.org
hostmaster.search.org. (55 86400 3600 604800 86400)
```

If any of your suspect's name servers are configured to allow you to get this information, it is very useful for your case board.

Once the range of IP numbers of investigative interest is determined, the IP numbers can be checked in the registry of Internet numbers to see who owns them. I again use whois on a Linux system for this. An example of the whois lookup on the dynamic IP address where www.mayfield.org is running at the time of this writing is as follows:

```
[Querying whois.arin.net]
[whois.arin.net]
Adelphia Cable Communications ADELPHIA-CABLE-6
  (NET-68-232-0-0-1)
                    68.232.0.0 - 68.235.255.255
Adelphia 68-234-224-0-Z7 (NET-68-234-224-0-1)
                    68.234.224.0 - 68.234.255.255
```

```
# ARIN WHOIS database, last updated 2004-01-19 19:15
# Enter ? for additional hints on searching ARIN's
WHOIS database.
```

I would typically use a tool to ping the IP range of interest to determine whether any hosts are answering, and then I would perform a port scan on the hosts to determine what services might be running. At the time of writing, it's not possible for law enforcement to exploit security vulnerabilities of services running on the suspect's hosts for further intelligence without a search warrant. However, this restriction does not usually apply to agencies gathering national security intelligence.

In short, the goal of the intelligence step of the investigation is to place data related to the case in front of the investigator in a format by which conclusions can be drawn as to what further steps are needed in the investigation to close the case.

VI. Determining the Critical Success Factors for a Case

For the purposes of this chapter, critical success factors are defined as the minimum number of things that must be done, and done well, to successfully close the case. To successfully close a case, the investigator needs to define what success is for the case. In some investigations success might be defined as demonstrating the facts of the case to a judge, jury, or decision maker. Success may also be defined in terms of handoff to a prosecutor or in obtaining convictions. In one case investigated, success was defined as being able to remove and prosecute a mainframe system administrator for embezzlement without the victim's online gaming system going down. This was the first case I worked where protecting the victim's computer system from the suspect had a higher priority than convicting the suspect. If the victim's mainframe gaming system were to have gone down during the case, over half of an entire state's online gaming machines would have become inoperable. Defining what will allow the case to be successfully closed clarifies the investigator's mission. In the this example, the critical success factors were:

1. Prevent the suspect from sabotaging the system by arresting him and shutting off his access to the system.
2. Immediately back up all data necessary for the operation of the system so that the system could be restored if it did go down.
3. Find evidence of the alleged embezzlement in the system transaction records.
4. Document the evidence in an easy-to-understand format.

ering Critical Evidence

time spent by a computer crime investigator is devoted to collecting documenting evidence. The intelligence phase of the investigation
allows the investigator to make good guesses as to where and in what form
electronic evidence may exist. This information is necessary for search warrants and the subpoena of records. Some examples of where critical evidence
might be located are as follows:

- Home and office computer storage media — hard disks, floppy disks, magnetic tape, memory sticks, optical disks, and other storage devices
- Voice mail or answering machines
- Newsgroup postings
- Fax machines
- Personal digital assistants (PDAs)
- Off-site backup — for example, most businesses store data backup media at an off-site location
- User account logs and records — e-mail, Hotmail, eBay, Yahoo, and instant messenger
- Remote server logs — chat, Web, and others
- Internet access provider logs
- Network storage — can be based on a local area network (LAN) or the Internet

It is very important to obtain computer logs as quickly as possible, such
as which subscriber to an Internet service provider had a certain IP address
at a specific time, because many businesses do not keep this information long.

After getting a search warrant signed, the investigator is ready to execute
the raid.

IX. The Raid

When executing a search warrant, the priorities for the computer crime
investigator are as follows:

1. Public and officer safety
2. Protect and preserve the court's evidence
3. Accomplish these objectives with the minimum intrusion into the suspect's rights, privacy, and business

There are three basic strategies that can be used to secure evidence at a
site:

Figure 4.2   A typical computer crime scene during a search warrant raid.

1. Verify that the evidence is present, document it, and leave.
2. Make a forensic copy of the data storage media and leave with the forensic copy.
3. Seize the computer hardware and media for later examination in a computer forensic laboratory.

Most experts recommend using the third strategy for all cases when possible.

An example of the first strategy — document evidence and leave — was an Internet obscene-pornography case investigated in Los Angeles. This was a membership Web site where members joined using a credit card payment and then were given an access code to an area of the Web server that contained obscene pornography. The investigators used an undercover identity and credit card to join the membership and enter the Web site. The obscene pornography images were photographed on the investigators' screen and saved to files; hash codes of the files were created; and the IP address of the server was logged. After obtaining a search warrant, the server location was raided and the server shut down. The server computer was then booted from the investigators' examination utility disk. A search utility was used to search the server's hard drive for the undercover credit card number. The investigators' account and credit card transactions were found on the suspect's server. This information was photographed on the screen and copied to a file. The search utility was also used to find the obscene-pornography files, which were also photographed and copied to a file, and hash codes were generated for the files. The server was not removed from the site. A forensic copy of the media was not made. The suspect was arrested on the basis of this evidence alone, and a conviction resulted. In short, establishing that the suspect owned and operated the server and that the violations were documented on the server were sufficient for this case.

This first strategy may be the investigator's only choice in situations where the computer system has terabytes of disk storage and cannot be forensically copied in a realistic amount of time, or if the amount of system hardware is so large that it cannot be realistically booked into an evidence room. It has the disadvantage that the investigator is working without a safety net, and if something goes wrong and the data is corrupted or lost, the investigator has no fallback position. Additionally, this strategy limits the time available to search for evidence to the amount of time the raid team can remain at the site. Using this strategy, the raid team must include members who are technically capable of dealing with the hardware, operating systems, software, and surprises encountered at the search warrant site. Evidence obtained through this strategy may also be open to more legal challenges by the defense than evidence processed through a forensic laboratory.

An example of the second strategy — make a forensic copy and leave — was a case involving a Web site–hosting company. In this case, multiple legitimate business Web sites were located on the same Web server along with one Web site containing obscenity violations. A critical success factor for this case was to collect the evidence necessary for the case without unduly impacting the legitimate Web sites hosted by this business. To accomplish this, the investigator obtained a search warrant, raided the site, shut down the server, and used a hard drive duplication utility to create a forensic copy of the server's hard drive. Then, the server was returned to service with minimum downtime for the legitimate Web sites. The evidence necessary for the case was successfully recovered from the forensic copy in a police forensic laboratory.

This second strategy has the advantages of limited disruption of the site and minimal amount of hardware to be accounted for and booked into evidence. In practice, an investigator using this strategy might wish to make two forensic copies of the hard drive — one copy to place back in service and one copy for forensic examination — and book the original hard drive into evidence. This strategy has the disadvantage that some of the suspect's software may be difficult to operate without the specific hardware of the suspect's computer. For example, if the suspect has multiple disks using a RAID controller board, the investigator is likely to need the same controller.

The third strategy — seize the computer hardware and media for later examination — is called "bag and tag" by seasoned investigators. This is because the computer, cables, and peripherals are labeled (tagged); disassembled into manageable pieces; placed in bags; and transported from the site for later examination. The evidence is then recovered in a computer forensic laboratory.

This third strategy has the disadvantage that it requires a lot of effort to take down, transport, and perhaps reassemble some systems. There is also some risk of damage to the system during handling and transport. There is sometimes a long backlog of cases waiting their turn to be processed in the computer forensic laboratory. These considerations are usually outweighed by the advantage of being able to do the evidence recovery in a controlled environment and having the suspect's hardware for any device-dependent software. The investigator also has the luxury of being able to spend more time recovering the evidence than is usually available at a search warrant site.

X.   Processing: Critical Evidence Recovery from Electronic Media

Regardless of which strategy an investigator uses to secure evidence at a site, the investigator still has the tasks of identifying and recovering evidence stored as electronic media. One example source for systems and assistance in this step is CyberForensic Associates, of Garden Grove, California (www.cyberforensic.com). It is important for the investigator to keep the chronological case log up to date during this phase of the investigation. At the time of this publication, most cases will involve critical evidence recovered from computer hard drive examination. It is beyond the scope of this chapter to cover the subject of forensic hard drive examination in detail; however, a computer crime investigator should be familiar with the following concepts and utilities associated with them.

1.   Drive Duplication Utilities

This is software that makes a forensic copy of a hard drive. It is critical that this utility makes an exact copy of the drive at the binary level and has been tested and proven to do so. Whenever possible, the investigator does not examine the original disk because of the possibility that the drive might crash or be unintentionally altered by the investigator.

2.   Search Utilities

Search utilities allow an investigator to find occurrences of a pattern of characters on electronic media. Examples might be a credit card number or the word *insurance* in a homicide case. The search utility allows the investigator to find all occurrences of the search pattern on the media. This helps the investigator to zero in on information of possible relevance to the case. One of the tasks of the investigator is to create a list of search words or patterns relevant to the case to be searched for during the evidence recovery process.

3.   Graphic and File Viewer Utilities

There are a number of programs that allow an investigator to view the information on electronic media. These utilities format the binary information on the media into a picture or document so that it is recognizable. The best of these utilities will allow the investigator to view virtually any file type in its intended display format. The kinds of files of interest to the investigator vary depending on the case type. For example, in an obscenity case the files of interest are likely to be picture format files.

4.   Recovering Deleted Evidence

When a suspect deletes information on a computer, it does not disappear. In most operating systems the deletion process just makes the space on the disk that the information occupied available for other information. Some operating systems use the concept of a recycle bin for deletion from which deleted files can be recovered. File recovery utilities allow the investigator to retrieve the deleted information if it has not been overwritten by other information. If the deleted information has been overwritten, it is still possible to recover the overwritten information by disassembling the hard drive and recovering the overwritten data directly from the magnetic disk media with specialized lab equipment. At the time of publication, this magnetic-force scanning recovery process is not typically available or realistic for law enforcement investigations. There are also file-overwriting utilities that, instead of using the operating system's deletion process, directly overwrite the information on the disk with a binary pattern up to 35 successive times. If properly used by a suspect, these file-overwriting utilities can make the information unrecoverable.

5.   Disk Utilities

Evidence can sometimes exist on a hard drive in areas not used by the file system. *Slack space* refers to an unused area of a disk after the end of one file, before the start of the next file. This area can contain information from a previously deleted file. Information may also exist on the disk in unallocated space, parts of the disk marked as bad sectors, or in other partition types. Disk utilities allow the investigator to examine these areas.

6.   Hash or Checksum Utilities

A hash or checksum utility uses every bit of a file to compute a unique result for the file. The checksum result for a file can be used to see whether any bits in the file have changed. If just one bit of the file changes, approximately half of the bits of the checksum will change. This is useful for the investigator to identify files and to demonstrate that a file has or has not changed. One commonly used checksum algorithm is named MD5. There is a database of MD5 checksums of known system files and known child pornography violations. An investigator can compute MD5 checksums for all the files on a disk being examined and then compare them to the database. The suspect system files that match do not need to be examined further, because there is a very high probability that they are just operating system files. If any of the MD5 checksums match against the known child pornography database, there is a very high probability that the investigator has found a violation.

7.   Passwords and Encrypted Media

Encryption is a process of scrambling information so that it is not recognizable without descrambling it. It can also be used for authenticating information and verifying that information is correct. Passwords and encryption are obstacles for the computer crime investigator that can be difficult to overcome if the investigator is not prepared for them. Password crackers and cryptanalysis utilities are commercially available that employ a variety of algorithms to gain access to the system or encrypted information. The success rate of these utilities varies depending on the type of encryption used and how good a password or key was chosen by the suspect.

A more reliable way to deal with passwords and encryption is to recover the password or the encryption key from the suspect by using the system. This can be accomplished in several ways. (1) A hardware or software keystroke logger can be installed on the suspect's computer. This records all of the keystrokes made by the suspect on the computer keyboard, including passwords and encryption keys. Both hardware and software keystroke loggers are readily available to investigators. (2) A surveillance pin camera can also be installed over the suspect's keyboard and good guesses can be made about passwords and encryption keys from the recorded movement of the suspect's fingers on the keyboard. However, before employing these methods, the investigator needs to determine whether a federal wiretap warrant is required. It is sometimes possible to recover encryption keys from RAM memory.

8.   Evidence Recovery from RAM Memory

One case I investigated involved organized-crime gambling violations. The intelligence phase of the investigation, through an informant, indicated that bets were being taken by telephone and entered into a computer employing a RAM drive. *RAM* refers to random access memory on computer chips and is different than magnetically stored information on the hard drive. RAM is usually composed of junctions that hold a binary one or zero as long as power is supplied to the memory chip. A RAM drive is a utility program that uses a portion of the computer's chip memory as if it were a disk to store information. The suspect believed that if there was a police raid, they could turn off the power to the computer and destroy all evidence of the crime. One critical success factor of this case was to raid the location and get to the computers before the suspects could remove power from them. This was accomplished by using a utility program on a floppy disk to copy the contents of all of the RAM to a zip disk plugged into the parallel port of the suspect's computer. The betting evidence was later recovered from the zip disk.

Most people believe that when RAM is powered down it is not possible to recover the information stored in it. However, equipment does exist that can determine what state the RAM was in when it was powered down, depending on how much time has elapsed since the power was removed, the temperature of the chip since power was removed, and how long the memory cell was in the same state before power was removed. This equipment is not readily available to law enforcement at the time of this publication. For the time being, if evidence critical to the investigation is in RAM, the investigator needs to get to the computer while it is powered on.

9.   Forensic Suite Software

There are a few software packages available that attempt to combine all of the investigative utility functions into one program. These programs can duplicate drives, search media, format, view files, recover information, and even help keep the case log. One of the biggest advantages to these forensic software packages is the availability of training and support for the investigator. However, an investigator who uses one of these evidence recovery software suites still needs to be aware of alternative utilities in the event a situation occurs that the software is not designed to handle.

10.   Network Drive Storage

On networked computer systems, the evidence of interest to the investigator may turn out to be stored anywhere on the network. This greatly increases the amount of intelligence the investigator needs in order to make a good guess on the location for the search warrant, because the evidence might not be in the same location as the suspect. Additionally, Internet services exist where someone can use disk storage space on a remote system as though it were a local hard drive. With this technology it is only a matter of time until some investigator executes a warrant at a site of suspected criminal activity and finds that the critical evidence is stored through the Internet on a server in another country under a crypto-analytically secure protocol.

XII.   The Investigator as a Determined Intruder

In the early 1990s I was working on a bulletin-board system and pilot Internet access for my students at Pepperdine University. During this project I came to the realization that only a subset of humanity could be prevented from gaining access to an information system, and only a subset of humanity could be successfully given access to an information system. This is because of system cost. Paradoxically, in terms of system cost, the most determined intruder is the same as the least capable user. It takes infinite money to stop the most determined intruder, and it takes infinite money to give access to the least capable user.

The computer crime investigator is a determined intruder with a long time horizon, significant technical resources, and the funding of a government. It is very expensive to deny an investigator access to the information assets of a system. Mayfield's Paradox demonstrates that if the investigator is determined enough, it is unrealistically expensive to deny the investigator access to a system. Determination gets evidence.

XIII.   Mayfield's Paradox

Mayfield's Paradox states that to keep everyone out of an information system requires an infinite amount of money, and to get everyone onto an information system also requires infinite money, while costs between these extremes are relatively low. I first observed this paradox in 1991 and began to lecture audiences about it in 1993 after joining the LAPD. The paradox is depicted as a U-curve, where the cost of a system is on the vertical axis, and the percentage of humanity that can access the system is on the horizontal axis.

Acceptance of this paradox by the information security community was immediate, because it was consistent with the professional experiences of this group. Mayfield's Paradox points out that, at some point of the curve, additional security becomes unrealistically expensive. Conversely, at some point of the curve, it becomes unrealistically expensive to add additional users.

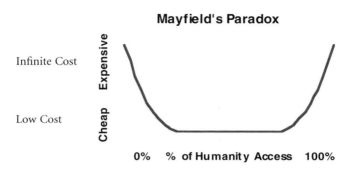

Percentage of Humanity That Can Access the System

These professionals began using this model to rationalize budgetary decisions both for security expenditures and for additional user capacity. Mayfield's Paradox is a simple concept model predicting real-world observations. The implications are that systems administrators and information professionals will never be able to keep everyone out of their systems, and, paradoxically, they will never be able to get everyone on their systems either. The University of Southern California's Department of Mathematics has developed two independent mathematical proofs of Mayfield's Paradox. Information about Mayfield's Paradox is available at: http://www.mayfield.org.

XIV.   Chain of Custody

Once the critical evidence has been recovered, the investigator must be able to demonstrate that evidence was accurate when recovered, and be able to demonstrate the chain of possession of the evidence from the time it was recovered up to the time it was introduced as evidence to the court.

XV.   Exhibits, Reports, and Findings

Earlier in this chapter the concept of viewing computer crime investigation as a system with case inputs, processing, and outputs was introduced. The output of the computer crime forensic investigation is decisive evidence for the court in the form of exhibits, reports, and findings. It is important for the investigator to communicate the facts of the case in the simplest terms. Each fact and conclusion requires supporting exhibits. The investigators chronological case log is a valuable resource for writing case reports.

XVI. Expert Testimony

It has been my experience that if the investigator does a good job on the investigation, there is no need to testify on the case, because the suspects agree to a plea bargain rather than go to trial in the face of overwhelming evidence. However, the investigator needs to be prepared to be called by the prosecution as an expert witness.

To be qualified as an expert, the court must find that the investigator has knowledge or expertise beyond that of a layperson, or that the investigator possesses information that can clarify the issues before the court. The investigator may wish to keep a one-page summary of his or her qualifications, sometimes referred to as a hero sheet, ready to give to the court for this purpose.

The real value of the investigator as an expert witness to the prosecution is that the investigator's opinion can be entered in the court. Opinions can differ, and the defense will find one that differs, if possible. There are many tips for the investigator to be an effective expert witness that are beyond the scope of this chapter. A good investigator can find them on the Internet.

XVII. Summary

In this chapter a computer crime investigative strategy has been presented consisting of the following steps:

1. Determine whether there is probable cause that a specific crime has been committed.
2. Determine what jurisdiction has authority to investigate the case.
3. Gather intelligence about the case.
4. Determine the critical success factors to close the case.
5. Gather critical evidence about the case.
6. Prepare exhibits, findings, and reports for prosecutors.
7. Provide expert testimony, if needed.

This strategy has tried to focus on the minimum steps and efforts to successfully clear criminal cases where critical evidence is associated with computer usage or storage. Although this strategy evolved in the criminal investigation environment, elements of it have successfully been applied in civil and corporate investigations. Utilities used by the computer crime investigator were presented in functional terms, because specific tools and utilities are in a period of rapid development and change. Case examples were presented to illustrate that a growing percentage of ordinary crimes have evidence in computer environments, and that computer crime presently involves policing in a rapidly changing technological environment. Mayfield's Paradox established that the determined computer crime investigators could make it unrealistically expensive for anyone to deny them access to a system.

Credits

The author wishes to thank the Los Angeles Police Department, the Torrance Police Department, the Redondo Beach Police Department, the Marion County Sheriff's Department, the Nevada Gaming Control Board Enforcement Division, and others as sources for examples in this chapter and/or for their review and comments.

Computer Forensics & Investigation: The Training Organization

5

FRED B. COTTON

I. Overview

The training of forensic personnel is of critical importance to agencies faced with the ongoing investigation and prosecution of computer-related crime, as well as to private sector security personnel who are tasked with private investigations that may result in job actions or criminal charges. The development of a comprehensive training organization is not a trivial task and must be fully supported at the highest levels of the organization for it to be effective. The components of a successful training organization are the topic of this chapter.

The rapidly changing technology sector produces new variations of products every day. Any of those products can become critical evidence in a technical investigation depending on the manner in which they are utilized to commit a crime or other unauthorized act. Staying abreast of the changing technology environment is a constant challenge to the computer crime investigator or forensic examiner. This need for updated information requires that the training organization constantly research technology advances and look at them from the perspective of an investigator or forensic examiner.

II. Hands-on Training Environment

Adults learn best by facing challenges and by solving problems in a hands-on training environment that closely simulates their real-world job skills. This simple fact is lost on many training organizations that attempt to teach technical subjects through lecture and theory without the benefit of practical hands-on exercises.

The development of a hands-on training environment requires capital expense on the part of the training organization in the form of computers, networks, hardware, software, maintenance, and upgrades over time. Although expensive initially, the benefits of such a capital outlay far outweigh the initial and ongoing costs.

When considering a hands-on training environment, the training organization should closely evaluate the type and level of training being considered. Advanced forensic training courses or courses involving highly technical subject matter, such as intrusion investigation, require sophisticated networked computer systems and security appliances that can be accessed by students and are not a part of the production information infrastructure of the training organization itself. This setup protects the production environment from damage while still affording students access to the inner workings of an enterprise system.

Equipment can be purchased, leased, or donated. Regardless of the acquisition method, it will require ongoing maintenance for both the hardware and software components. If a piece of equipment or a software program is a critical part of a particular course, then that course budget must provide for its ongoing maintenance and upgrades over the life cycle of the equipment and for the life cycle of the course, respectively.

It is all too easy to become hardware rich in a training environment by purchasing hardware so specialized that it cannot be used across multiple programs. Although there are times when limited-use equipment is critical to the development of a core skill set for a trainee, training organizations must look for flexibility in the equipment they purchase. The nature of the training the organization conducts will dictate the type of equipment they purchase. A fixed training center has the advantage of being able to use large systems with a lot of capability in the form of multiple drives, complex networks, and multiple security appliances in fixed racks. If the training center is to be portable, then weight, size, and connectivity become more of an issue. Consider the intended venue prior to the purchase of a computer training center and select equipment that is best suited for deployment in that venue.

The development of a mobile training center adds several dimensions to the equipment specification process. The use of laptop computers can limit the degree to which forensic training can be delivered at remote sites but may be fine for investigative training courses. The use of Shuttle-type systems may be better suited to mobile forensic training. These units are, however, bulkier and require a larger shipping system. The additional bulk and shipping adds expense to the course that must be weighed against the enhanced hands-on capability.

Computers draw power from a wall circuit, and a computer laboratory draws a lot of power from a circuit. The power requirements of a 40-computer mobile training center must be closely estimated and a suitable site found that supports the space and power needs of such a center. When the presentation equipment, such as projectors, and the network equipment are added to the mix, the mobile lab may overwhelm the power available at the host site. These issues must be addressed ahead of time when choosing the remote site.

The training organization has a sizable investment in any mobile training center. Hotels and other venues may not have absolute control over staff access to large conference rooms and classrooms. Advanced arrangements must be made to address the security of the mobile equipment when it is on-site after hours. Rooms that have limited access and can be locked securely at night should be used during mobile training classes. It may also be advisable to hire overnight security for the equipment to prevent theft or damage.

Network connectivity is another concern when deploying mobile computer training facilities. Training organizations that utilize remote sites must carefully coordinate with the Internet service provider at the site to ensure appropriate connectivity and sufficient bandwidth for the mobile training operation. For most law enforcement investigative training classes, the issue of filters and restricted Internet access should also be addressed. Many Internet service providers servicing hotels and remote training sites use filters or firewalls that prevent access to objectionable areas of the Internet. It may be important as part of the training curriculum to have students access areas of the Internet where they will be doing their investigations. If so, the filters and firewall rules must be altered to allow such access. If done properly, mobile training centers can provide a platform for outreach to students who may not otherwise have the opportunity to receive hands-on computer investigative or forensic training.

The acquisition and configuration of equipment is secondary to the practical application of that equipment in the training environment. Having the proper equipment in place only provides the instructor with a platform for learning. The ways in which that platform is utilized in the learning process makes the difference between an effective training program and a static computer show.

Whenever skills are being taught to trainees, those skills should be reinforced with hands-on practical exercises designed to illustrate the practical application of the skill. A great deal of thought must go into the design and conduct of practical exercises to ensure that they are relevant and reflect problems being faced in the real job environment. Additionally, a series of integrated practical exercises should be used to help build and reinforce a set of skills that can later be deployed in the field.

It is never a good practice to use unreasonable or unsolvable practical exercises. This is particularly true when the exercise does not reflect scenarios likely to be encountered in the field. The practical exercise is a tool to help the trainee or student enhance their skill set and can be used very effectively when it is integrated into a building-block approach to attain the desired skill level. The "gotcha" or "ambush" practical exercise is rarely, if ever, useful unless the goal is to make the trainee or student shy away from a particular activity.

III. Course Design

The development of a comprehensive course map is of critical importance to today's technology crime investigator, forensic examiner, or other criminal justice professional. Each discipline has a set of core requirements that also apply across the other disciplines. Each discipline also has specialized requirements that apply to it alone. A course map provides a guide for integrated course development and lays out a long-term training strategy aimed at developing both general and discipline-specific skills and knowledge.

The first step in designing a course map is a comprehensive look at the specific job requirements of the trainee. The course designers must take the time to sit down with subject matter experts and practitioners in the field and have them describe the skills necessary to properly perform their job. The most common method of doing this analysis is through a facilitated meeting of subject matter experts who can articulate the daily requirements of their profession.

Once documented, the course design team can look at each required task and break it down into its core skills and knowledge elements. These elements can then be arranged in a presentation time line designed to teach core skills and knowledge in a logical order that builds upon basic concepts to develop increasingly advanced topics. Only then can the estimate of time be considered; the time necessary to develop the skills and knowledge satisfactorily dictates the length of a particular course and its place in the overall course map. Training organizations should not attempt to force training into preconceived time slots without ensuring that those time slots are sufficient to teach a particular set of skills and knowledge.

When considering a course map, it may be advantageous to review existing training programs and courses in view of the identified skills and knowledge required, then those courses and blocks can be integrated into the overall course map where appropriate. A training organization should concentrate course design resources on the development of training where a need exists as opposed to trying to duplicate courses that have already been developed by another training organization.

Feedback from the field is a critical component of the course design. A training organization should conduct a regular review of training currency in cooperation with subject matter experts in the field. A course design review committee composed of trainers, training managers, and practitioners should meet regularly to assess the effectiveness of the training program and the currency of the course map. A competent committee should review the curriculum and recommend modifications. Any modifications should be considered in light of their long-term relevancy to the core training program. Information needs that fall short of the long-term impact threshold should be addressed as part of a series of specialized training briefings or update training seminars.

IV. Specialized or Update Training

Technology development is rapid, and new technologies are constantly changing. Thousands of new products are introduced to the consumer markets each day, and many products find their way into criminal hands or are co-opted for criminal purposes. In spite of the many different new products being developed and brought to market, there are often underlying trends driving the development. Whenever a criminal use of technology can be identified as following one of the underlying trends, that trend should be considered as part of the core training requirements. Whenever a criminal use of a technology is emerging, it is best addressed initially through specialized or update training.

Specialized or update training can be described as a presentation of information about a new technology or crime trend that is emerging and has not matured. These presentations are generally not formal training courses but rather opportunities for practitioners to receive specific information about a new technology or updates on recent changes to existing technology that may impact investigations or forensic examinations. Many times, training is available from industry professionals familiar with specific technologies. Training may also be obtained by inviting other investigators or forensic examiners who have encountered the technology in the field to speak about their experiences. The training may consist of attendance at industry product training seminars and technical courses that are not designed by or conducted by the agency training organization.

Whenever outside training programs are used, care must be taken to assess the level of training being presented and its usefulness to the trainee.

This is often difficult because the curriculum is not always open for examination or review due to proprietary interests. Sometimes a facilitated meeting with a technology vendor that involves less formal presentation and more question and answer is more effective for those learning about a new technology.

The development and participation in a public-private sector partnership organization can also serve to assist training organizations in providing specialized or update training forums. Task forces such as the New York Electronic Crimes Task Force, funded through the United States Secret Service, use quarterly meetings to provide specialized or update training by inviting guest speakers from technology-related organizations to present information on emerging technologies. Follow-up question and answer time can provide a good information foundation upon which to conduct further research and delve deeper into a new technology or emerging crime trend.

Specialized or update training conferences are another good way to disseminate information to in-service personnel about new and emerging technologies and crime trends. Peer networking and access to experts in a conference setting provide the computer investigator or computer forensic examiner an opportunity to update their skills and knowledge of new or emerging technology and crime trends.

Case agent debriefing is a good way of providing source material for specialized or update training. Whenever practitioners are confronted with a new or emerging technology or crime trend, there is usually an individual or group of individuals who must take the initiative to develop a protocol for addressing the problem. Identifying these individuals and debriefing them on their solutions often produces valuable specialized or update training information. The experience of others, good or bad, is valued information for specialized or update training.

Suspect debriefings can also provide a wealth of information for update or specialized training. Many times, suspects who are convicted of a criminal offense involving a unique or emerging crime trend are willing to be debriefed as a condition of their sentence or probation. These debriefings can yield valuable insight into the methods of operation of criminals and assist training organizations in developing investigative training skills to combat the crime problem.

When conducted regularly, many of the new topics can be combined into specific tracks of interest. In this way, practitioners can be exposed to a wide variety of updates and specialized training that otherwise would not be included in their core skills training programs. If the new technology or emerging crime trend develops into a longer-term crime problem, the information gleaned through specialized or update training can form the basis for a more formalized addition to the course map and inclusion in the core training curriculum.

In any program where ongoing, specialized, or update training is conducted, the need for timely research is critical. Access to research material is required as well as having time and manpower available for the research component. If instructional staff is expected to conduct independent research, sufficient time must be allotted outside of the classroom to conduct and validate the research. Subscriptions to significant industry publications, legal resources, and databases applicable to the training under development are a key component to effective programs. If research assistance is available using staff research assistants or interns, the research must be closely supervised and validated before it is used in the training environment.

Regular exposure to information about emerging trends and new products provides the practitioner in the field the tools necessary to broaden their skills and knowledge and gain insight into changes affecting their blocks of instruction.

V.   Personnel

The key to any successful training operation is the selection of personnel. There are many people in the world who know voluminous technical data and information, but there are very few who can reduce technical data and information to understandable and *retainable* levels. This rare combination of skills is very difficult to assess in most formal hiring practices. It is critical that good trainers possess a high level of curiosity and thirst for knowledge about the topics they are to teach. Without a passionate interest, teaching becomes rote recital and uninspired.

When teaching technology crime topics, the synergy between instructors can have a dramatic impact on the students in the class. Merging instructors from diverse disciplines into teaching teams has proven to be a very effective approach not only for student learning but for instructor development as well. This is particularly true when the instructors work closely together on a full-time basis as part of the organization staff. The continuity of the training material presented is greatly improved and the credibility of the training course is greatly enhanced when a complete desirable skill set is represented across the instructor base where each instructor contributes a level of expertise to the instructional team in a specific discipline.

The diversity of skills cannot always be maintained on full-time staff in any training organization. It is therefore necessary and desirable to contract with independent instructors and practitioners outside the training organization to provide instructional services not available through the staff instructors. Training organizations can incorporate high-level and advanced instructional blocks into their programs through the use of outside experts.

The advantages are obvious, but the difficulties of these arrangements are sometimes subtle.

The difficulties associated with contract instructors involve two main issues: (1) continuity, and (2) availability. If not addressed, either of these issues can make or break a training program that relies too heavily upon outside nonstaff instructors.

Continuity refers to the smooth flow of learning for the student throughout the length of the training course. This is difficult to achieve when a contract instructor does not work closely with staff instructors to coordinate their instructional blocks. If the instructional staff is not familiar with the content of each other's blocks, the student receives a fragmented information flow that does not smoothly build upon previous learning blocks and can result in large gaps in the student's skill and knowledge. To overcome this limitation, contract instructors must communicate clearly with staff instructors and ensure that they fully cover the student learning objectives required of their respective blocks with a full understanding of how their block fits into the design of the overall course.

Availability is another critical issue when nonstaff instructors are utilized in a training program. Many of the best in any field have very busy schedules. This is particularly true when the nonstaff instructors are from environments such as law enforcement that require their availability for emergencies on short notice. Add to this the difficulty in finding qualified instructors in some critical disciplines, and the possibility of having depth in the instructional staff becomes very slim. Advanced planning and notice of instructional dates, times, and locations is always a good practice when employing contract instructors. It does not, however, guarantee their availability for your program. Contractual agreements are a more formal mechanism for addressing the issue of availability. Contracts still require careful crafting because they are legally binding on both parties in most cases.

Another staff concern for a good training organization is the clerical support for the organization. The clerical staff is responsible for keeping the flow of administrative tasks on time and at the proper location. A master calendar is a very important component that must be maintained by competent clerical staff. Everything must be planned around the start date for a particular course. Additionally, the clerical staff members are the first people encountered by the trainees and other clients. They must present a professional appearance and demeanor as well as be polite and helpful in all situations. Good clerical support can head off many potential problems before they become actual problems. Proper coordination of tasks and deadlines helps to ensure successful training programs.

Currency is always an issue for any training organization. Instructors are constantly requiring updated information on instructional topics and, because of the pressures of aggressive training schedules, almost never have sufficient time to update topical areas. This is where the research assistant is a valuable asset to any training organization.

The staff research assistant can provide valuable insight into new and emerging issues by researching the topical areas and reporting their research to the instruction staff for review and inclusion into the training curriculum. This does not relieve instructors from maintaining their professional skills and knowledge, but it can help reduce information overload by directing relevant and useful information to instructors on their respective topical areas. Directed research can be easily coordinated with the instructor, and the assistant can help maximize the instructor's time.

Interns also fill a valuable research role when assigned to a program as part of their educational experience. This cost-effective way of supporting the program has many benefits but can also be fraught with error and misinformation if the interns are not closely directed and supervised in their research efforts. Interns are generally students who are undertaking an education in a related discipline and are willing to work closely with a training organization to enhance their learning and understanding of the discipline. Given the fact that they are students, their level of expertise in the field is likely limited and their research and conclusions must be closely reviewed for accuracy. When properly directed and supervised, interns can bring a new level of effectiveness to a program by looking at problems through fresh perspectives.

Developing and enhancing the skill sets of staff instructors is of critical importance to any fully staffed training organization. Although this is easily said, it is often difficult to do in practice due to the ongoing demand for classes and the heavy workloads placed upon instructors. Training organizations need to look at innovative ways to help instructional staff build and maintain skills and knowledge. The following are a few resources that may go beyond the normal formal training classes for instructor development:

1. Develop liaisons with working investigative units and task forces in the local area. These liaisons and informal relationships not only help develop the instructor's skills but can also familiarize them with practical application of the skill they are teaching in the classroom and breach the gap between theory and practice.
2. Training organizations may also convene focus groups composed of subject matter experts to look at training needs and to identify specific job descriptions that can be used to identify critical skills and knowledge elements.
3. Instructional staff may review surveys and trend analysis from both the government and private sector to help identify trends in technology crimes and investigative techniques.

4. Meetings with futurists can add a new dimension to the skills of individual instructors by exposing them to the process of looking at future trends and driving factors in the technology crimes discipline.

5. Peer networking is important to instructor development. Instructional staff should also be encouraged to join professional organizations and associations to help improve their contacts and knowledge base. Attendance at industry conferences and trade shows are important components for instructor currency. Additionally, attendance at specialized training, as well as instructional skills workshops serve to round out the development of the instructional staff.

6. Instructional staff meetings held on a regular basis provide a forum for staff instructors and contract instructors to coordinate their training sessions and exchange ideas to improve the continuity of the courses being offered. Advanced agendas are important, and meetings should be held with distinct goals in mind.

7. It may be beneficial to attend conferences and meetings hosted by the computer underground, as well as to monitor underground postings, publications, and Internet sites. These contacts and monitoring provide valuable insight into the methodologies and technical sophistication of the computer criminal.

A well-trained and proficient instructional staff is the core asset of a training organization. Investment in their proficiency pays large dividends for the student and the program itself.

VI. Equipment

Training operations designed to teach computer technical skills should be conducted using computers and software likely to be encountered in the field. This single requirement of training operations is one of the costliest parts of the training program. Although computers are relatively inexpensive, peripherals, software, and upgrades are critical cost items in equipping the training program.

The deployment of computers requires a great deal of thought and preparation. The types of computers purchased will depend upon the software and operating systems that will be run upon them and the manner in which that software will be utilized in the lesson plan. There are benefits to purchasing the best systems available with the goal of getting the longest life cycle out of those systems. Rapid advances in software programs require constant upgrades and maintenance. An efficiently run training center requires imaging software to ensure that the systems can be set up quickly and reloaded quickly before and after class, or during class in the event that a student inadvertently damages the software setup on a system. This requires networking software and hardware designed to restore systems as well as to allow systems to share information and access outside networks.

When designing a computer training lab, careful thought should be given to maintaining the greatest amount of flexibility within the lab. The greater the flexibility, the wider use the lab can be put to. Decisions such as whether or not to use a fixed training center or a mobile training center need to be carefully weighed as well. There are several factors that should be weighed when deciding upon either a fixed or mobile training center.

Fixed training centers have the advantage of being stationary, so the network settings do not change and neither do the requirements for power outlets and phone lines. Fixed audio and video systems and other classroom necessities can be preset. Once set up, they are easily configured and coordinated. The layout of the classroom is predictable so instructors and students work in familiar environments.

Mobile training centers add a broader dimension to the training operations in that they can bring advanced training to the field where the need exists. This can generally be done with lower cost to the students or client agencies because the travel costs are borne by the presenter. Even with increased tuition cost to cover the cost of moving a mobile center and the related instructional staff, the cost per student for the training is still reduced, which makes it an attractive alternative to fixed centers.

The design and configuration of a mobile training center presents unique challenges to the training organization. When deployed as a mobile training center, systems must be limited by size, weight, and portability. Additionally, networking issues are increased exponentially whenever the lab is transported to a strange location where it must be integrated into a strange network.

To overcome these issues, mobile training centers are usually networked on a private network and connected through one or more routers using some form of network address translation. Advanced coordination with the host site is required to make this type of system work. Additionally, there are power concerns when bringing 20 to 40 computers onto a site such as a hotel. Computers, monitors, routers, and other peripherals in a single room may overload available power. Again, advanced coordination is essential to the success of the training organization in these situations.

Physical security of the mobile training lab is another area of concern when it is deployed in the field. Hotels do not always secure conference rooms after hours against entry by employees, and thefts may occur. If there are no physical security restraints to prevent equipment theft, uncontrolled access to the training conference rooms may not be desirable. Hotels with the ability to provide physical door lock devices or that are willing to provide the training organization with exclusive access to the conference rooms are desirable. Training organizations may need to purchase security devices designed to secure the mobile computers onto tables to discourage their removal. Hiring physical security guards locally may also be worthwhile insurance against theft or tampering. Security costs must be set appropriate to the equipment being used.

Peripheral devices are important to both the fixed and mobile training centers. Monitors, keyboards, mice, CD or DVD burners, and printers must be transported or otherwise made available in the classroom. Specifications for purchase of these devices require preplanning to maximize their usefulness in a wide variety of training scenarios.

The most significant expenses in the computer training center are the cost of software and the appropriate licensing associated with using that software in the training environment. Depending upon the nature of the training program and its impact upon the industry as a whole, software grants and donations can help defray the cost of maintaining a lab. Some software companies provide grant programs designed to assist education and training organizations through the use of software for students. Regardless of whether it is donated or purchased, software licensing must be closely controlled and documented by the training organization.

Specialized or niche market software may be required to provide realistic training in the field. This specialized software is very expensive and may not be available in affordable large quantities unless the training organization has carefully budgeted for the purchase and maintenance of software and licenses. Many of these programs come with copy protection and restricted-use token or dongles, and appropriate licensing must be purchased. The use of these programs should be controlled closely in the classroom.

Software licenses like shareware and freeware must be carefully evaluated to determine whether or not they are applicable to classroom use. Evaluation licenses may provide additional functionality with reduced cost. Another software source is government software that may be available at little or no cost to the training organization. If the training organization has the resources, custom software can be tailored to specific classroom needs but is usually the most expensive option for anything but the smallest utility programs.

As a rule of thumb, the fastest and most advanced computer training lab has a 2-year lifetime if it is used to train field practitioners. Most training organizations will stretch this to 3 years, but attempts to stretch it beyond that result in unrealistic training that has limited application in the field and an inability to demonstrate hands-on application of advanced topics.

VII. Materials

Aside from the main computers in the training centers, a host of other related equipment must be budgeted for and purchased. Many training organizations and individual instructors still use VHS video, and a lot of training material is still being developed in this media format. The wide acceptance of DVD and the availability of DVD burners will likely move production to this media, replacing VHS tape. Streaming video over a LAN (local area network), as well as over the global Internet require additional equipment and network resources beyond those normally found in a training lab. Some of the additional resources that may be needed include specialized broadcast software and high-bandwidth network connections.

Hands-on training also requires exhibits and components that can be used to hand around to students in class to illustrate lesson topics. Items such as evidence from deposited cases and inoperative hard disk drives and circuit boards make excellent instructional props. Training organizations should maintain a supply of parts that are no longer useful in production computers. These hand-around props provide students with hands-on experience and an opportunity to see the inner workings of the computer as part of their training experience.

Resource lists for students and instructors provide a wealth of information for reference in both the classroom and instructor research. A list of current resources on the Internet should be maintained and provided to students and instructors. Class exercises can also be enhanced by research assignments involving Web resources.

Some resources may require subscriptions and access fees. These costs must be evaluated and prioritized appropriately based upon their usefulness to the training programs being taught. A reference library should be developed and maintained with a combination of subscriptions, Web resources, books, and publications related to the topics of instruction. Shared library resources are still the mainstay of instructional development, and the better the resource materials, the better the training content.

VIII. Funding

Most training operations are supported by a line-item budget and must compete for scarce resources with other programs and activities throughout the agency. If designed and conducted properly, training can be a very cost-effective component of any organization. The return on investment in training is very high and has a wide impact on all other parts of the organization. A comprehensive cost-benefit analysis should be undertaken to document these residual benefits to the organization. This analysis will be helpful for continued budget justification.

Another funding source for training programs is the grant process. Grants are available from both government and private foundations and are offered to address specific problems. For example, if the problem being addressed is targeted at forensic evidence and has a training solution, it may be a good source of funding to develop and present computer forensic training.

Large corporations and private organizations are often victims of technology-related crimes and may donate funds or other resources to help address this crime problem. Training is a good tool for them to use to address a problem that affects them directly. The public relations benefit to the corporation is an additional bonus for these corporations and organizations. Donations of equipment, funds, software, and instructor availability are all very valuable to a training organization and may help make the training more cost-effective.

Some training classes are self-supporting in that the costs for the training and related equipment are included in a course tuition paid by attendees. These funding sources are adequate, providing that the development time and other operational requirements are addressed as part of the course budget.

Hybrid funding options involve a combination of grants, donations, and tuitions to cover training operating expenses. Having multiple sources of funding is essential to any training organization and must be constantly maintained and developed at the highest levels of the organization.

IX. Record Keeping

Training organizations often provide curriculum for students in furtherance of an advanced degree, a certification, or a mandated core competency program. The training organization is responsible for tracking courses, content, instructors, and attendees as part of their overall training record system. Although this seems like a very basic function, not all training organizations have a good record-keeping system. The lack of such a system may open the training organization up to legal liability in cases where the training provided to a criminal justice professional is called into question as part of an investigation.

The concept of vicarious liability is not new to the justice system. Lawsuits often target corporations and government agencies, holding them responsible for the actions of their employees. This concept extends to training programs. If an employee was trained and took some action that caused injury to another party, the training content may be called into question in the courts. A well-designed and maintained record system for training programs can help clarify the issue and may serve to show that the agency has a reasonable and prudent approach to employee training. A well-documented program may also protect the agency by showing that the injurious act was not consistent with training.

To properly document a program, the training organization must consider the parts of a training program that are subject to change and loss over time. These parts include individual trainee records, class lists, class schedules, content change control, and legal review.

Attendees or students are the reason training organizations exist. They are the raw material with which training programs work. Documenting identity and attendance is critical to student careers and should be carefully tracked. The attendee's name, address, unique identifier, and contact information should be maintained and linked to the training programs attended. Anytime personal information is kept on a student or attendee, the training organization must protect that information from unauthorized disclosure or compromise. At any time, a training organization should be able to produce records establishing the courses a student has attended, their grades, and the content taught to them in that course as well as the instructor(s) who taught the information.

Class rosters are an important document that should be maintained by the training organization. Class rosters are a cross-reference to individual students and are important to faculty and students alike, especially when it comes to networking between students later. Rosters of attendees assembled by class also provide demographics for a particular course and are useful in marketing a particular course.

An ongoing calendar provides scheduling of tasks and preparation necessary to coordinate training resources. The calendar also represents the time lines for planning course preparation and presentation. Classrooms, computer labs, instructors, and other resources must be carefully managed so the training operation can run smoothly and efficiently. Classes should be scheduled at least 6 weeks in advance to allow attendees time to register and adjust their schedules. Coordinated automated calendar systems allow personnel and resources to be scheduled in advance. This helps avoid conflicts. If properly categorized, the calendar can provide a documentation of the organization's work efforts over a set period and can provide valuable information for reports and budget justification documents.

Course content is dynamic in computer forensic and investigative classes. It is important that training organizations adopt a system of change control that allows them to manage changes to course curriculum and to document those changes as part of their records-keeping responsibility. It is important that changes in curriculum be documented and previous iterations maintained for future historical and legal reference. Changes in core curriculum should not be allowed without justification, documentation, and review.

Without these processes in place, course content cannot properly be maintained. At the same time, care must be taken to provide a means to quickly and efficiently implement changes to core curriculum on a timely basis when needed.

Other records should be maintained because they serve some operation need. Training organizations must be careful not to create a records bureaucracy and should limit record keeping to records that fall into one of the following categories:

1. The record is legally required.
2. The record is operationally necessary to provide training.
3. The record provides valuable information to assist the training organization in program development
4. The record provides budget justification.

Efficiency and accuracy are the keys to a good training records system, and careful thought must go into the records system design and maintenance.

X.   Testing and Certification

The effectiveness of a training program is measured in the ability of the students to demonstrate the required skills and knowledge in the tasks being taught. Testing is part of the feedback loop that allows training organizations to assess their effectiveness and monitor the need for change.

Testing student knowledge and skills is not a trivial endeavor. The design of the testing instrument or practical exercise is critical to its accuracy as a feedback tool. The test should accurately challenge the student to demonstrate competency in the skills or knowledge taught in the course curriculum. The test or exercise must be unbiased and relevant in real-world situations. Positive exercises that present real-world problem solving are the most effective in computer forensic and investigative training. Basing exercises on actual situations allows the student to work through the problem and develop skills that will have value in the field. Basing exercises on unrealistic problems does not help students later when they try to bring their skills and knowledge to bear on real problems in the field.

Unfortunately, it is not uncommon for exercises and tests to involve the use of booby traps and other surprise tactics. These tactics should be avoided most of the time and, if used, should be used judiciously with the express purpose of discouraging certain actions by the student. Any exercise must be carefully debriefed with the student in a very positive manner. If handled and debriefed properly, exercises can help the student apply their newly learned skills and knowledge to practical problems. If handled improperly, they can have a serious negative impact on the training experience and can discourage students from further developing their skills and knowledge in the field.

Training organizations have struggled with the issue of certification of students in the computer forensic field for many years. There is still a great deal of debate over the proper approach to certification. The concept of certification implies that a student received training in skills and knowledge and attained a specified level of competency. Competency is demonstrated through testing, and the student receives a certificate stating that they are competent to perform tasks involving those skills and knowledge. Certification implies the development of measurable standards and some form of independent vetting of those standards. This, by its very nature precludes the training organization itself from also filling the role of standards body because of an inherent conflict of interest. The conflict arises from the training organization accepting tuition for the training session and then being reluctant to fail a marginal student because the student has paid for the certification training.

If the training organization cannot ethically set and certify certification standards, then there must be another independent body of peers tasked with setting the certification standard and ensuring that it is maintained. This independent body should have representatives from the field who are competent in the skills and knowledge required to perform their jobs. The standards they set must reflect core competencies that are realistic and represent the actual work to be performed. Formal standards organizations may include state peace officer standards offices, industry associations, and academic standards bodies. A proper standards body will develop standards that have been vetted through a peer review process open for comment and review by all professionals in the field. The impartial standards are desirable because any certification may later be examined by a court of law for reasonableness and accuracy. The credibility of the certification is therefore reliant upon the credibility of the standards body.

Training organizations should not attempt to become self-certifying, because the validation of such a certification is questionable in its ethics. Self-certification programs should be suspect particularly when there is a product or profit motive involved.

XI. Summation

In the field of computer forensics and investigation, the training organization plays a critical role in the core competency of the field as a whole. A properly designed and run training program with competent testing and feedback can dramatically improve the competency of the criminal justice practitioner in the field. Although it may appear that these programs are expensive at first glance, any in-depth look at the cost-benefit analysis will show that training programs provide an admirable return on investment in the form of a competent workforce as well as a better, fair, and just criminal justice system.

Internet Crimes Against Children

6

MONIQUE MATTEI FERRARO, JD, CISSP WITH
SGT. JOSEPH SUDOL

I. Background

Soon after the Internet started to become widely available, law enforcement
started arresting people for using it to exploit children.* The growth of the
personal computer industry allowed average consumers to bring the Internet
into their home. Faster Internet connections and cheaper computers bring
thousands of new users into the fold every day. The development of hypertext
markup language (HTML) that occurred at about the same time that personal
computers started to become more widely available, made the Internet much
more user-friendly and made the World Wide Web possible.** Development
and refining of scanner and digital photography technology created a whole
new way for people to create and exchange child pornography. Meanwhile,
new chat and instant messaging technology created the possibility of communications absolutely unknown before the late 1990s.

These seemingly innocuous advances in technology spawned an entirely
unprecedented growth in the creation, distribution, and possession of child
pornography. At the same time, it gave preferential sex offenders access to
millions of new victims. A brief history of how children were exploited before
the Internet became ubiquitous is in order before we can move on to an
exploration of how Internet features are used to exploit children and what

---

* The first arrest for using the Internet to obtain child pornography one author knows of
happened in 1992, although undoubtedly there were earlier arrests.
** Hypertext markup language was developed by Tim Berner-Lee in 1990.

is being done about it in the United States. A discussion of child pornography will precede an overview of enticing minors to engage in sexual activity.

Frequent travelers of the information superhighway might be shocked to learn that child pornography was rarer than hens' teeth in the 1980s. During the 1970s, child pornography began to proliferate in adult bookstores throughout the United States. However, the pictures were of low quality and the product was expensive. In the 1970s and 80s, when 8-millimeter films were popular, a child pornography film cost hundreds of dollars. It was expensive to buy child pornography, because it was illegal and because the primary way to buy it was in adult bookstores. Obscenity and zoning laws at that time confined commercial adult bookstores to seedier areas of cities — places that the average suburbanite would hesitate to go. That made it fairly easy for law enforcement to crack down on distributors. They would go to the local adult bookstore, and if they found child pornography there, they would arrest the owner (Burgess 1984).

In the days before chat rooms and instant messaging, *preferential sex offenders* found their victims at playgrounds, school, church or campouts. The *preferential sex offender* would choose his or her career and leisure activities in order to be closer to potential victims. Favored careers included teachers, bus drivers, and clowns. Leisure activities included coaching, leading scout troops, mentoring — anything that would involve close contact with children over long periods of time. The length of time for exposure to the potential victim is important in order to nurture a relationship.

Although there are certainly individuals who favor instant gratification with the child victim, such contact comes at a price. The offender will not have the advantage of trust, so the child may fight, and if the offender doesn't kill the child, the child might tell and be believed. If the child fights, the possibility of detection and apprehension is increased. Also, if the child fights, the offender may need to use force in order to get what he wants. If force is used, the penalty is higher for the crime, there is more physical evidence, and it becomes more likely that the child's account of the incident and identification will be believed. So, the *preferential sex offender* who wished to elude the authorities and continue his activities groomed his victims.

Grooming refers to the process of gradually breaking down a child's resistance to engage in sex with the *preferential sex offender* (Lanning 2001). Over time, the offender befriends the victim, gains his or her trust, and gradually introduces the idea of a sexual relationship. This is accomplished by talking about sex, perhaps showing the child pictures or movies of adults, children, and children and adults partnered in sex. Some offenders introduce cartoons depicting sex. The offender might say things like, "She looks like she's having fun, doesn't she? Would you like to try having some fun? I could show you." The process of grooming a potential victim may take months or even years and requires that the offender have access to the child. In the physical world, access is limited to times when an adult has physical access to the child.

The dawn of the Internet age brought tremendous advances in many areas. The impact the Internet has had on child exploitation cannot be over-stated. Even without the Internet, technology has advanced in the past 25 years that has removed all of the traditional barriers to creating, distributing, and possessing child pornography (Ferraro and Casey 2004). Before the Internet, pictures had to be developed either on one's own or by a laboratory. Developing film requires at least some level of expertise and expense. Of course, Polaroid cameras and film made it possible to create child pornography as far back as the 1960s; however, distribution of the pictures was difficult because Polaroids of the time did not lend themselves to duplication. Many child pornography and child sex assault investigations were initiated when a film processor alerted law enforcement to suspicious photographs.

Today, the availability of very low-cost digital cameras, video, and scanners makes it possible to create child pornography without ever involving a third party. Digital cameras do not require processing. An image captured by a digital camera can be instantly uploaded to the Internet — e-mailed, posted to a newsgroup, displayed on a Web page, or shared through a peer-to-peer application or Web site. Rather than having to put on a trench coat and hiding under a wide-brimmed hat to skulk into a seedy part of town, anyone seeking child pornography can access it for *free* with the click of a mouse. Accessing some newsgroups or Web sites, one can see and download a nearly limitless number of pictures and videos depicting every sort of sex between children, between children and adults, between children and animals, and everything else under the sun (Ferraro and Casey 2004).

Despite the availability of free child pornography, there are those whose appetites are not sated. A few consumers seek out new pictures and specific types of children committing specific types of sex. These consumers pay for access and downloading of pictures. As evidenced by the number of large-scale, multinational investigations of Internet-based child pornography pay sites, there is no shortage of people who will pay for access to child pornography.

There is something about the Internet that insulates it in a shroud of assumed privacy (Ferraro and Casey 2004). For whatever reason, people believe that whatever they do on the Internet is private. This impression pervades even though no one ever told people that their Internet transactions would be private. How many people would you guess actually ever read their Internet access agreement received when they subscribed to an online service? Sometimes the Internet access agreement says something ominous such as, "I acknowledge that by clicking on the 'accept' button that I have read and

I accept the terms of this agreement. By accepting this agreement, I relinquish all rights to privacy regarding the contents of all communications and the nature of all transactions any user of this account conducts." Oops! (Are you certain that your Internet access agreement does *not* contain the above clause?)

Nonetheless, people assume that whatever they do on the Internet is anonymous and private. This notion endures no matter where the person is. At home, at work, at an Internet café, a library, a mall Internet kiosk — people think that they are in a private world where no one else is watching them, and they become outraged at the thought that anyone might be watching them. Likewise, they believe that no one will hold them accountable for what they do. It is almost as if everything is make-believe. But, anyone in law enforcement or in the helping professions who has dealt with the victims of child pornography and Internet enticing knows that the virtual world of the Internet leaves behind many real victims. Using the Internet to exploit children is a particularly heinous crime that often leaves hard-to-heal scars.

Before the Internet, the biggest technological development to affect *preferential sex offenders* was the citizens' band (CB) radio. In the late 1970s and early 1980s when CB was popular, offenders enjoyed access to children they had never known before. The CB allowed them to talk to kids and get to know and groom them. But the CB only carried a radio signal a short distance — several miles with an average antenna. Ham radio carries a much stronger signal that can reach internationally. However, the skills, expense of equipment, and licensing required to operate a ham radio is much higher than for CB access. Internet chat rooms reach children all over the world, and more children access the Internet than ever used the CB or ham radio.

According to the United States Department of Commerce, children and teenagers use computers and the Internet more than any other age group. "Ninety percent of children between the ages of 5 and 17 (or 48 million) now use computers [and] seventy-five percent of 14–17 year olds and 65 percent of 10–13 year olds use the Internet" (United States Department of Commerce 2002). A study by the University of New Hampshire of children between the ages of 10 and 17 found that 20 percent, or one in five of the children using the Internet had been solicited for sex in the past year (Finkelhor 2000). Of course over time, the probability that a child will be exposed to explicit sexual content or solicited for sex by a *preferential sex offender* increases geometrically — the probability of solicitation is 20% in 1 year, but over a 2-year period the probability rises to 40%, and so on. (See Figure 6.1)

Using the same sample, researchers further explored the characteristics of preteens and teens that developed romantic relationships using the Internet (Wolak 2003). Researchers found that both boys and girls who have problems, are troubled, or are alienated from their parents were more likely to form

A *preferential sex offender* is a person who prefers to have sex with minors. A minor is a person under the age of sixteen.

Computer Assisted, or *Internet Child Exploitation* includes *Child Pornog*raphy and *Enticing a Minor to Engage in Sexual Activity*.

Child Pornography is the depiction of a person under the age of sixteen engaged in sexual activity (for example, intercourse, lascivious exhibition of the genitals, masturbation, fellatio or cunnilingus).

Enticing a Minor to Engage in Sexual Activity means the use of the Internet or interstate facility to persuade a person under the age of sixteen to engage in sexual activity that would be a crime if attempted or completed. In many places, it is a crime for a person under the age of sixteen to have sex with a person more than two years older than them. It is also a crime in many places for a person more than two years older than the other person to have sex with someone under the age of fourteen. In most places, it is a crime to force sex on a minor.

Figure 6.1   Definitions related to Internet child exploitation.

close online relationships. The researchers hypothesized that troubled teens may be more likely to seek out support and nurturing relationships through the Internet, whereas better adjusted teens find satisfying relationships in the offline world. (See Figure 6.2)

II. Computer-Assisted and Internet Crimes Against Children

There is no question that the Internet has created a new and effective means of manufacturing, distributing, and storing child pornography. The Internet has made access to unprecedented numbers of potential victims of preferential sex offenders possible as well. This next section discusses how offenders use technology to perpetrate their criminal activities.

As discussed earlier, child pornographers use whatever technology becomes available as soon as it is available to manufacture, distribute, and store illicit images of children. Some Internet features lend themselves to trafficking in child pornography more readily than others. In his seminal

Based on interviews with a nationally representative sample of 1,501 youth ages 10 to 17 who use the Internet regularly

- ❖ Approximately one in five received a sexual solicitation or approach over the Internet in the last year.

- ❖ One in thirty-three received an aggressive sexual solicitation—a solicitor who asked to meet them somewhere; called them on the telephone; sent them regular mail, money or gifts.

- ❖ One in four had an unwanted exposure to pictures of naked people or people having sex in the last year.

- ❖ One in seventeen was threatened or harassed.

Approximately one quarter of young people who reported these incidents were distressed by them.

Figure 6.2   Some statistics for child exploitation. (*Source:* Finkelhor, 2000.)

work on Internet child pornography, Philip Jenkins details the extensive and clandestine network of child pornography traffickers in *Beyond Tolerance* (2001). The book follows traffickers who set up Web sites, e-groups, newsgroups, and file transfer protocol (FTP) sites; post the password; and then take the site down and put it up elsewhere to avoid detection. Jenkins followed more sophisticated traders whose detection eludes the average law enforcement officers. Most child pornography manufacturers, distributors, and collectors are much lower-tech and less concerned with avoiding detection (Ferraro and Casey 2004; Lanning 2001).

The most prolific source of child pornography on the Internet is newsgroups. Some distributors download images from newsgroups and resell the CDs and DVDs that they make. Newsgroups are the distributor's sole source of illicit material (which, by the way, they download for free). There is no shortage of newsgroups that cater to those who have a sexual predilection for children of any age.

Web sites are another popular method of trafficking in child pornography. Given the ease of trading images via other methods and that setting up a Web site is more labor-intensive, Web sites trading child pornography are most often pay sites. As all fraud and white collar crime investigators know, whenever money is involved, the best method of finding the offender is to follow the money. The most expansive, high-profile, multijurisdictional child pornography cases started by investigators taking down a pay Web site. Perhaps the largest and most fruitful Web site–based investigation began in 1999 when the Dallas, Texas, police department seized the Landslide Web portal and arrested the Reedys, a married couple who made millions of dollars operating a Web service that charged customers for viewing adult and child pornography Web sites.

Using the information gained from the Landslide Web servers, the United States Postal Service and the Dallas police extracted identifying information for the child pornography Web site customers and launched a multijurisdictional investigation that continues to provide intelligence today. The investigative effort was dubbed "Operation Avalanche." Because the Landslide sites required information for billing, subscribers supplied a valid credit card number, billing address, and name. Tracing back through the credit card number, law enforcement was able to identify a large number of the subscribers. The affirmative action on the part of the subscriber — requesting a certain Web site and paying for it — tended to prove that their actions were made knowing the content and character of the images sought. (See Figure 6.3)

E-groups were once a popular method of exchanging child pornography (Ferraro and Casey 2004). The federal law that requires Internet service providers to report child pornography* has reduced the use of e-groups for trafficking in images considerably. Also, the highly publicized "Operation Candyman" conducted by the Federal Bureau of Investigation (FBI) in conjunction with other law enforcement agencies has increased users' and Internet service providers' awareness to this type of activity. (See Figure 6.4)

File Transfer Protocol servers (FTP) are most often used to distribute or collect large quantities of images. An FTP site can be advertised to users in many different ways, such as on a newsgroup, an e-group, a Web site, or listserve. In many cases, the FTP server is protected by a password that is changed often or shared with only known members of a community (Jenkins 2002). Quite frequently, Internet Relay Chat (IRC) is the means used to advertise an FTP site. In order to download images, the FTP owner will either charge money or, more likely, require that the downloader upload a certain number of images per number of images downloaded. For example, the ratio of images required might be to provide one for every five downloaded. This ensures that the downloader is not a law enforcement agent, because law enforcement officers are generally not allowed by policy to distribute child

---

* (42 U.S.C. § 13032 states, "Whoever, while engaged in providing an electronic communication service or a remote computing service to the public, through a facility or means of interstate or foreign commerce, obtains knowledge of facts or circumstances [ ] involving child pornography [ ], [ ] shall, as soon as reasonably possible, make a report of such facts of circumstances to the Cyber Tip Line at the National Center for Missing and Exploited Children, which shall forward that report to a law enforcement agency or agencies designated by the Attorney General. [ ] A provider of electronic communication services [ ] who knowingly and willfully fails to make a report [ ] shall be fined — [ ] in the case of an initial failure to make a report, not more than $50,000; and [ ] in the case of any second or subsequent failure to make a report, not more than $100,000." 42 U.S.C. § 13032 (2003).

Internet Crimes Against Children Task Forces in Operation Avalanche

Attorney General John Ashcroft and former Chief Postal Inspector Kenneth Weaver

announced in August 2001 the successful conclusion of a two-year investigation that

dismantled the largest commercial child pornography enterprise ever uncovered.

Following the "take down" of Landslide Productions, Inc., a multimillion-dollar child

pornography business, 30 federally funded ICAC task forces throughout the United States

partnered with U.S. Postal Inspectors to launch Operation Avalanche. This proactive,

undercover investigation resulted in an unprecedented sentence of life in prison for

Landslide's owner, the execution of over 160 state and federal search warrants across the

country, the arrest to date of more than 120 offenders for trafficking child pornography

via the U.S. Mail and the Internet, the identification of child molesters, and the rescue of

child victims.

The Internet Crimes Against Children (ICAC) Task Force Program was created in 1998

by a Congressional mandate. Administered and funded through the Department of

Justice's Office of Juvenile Justice and Delinquency Prevention (OJJDP), ICAC provides

grants to state and local law enforcement agencies, which use them to build regional task

forces that address and combat Internet-related crimes agains tchildren.

Operation Avalanche began in 1999, when Postal Inspectors discovered that a Ft. Worth,

Texas, company, Landslide Productions, Inc., operated and owned by Thomas and Janice

Reedy, was selling child pornography Web sites. Customers from around the world paid

monthly subscription fees via a post office box address or the Internet to access the

hundreds of Web sites, which contained extremely graphic child pornography material.

Figure 6.3   Operation avalanche.

Ft. Worth Postal Inspector Robert C. Adams and Dallas ICAC Task Force Detective Steven A. Nelson teamed together to initiate what would become a child exploitation case of unprecedented magnitude.

During the investigation, while Landslide Productions was still in business, the National Center for Missing and Exploited Children's Cyber Tipline received more than 270 complaints from people around the world related to the Landslide case. All credible complaints were forwarded to investigators.

Postal Inspector Bob Adams obtained federal search warrants for the business and personal residence of the Reedy's. The warrants were executed by a task force of 45 officers and agents. They served seizure warrants on Landslide's bank accounts and two unencumbered Mercedes Benz vehicles valued at more than $150,000—and purchased with the Reedy's ill-gotten gains. Landslide was a highly successful financial enterprise, at one point taking in over $1.4 million in a single month.

After reviewing volumes of seized evidence and subpoenaed financial records, the Reedy's were indicted in federal district court on 89 counts of conspiracy to distribute child pornography and possession of child pornography. Following a one-week jury trial, the Reedy's were convicted on all counts as charged. Thomas Reedy was given an unprecedented sentence of life in prison, and his wife Janice received a 14-year prison sentence.

Putting Landslide Productions out of business and the Reedy's behind bars struck a major blow to the global child pornography industry, but the investigation did not end there. Using intelligence gained from Landslide's customer database, Postal Inspectors joined with 30 federally funded ICAC task forces across the country and, with legal guidance

Figure 6.3 (continued).

from the Department of Justice's Child Exploitation and Obscenity Section, designed and implemented a nationally coordinated, undercover operation.

Working out of the Dallas ICAC Task Force office, Postal Inspectors and other investigators initiated undercover contacts with the most egregious suspects. As cases were developed, the suspects were passed off to other Postal Inspectors and ICAC task forces throughout the United States for further investigation. Investigators obtained and served search warrants, seized huge volumes of child pornography images and materials, identified child molesters, and rescued victimized children from further sexual abuse. To date, over 160 search warrants have been served and more than 120 child sex offenders and pornographers have been arrested.

In one instance, Postal Inspectors and ICAC Task Force investigators searching the home of a 36-year-old computer consultant in North Carolina found videotapes he had produced depicting the sexual abuse of a number of young girls, one of whom was only four years old. The offender recorded the activities with a pinhole camera he had hidden in a bedroom smoke detector and which was connected to a VCR and a computer. On August 7, 2001, the man was sentenced to 17 and 1/2 years in federal prison on various charges of sexual exploitation.

Figure 6.3 (continued).

pornography, even in the course of an undercover operation. At the same time, the practice ensures that the FTP operator has a constant influx of new images both to distribute and to consume for their own pleasure (Ferraro and Casey 2004).

Regular e-mail, instant message utilities, and chat rooms are also frequently used methods to distribute child pornography. More often than not, the number of images transferred using these methods of communications are small due to the relatively large size of picture files. Quite often, the child pornography images are sent either to other preferential sex offenders or pedophiles or to a potential victim the offender is grooming (Ferraro and Casey 2004).

Operation Candyman Statistics
Occupations of Operation Candyman Arrestees

Albany: 1 subject — **school bus driver, registered foster parent**
Baltimore: 8 subjects — **member of clergy**
Denver: 1 subject
Houston: 1 subject
Las Vegas: 2 subjects — **teacher's aide at a preschool and day care**
Little Rock 1 subject — **respiration therapist - committed suicide**
Los Angeles: 3 subjects
New Orleans: 1 subject
New York: 1 subject — **landscaper**
Norfolk: 3 subjects
Philadelphia: 7 subjects — **child photographer, guidance counselor , and member of clergy**
Phoenix: 1 subject — **correctional officers/camp counselor**
Pittsburgh: 1 subject — **law enforcement personnel**
Richmond: 1 subject
St. Louis: 7 subjects — **student, contractor/handyman, sales representative, self-employed/
advertising, custodian/janitor - hospital**
San Diego: 1 subject — **law enforcement personnel**

Figure 6.4   United States Postal Service web page. (*Source:* FBI, Innocent Images Initiative, http://www.fbi.gov/pressrel/candyman/accompoccu.htm)

Similarly, instant messaging, chat, and regular e-mail are favored mediums of preferential sex offenders to court potential victims (Ferraro and Casey 2004). Chat services are available from many sources. America Online is a very popular source of online chat, as is IRC — a facility that may be downloaded for free. Many other service providers such as Yahoo!, MSN, and a host of other Web sites offer free chat. Instant messaging, mostly America Online Instant Messaging (AIM), usually comes bundled with software in new personal computers. AIM is free and can be used with any Internet service.

Preferential sex offenders haunt online chat rooms looking for potential victims. Just as they used to frequent arcades, public pools, parks, and playgrounds, preferential sex offenders troll the Internet chat rooms because they know that is where potential victims will be (Ferraro and Casey 2004). Chat rooms, in particular, are furtive hunting grounds for offenders. The chat technology lists each participant in the room and offers the ability (usually) to obtain further information about the parties by accessing a profile. A *profile* is a database containing user-entered information about the user's location and interests. The user may enter as much information or as little information as they like.

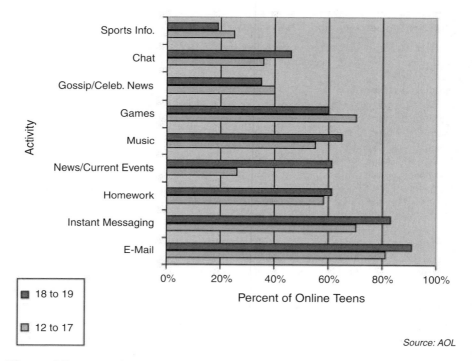

Figure 6.5   Use of the internet by teens, by category. http://cyberatlas. inter-net.com/big_picture/demographics/article/0,,5901_961881,00.html#table.

As one might imagine, the amount of personal information that a child enters into a profile is directly related to the amount of supervision provided while they access the Internet (Ferraro and Casey 2004). Any preferential sex offender with even a modicum of insight can detect that a youth with a profile chock-full of personal information is at the least not closely supervised and quite often a potential target. There have been several sexual assaults that began with Internet enticing in the small state of Connecticut over the past 2 years alone. In one case, a 13-year-old met a man who she believed was a prospective babysitting employer but instead was a sex offender who brutally raped her.

The two met online in a chat room. The offender discovered through the girl's profile that she was looking for a babysitting job. The girl provided her telephone number in the profile, along with the town and state in which she lived. Using a reverse directory database, the man looked up the subscriber information for the telephone number and other Internet databases to discover the girl's address and the name of her mother. Over the course of several conversations, the man persuaded the girl that he knew her mother and that it would be safe for her to meet him at the local library. On arriving at the library, she immediately recognized that the man was not a prospective employer but was likely a stranger seeking to hurt her. Unfortunately, instead of contacting a parent or a trusted adult, such as the librarian or a police officer, the girl decided to walk home. The man followed her, dragged her into the woods, raped her, and left her tied to a tree (Personal knowledge 2003). Fortunately for the victim, a passerby discovered her and she survived the ordeal. Unfortunately, another 13-year-old girl who lived 20 miles away was not as lucky.

Christina Long was 13. She was active in her church and a cheerleader at school. But she also had an active romantic and sexual life through the Internet. She met Sol dos Reis in a chat room online. Their relationship led them to meet at the mall where they engaged in sex in his car in the parking lot. Dos Reis strangled the girl then tossed her body on the side of the road. Christina Long left behind a home page filled with pictures of herself and details of her life along with tales of her sexual exploits. Her guardian maintained that she discussed Internet safety with the girl but notwithstanding her attempts to keep Christina safe, the girl engaged in risky and ultimately deadly online activity. Christina Long's guardian had no idea what she was doing online nor did she suspect that anything untoward was taking place in Christina's life (CBS News 2002).

Figure 6.6   The Cybertipline provides a way for people to report suspicious online activity. Saul Dos Reis, left, in 1997 yearbook photo, and Christina Long, undated family photo. (CBS/AP) http://www.cbsnews.com/stories/2002/05/31/national/main510739.shtml

Both victims in the foregoing examples provided substantial personal identifying information online. In both cases, the amount of personal information the girls provided was like a beacon drawing sex offenders to them. In the wake of Christina Long's murder, many have blamed the victim. She may have been more at-risk than other teens, but anyone who takes a tour of the online chat rooms and explores local profiles will see that there are very many minors who reveal large amounts of personal information in their profiles. Exploring further, one will find that those who provide substantial personal information about themselves are quite willing to talk to strangers who approach them online. Blaming the victim is a frequently used defense mechanism that helps to assuage the panic and guilt we feel when a child falls victim to a preventable fate (McGrath 2004*). The blame is misplaced. Of course, a 13-year-old cannot be responsible for bringing on her murder. When faced with that statement, those seeking to blame will retreat to blaming the guardian. The girl's guardian "should have known," or did not supervise the girl closely enough. The victim was from a broken home. That must explain it. But it doesn't explain why Christina Long was murdered, and it doesn't explain the increasing numbers of teens and preteens who are sexually victimized by adults they meet through Internet communication. If that reasoning justifies Christina Long's murder, then so many other children fit similar circumstances — guardians who don't know everything their 13-year-old charge is doing online; guardians or parents who don't supervise every Internet transaction their 13-year-old makes; children from interracial families — the description could fit almost any teenager in the twenty-first century. The fact is that, but for safety education, supervision, and the grace of God, many of our youth today are potential victims (McGrath, 2004).

III. Law Enforcement Efforts

Now that the types of crimes and how the Internet and computers help to facilitate their commission has been discussed, the final topic of this chapter is what law enforcement is doing to stop computer-assisted child exploitation. Criminal law has been an area reserved for state and local enforcement since the formation of the union. The federal government enjoyed limited jurisdiction over crimes with a patently federal connection — acts such as espionage, treason, tax evasion, and counterfeiting. It has been only since the population has become more mobile that the Commerce Clause of the United States Constitution has been invoked to justify federal incursion into areas of the criminal law traditionally reserved for the states, counties, and municipalities. The Mann Act was the first federalized sex crime (18 U.S.C. 2421). Enacted in 1910, the Act was aimed initially at the white slavery trade and forced prostitution. At the time, offenders would kidnap women and transport them across state lines for the purpose of forcing them into lives of prostitution. Crossing over a state line gave the act a federal nexus because there was a connection to interstate commerce. Congress, and Congress alone, is vested with the power to regulate interstate commerce. It was difficult or impossible for local and state authorities to locate and extradite suspects, and federal law enforcement had more resources and the ability to exact greater prison terms.

Since the Mann Act, the Commerce Clause has been used to justify federal laws prohibiting discrimination in public accommodations, and most recently enticing minors to engage in sexual activity using an interstate facility for the manufacture, distribution, or possession of child pornography (18 U.S.C. 2251, 2252, 2252A). The federal connection is that the Internet, by its very nature, is an interstate facility. Communicating using the Internet even from one location in your home state to another within the same state might send a signal through a server in another state. Everything conducted on the Internet, according to the thinking of Congress, invokes interstate commerce. Similarly, with the manufacture, distribution, or possession of child pornography — no matter how small or seemingly insignificant the piece of equipment used — if it's passed through interstate commerce, the federal government may take jurisdiction if the equipment was used to facilitate the crime. For example, if a person were to store images of child pornography on a CD and that CD was created in another state, then the CD passed through interstate commerce, and there is a sufficient federal nexus to justify federal jurisdiction.

Of course, the states and local governments also have laws against child pornography and luring minors into sexual relations. So, there exist multiple layers of possible criminal liability for a single given act. Whether the broadening of federal jurisdiction is intended to help the states or is a concerted effort to federalize the criminal law, the assistance available from the federal government in the area of computer-assisted child exploitation has created unprecedented multijurisdictional law enforcement efforts (Ferraro and Casey 2004). Among the most successful efforts are the FBI's Crimes Against Children Task Force and the Innocent Images Initiative, the Internet Crimes Against Children Task Force Program administered by the Department of Justice Office of Juvenile Justice and Delinquency Prevention, and the National Center for Missing and Exploited Children.

The FBI operates Crimes Against Children (CAC) Task Forces. Many of the field offices throughout the country have organized CAC task forces. The program aims to "develop a nationwide capacity to provide a rapid, effective and measured investigative response to crimes involving the victimization of children; and enhance the capabilities of state and local law enforcement investigators through training programs, investigative assistance and task force operations" (FBI CAC Web site 2003). CAC task forces recruit multi-disciplinary and multiagency teams, they promote sharing of intelligence information and specialized skills among all levels of law enforcement and provision of victim and witness services (FBI CAC Web site 2003). CAC task forces focus on crimes against children but do not exclusively concentrate on computer-assisted or Internet crimes against children.

The Innocent Images National Initiative is a component of the FBI's Cyber Crimes Program. Innocent Images is devoted to investigating computer-assisted and Internet-related crimes against children. The Initiative's primary focus is on *travelers*, those individuals who use the Internet to entice minors into sexual activity and travel across state lines to do so, and major manufacturers and distributors of child pornography (FBI Innocent Images National Initiative Web page 2003).

HISTORY OF INNOCENT IMAGES

While investigating the disappearance of a juvenile in May 1993, FBI Agents and Prince George's County, Maryland, police detectives identified two suspects who had sexually exploited numerous juveniles over a 25-year period. Investigation into the activities of the suspects determined that the adults were routinely utilizing online computers to transmit child pornography. Further investigation and discussions with experts, both within the FBI and in the private sector, revealed that the utilization of computer telecommunications was rapidly becoming one of the most prevalent techniques by which some sex offenders shared pornographic images of minors and identified and recruited children into sexually illicit relationships. Based on information developed during this investigation, the Innocent Images National Initiative was started in 1995 to address the illicit activities conducted by users of commercial and private online services and the Internet.

During the early stages of Innocent Images, a substantial amount of time was exhausted on commercial online service providers that provide numerous easily accessible "chat rooms" in which teenagers and pre-teens can meet and converse with each other. By using chat rooms, children can chat for hours with unknown individuals, often without the knowledge or approval of their parents. Investigation revealed that computer sex offenders used chat rooms to contact children. Chat rooms offer the advantage of immediate communication around the world and provide the pedophile with an anonymous means of identifying and recruiting children into sexually illicit relationships.

Figure 6.7   The history of the Innocent Images program. (Source: FBI, Innocent Images National Initiative Webpage, at www.fbi.gov/hq/cid/cac/innocent.htm)

Congress created the Internet Crimes Against Children (ICAC) Task Force program in 1998. Initially funding 10 task forces, the program has grown to fund 30 task forces around the country. The ICAC program encourages partnering and resource sharing among various levels of government — local, county, state, and federal — and promotes a multidisciplinary approach to attacking Internet crimes against children. Most of the ICACs have elements of community education, an investigatory component, and training for investigators and multidisciplinary partners.

Some task forces utilize a vertical prosecution model, in which a prosecutor or team of prosecutors is assigned to the task force and takes cases from their inception to their conclusion. There is no question that in complex cases, such as computer-assisted child exploitation cases, that vertical prosecution can have many benefits. The prosecutor has a thorough knowledge of the technology and common issues involved in the cases. Having a prosecutor involved from the very beginning, investigators benefit from legal counsel in an area of the law that is unsettled and tricky. Finally, the continuity of having one prosecutor assigned to a case throughout the process leaves less room for hasty, uninformed judgments regarding plea negotiations and sentencing. A prosecutor who is well-versed and experienced with an investigation and the ensuing criminal case is in a much better position to negotiate a just outcome and sentence.

The principle and critical drawbacks of vertical prosecution in computer-assisted child exploitation cases are that the expertise is centralized in only a few individuals and burnout often occurs in professionals who work closely with child exploitation cases. These issues are important to address because they are inextricably intertwined. Centralizing knowledge is acceptable if the rate of turnover is low. However, if turnover is high — as in the case with child exploitation — then expertise should be spread over other professionals. Even though the number of Internet crimes against children will not subside, but will likely increase, it is difficult to recruit prosecutors who have the inclination and aptitude to become expert in both child exploitation prosecution and the Internet and its related technology.

Some ICAC task forces devote considerable resources to developing electronic forensic evidence capabilities, whereas others concentrate on investigations. Each of the task forces is a wholly unique entity with its own set of goals and self-directed mission. The uniting force for the separate task forces is the ICAC Board, which provides policy guidance and determines investigative priorities. When a task force accepts funding, it agrees to abide by a few strict terms.

First, it must follow the ICAC guidelines for conducting undercover investigations. The ICAC guidelines for undercover investigations require that law enforcement officers adhere to high standards of online conduct and mandate that undercover operations receive prior approval from the ICAC Board. Among the requirements, officers may only use authorized equipment and Internet access methods to conduct undercover investigations. All targets and activity must be reported to a centralized database to ensure duplication of efforts is minimized.

Second, the task force must send a representative to the ICAC Board meetings. This is essential in order for the entity to be adequately represented. The ICAC Board approves undercover operations and decides policy issues. (See Figure 6.8)

By far the greatest resource for law enforcement is the National Center for Missing and Exploited Children (NCMEC). It has become the principal clearinghouse for information about computer- and Internet-assisted child exploitation. According to NCMEC's Web site, they set up the Child Pornography Tipline in 1987. Since then, they launched the Cybertipline in 1998 (http://www.cybertipline.org) to receive reports of online child exploitation. Since its inception, the site has taken more than 120,000 complaints of child sexual abuse, child pornography, and child sex tourism (NCMEC 2003). In 2003, NCMEC set up a virtual private network to assist in referring cases to ICACs and other law enforcement agencies that were reported under mandatory Internet service provider reporting laws.

IV. Conclusion

The future of Internet- and computer-assisted child exploitation is certain to be even more challenging than it has been to date. Advances in technology ensure that these crimes will be with us well into the future and will be increasingly difficult for law enforcement to battle and for the helping professions to treat both the victims and the offenders. The nature of the Internet — that it defies governance or regulation — makes tracking down those who exploit children using high technology a virtually* impossible task.

---

* Um, pardon the pun.

Active Internet Crimes Against Children Task Forces in the United St

■ Starting operations in spring of 1999 were the Bedford County, VA, Sheriff's Department; Broward County, FL, Sheriff's Department; Colorado Springs, CO, Police Department; Dallas, TX, Police Department; Illinois State Police; New York State Division of Criminal Justice Services; Portsmouth, NH, Police Department (including Maine State Police, New Hampshire State Police, and Chittendon County, VT); Sacramento County, CA, Sheriff's Office; South Carolina Office of the Attorney General; and the Wisconsin Department of Justice.

● Starting operations in spring of 2000 were the Delaware County, PA, District Attorney; Michigan State Police; Seattle, WA, Police Department; Utah Office of the Attorney General; Nebraska State Patrol; Connecticut State Police; Massachusetts Department of Public Safety; Las Vegas, NV, Metropolitan Police Department; Maryland State Police; and the Knoxville, TN, Police Department.

▲ Starting operations in summer of 2000 were the Alabama Department of Public Safety; Cuyahoga County, OH, District Attorney; Hawaii Office of the Attorney General; North Carolina Division of Criminal Investigation; Oklahoma State Bureau of Investigation; Phoenix, AZ, Police Department; Saint Paul, MN, Police Department; San Diego, CA, Police Department; Sedgwick County, KS, Sheriff's Office; and the Wyoming Division of Criminal Investigation.

---

*Note: The agencies shown are those participating in the program as of September 2001.

Source: "Protecting Children in Cyberspace: The ICAC Task Force Program" Medaris, Michael and Girouard, Cathy, Juvenile Justice Bulletin (United States Department of Justice: Washington, D.C, Jan. 2002) http://www.ncjrs.org

Figure 6.8 Active ICAC Task Forces in the United States. (*Source:* FBI, Innocent Images National Initiative Webpage, at www.fbi.gov/hq/cid/cac/innocent.htm)

References

18 United States Code. 2421.

CBSNews.com. The Two Faces of a Thirteen-Year-Old Girl. Online at: http://www.cbsnews.com/stories/2002/05/31/national/main510739.shtml.

Federal Bureau of Investigation Crimes Against Children Web page. Online at: http://www.fbi.gov/hq/cid/cac/crimesmain.htm.

Ferraro, Monique M., and Eoghan Casey. 2004. *Computer Assisted Crimes Against Children: Investigation, Prosecution, and Forensic Examination* (tentative title). Boston, MA: Academic Press.

McGrath, Michael, M.D. 2004. Online Victims. In *Computer Assisted Crimes Against Children: Investigation, Prosecution, and Forensic Examination* (tentative title), by Monique M. Ferraro and Eoghan Casey. Boston, MA: Academic Press.

Finkelhor, David, Kimberely J. Mitchell, and Janis Wolak. 2000. Online Victimization: A Report on the Nation's Youth. Alexandria, VA: National Center for Missing and Exploited Children.

Jenkins, Phillip. 2001. *Beyond Tolerance*. New York: New York University Press.

Lanning, Kenneth. 2001. *Child Molesters: A Behavioral Analysis.* Alexandria, VA: National Center for Missing and Exploited Children.

National Center for Missing and Exploited Children Web page. 2003. Online at: http://www.missingkids.com.

United States Department of Commerce, National Telecommunications and Information Administration. 2002. *A Nation Online: How Americans Are Expanding Their Use of the Internet.* Washington, D.C. Online at: http://www.ntia.doc.gov/.

Wolak, Janis, Kimberly J. Mitchell, and David Finkelhor. 2003. Escaping or Connecting? Characteristics of Youth Who Form Close Online Relationships. *Journal of Adolescence* 26:105–199.

Wolbert Burgess, Ann. 1984. *Child Pornography and Child Sex Rings*. New York: Lexington Books.

18 United States Codes 2251, 2252, 2252A.

Challenges to Digital Forensic Evidence

FRED COHEN

I. Basics

Digital forensic evidence is identified, collected, transported, stored, analyzed, interpreted, reconstructed, presented, and destroyed through a set of processes. Challenges to this evidence come through challenges to the elements of this process. This process, like all other processes and the people and systems that carry them out, is imperfect. That means that there are certain types of faults that occur in these processes.

A. Faults and Failures

Faults consist of intentional or accidental making or missing of content, contextual information, the meaning of content, process elements, relationships, ordering, timing, location, corroborating content, consistencies, and inconsistencies.

Not all faults produce failures, but some do. Although it may be possible to challenge faults, this generally does not work and is unethical if there is no corresponding failure in the process.

Certain things turn faults into failures, and it is these failures that legitimately should be and can be challenged in legal matters. Failures consist of false positives and false negatives. *False negatives* are items that should have been found and dealt with in the process but were not, whereas *false positives* are things that should have been discarded or discredited in the process but were not.

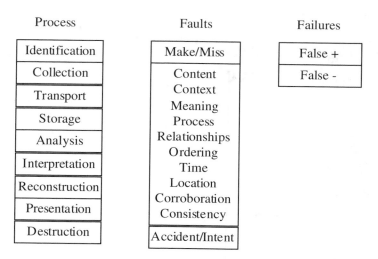

Figure 7.1 Possible faults in failures in the processes of interacting with digital evidence.

B.   Legal Issues

In the United States, evidence in legal cases is admitted or not based on the relative weights of its probative and prejudicial value. *Probative value* is the extent to which the evidence leads to deeper understanding of the issues in the case. *Prejudicial value* is the extent to which it leads the finder of fact to believe one thing or another about the matter at hand. If the increased understanding from the evidence is greater than the increase in belief, the evidence is admissible.

Part of the issue of probative value is the quality of the evidence. If the process that created the evidence as presented is flawed, this reduces the probative value. Impure evidence, evidence presented by an expert who is shown to be unknowledgeable in the subject at hand, evidence that has not been retained in a proper chain of custody, evidence that fails to take into account the context, or evidence falling under any of the other fault categories described in Figure 7.1, all lead to reduced probative value. If the result of these faults produces wrong answers, the probative value goes to nearly zero in many cases.

C.   The Latent Nature of Evidence

In order to deal with digital evidence, it must be presented in court. Because digital data is not directly observable by the finder of fact, it must be presented through expert witnesses using tools to reveal its existence, content, and meaning to the fact finders. This puts it into the category of latent evidence. In addition, digital evidence is hearsay evidence in that it is presented by an expert who asserts facts or conclusions based on what the computer recorded, not what they themselves have directly observed. In order for hearsay evidence to be admitted, it normally has to come in under the normal business records exemption to the hearsay evidence prohibition. Thus, it depends on the quality and unbiased opinion of the experts for each side.

D.   Notions Underlying "Good Practice"

One of the results of diverse approaches to collection and analysis of digital forensic evidence is that it has become increasingly difficult to show why the process used in any particular case is reliable, trustworthy, and accurate. As a result, sets of "good practices" were developed by law enforcement in the United Kingdom, United States, and elsewhere. The use of the term *good practices* is specifically designed to avoid the use of terms such as *standards* or *best practices*; this is because of a desire to prevent challenges to evidence based on not following these practices.

The real situation is that there are no best practices or standards for what makes one approach to digital forensic evidence better or worse than another. In the end, what works is what counts. Because the law and the technology are not settled, many things may work in different situations, and to choose one over another would only muddy the waters.

Throughout this chapter I will comment on good practice, how and why deviations occur, and their implications. It is important in challenging evidence to seek out deviations from good practice, but it is also important to seek out reasons that these deviations are meaningful in terms of the basis of the challenge.

E.   The Nature of Some Legal Systems and Refuting Challenges

In some legal systems, there are great rewards to those who challenge everything. The idea is to spread the seeds of doubt in the minds of the finders of fact. In presenting and characterizing evidence, care should be taken to not mischaracterize, overcharacterize, or undercharacterize the value and meaning of evidence.

There are valid and reasonable challenges to digital evidence, and those challenges must be addressed by those presenting it, but in many cases the challenges performed by court-recognized, but inadequately knowledgeable experts are just plain wrong. In my experience, such challenges are easily refuted and should be refuted.

Refuting clearly invalid challenges is often straightforward. In most such cases, ground truth can be clearly shown. As an example, when claims are made that the presence of a file indicates something unrelated to that file, a combination of manufacturers' manuals and demonstrations readily destroy the credibility of the evidence and the person giving it. In one such case, a court-appointed special master made assertions that were clearly wrong. The combination of documentation and demonstration showed this expert for what he was and made a compelling case.

F.　　Overview

The rest of this chapter will focus on identifying sources of faults that occur in and among elements of the process and ways that those faults turn into failures. The failures are then used to challenge the process. Challenges can be couched in terms of the process, the fault, and the resulting failure, and this makes for an effective presentation of the challenge.

II.　Identifying Evidence

The first step in gathering evidence is identifying possible sources of evidence for collection. It is fairly common that identified evidence includes too little or too much information. If too much is identified, then search and seizure limitations may be exceeded, whereas if too little is identified, then exculpatory or inculpatory evidence may be missed. The most common missed evidence comes in the form of network logs from related network components.

A.　　Common Misses

There is a great deal of corroborating evidence that can be sought from connected systems that produce log files, which can confirm or refute the use of a system by a suspect. If the evidence is not sought and the actions are in question, either in terms of taking place or in terms of their source, path, or content, the lack of intermediate audit trails may complicate the ability to definitively show what took place.

Other evidence that is commonly missed includes storage devices, networked computer contents, deleted file areas from disks, secondary storage, backups, and other similar information. Properly identifying information to be collected often fails because of missed relationships between computers and evidence in those computers. This evidence is oftentimes sensitive and is lost if not identified and gathered within a short time frame.

Relevant information is often located in places not immediately evident from the original crime scene. In cases where evidence is stored for long periods and can be identified as missing in a timely fashion, the fault can usually be mitigated by additional collection. The time frame for much of this information is very limited, particularly in the case of server logs, connection logs, and similar network-related information. The chain of custody issues for such evidence can also be quite complex and involve a large number of participants from multiple jurisdictions.

B.   Information Not Sought

In some cases evidence is not sought. For example, when one side or another looks for evidence in a case, they may decide to follow up or not follow up on different facets of the case, pursue or not pursue various lines of enquiry, or limit the level of detail or sort of evidence they collect. These represent intentional nonidentification of evidence. On the other hand, there are plenty of good investigators who miss all sorts of evidence for one reason or another. Evidence is often concealed and not found by investigators. Sometimes it is stored somewhere the investigators are unaware of or cannot gain access to. Sometimes the evidence is destroyed or no longer exists by the time it becomes apparent that it might be of value. These sorts of faults occur in every case, but they rarely rise to the level of a failure causing a substantial error in a case. People do their best or focus their attention on what they think is important, and sometimes they miss things. Time and resources are limited, so certain lines are not always pursued. That's just how the world is.

C.   False Evidence

On the other hand, there are also cases, rare as they may be, when evidence is made up from whole cloth. Although this is increasingly difficult to do in all areas, such evidence in the digital arena is exceedingly rare. Indeed, it is very hard to make up digital evidence and have it survive expert challenges, and I am aware of no case when this has been done. There are cases when the defense makes such a claim, and there are even cases when digital evidence has been found to not be adequately tied to the party involved, but no cases I am aware of have been successfully challenged on the basis that the evidence was constructed. Every claim of construction of this sort that I am aware of to date has been successfully refuted.

D.   Nonstored Transient Information

Any data that is not stored in a permanent storage media cannot be seized; it can only be collected in real time by placing sensors in the environment. Such evidence must be identified in a different manner than evidence sitting on a desk or within a disk. This sort of evidence must be identified by an intelligence process, and special legal means must be applied in many cases to collect this evidence.

E.   Good Practice

The general plan for good practice is to discover the computer(s) and/or other sources of content to be seized. To the extent that some source of evidence is not discovered, good practice is not followed. As a challenge, the sources of evidence not discovered may contain exculpatory content or other relevant material. It may seem obvious that anyone doing a search for digital evidence will try to find anything they can, but the technology of today leads to an enormous number of different devices that can be concealed in a wide variety of ways. Small digital cameras are commonly concealed in sprinkler systems, pictures, and similar places. A memory stick or SD drive can contain many megabytes of information and be the size of a fingernail or smaller. It is hard to find every piece of digital evidence, and harder still if it is intentionally concealed.

It is good practice to seize the main system box, monitor, keyboard, mouse, leads and cables, power supplies, connectors, modems, floppy disks, DATs, tapes, Jazz and Zip disks and drives, CDs, hard disks, manuals and software, papers, circuit boards, keys, printers, printouts, and printer paper. Also seize mobile phones, pagers, organizers, palm computers, land-line telephones, answering machines, audio tapes and recorders, digital cameras, PCMCIA cards, integrated circuits, credit cards, smart cards, facsimile machines, and dictating machines. All of these items may contain digital forensic evidence and may be useful in getting the system to operate again. A good rule of thumb is, "If in doubt, seize it."

III. Evidence Collection

Most evidence is collected electronically. In other words, the process by which it is gathered is through the collection of electromagnetic emanations. In order to trust evidence, there needs to be some basis for the manner in which it was collected. For example, it would be important to establish that it comes from a particular system at which the user sits. This implies some sort of evidence of presence in front of the computer at a given time.

A.   Establishing Presence

Records of activity are often used to establish presence. For example, users may have passwords that are used to authenticate their identity. These may be stored locally or remotely and will typically provide date and times associated with the start of access, as well as with subsequent accesses. The verification process provides evidence of the presence of the individual at a time and place; however, such validations can be forged, stolen, and lent. In some environments common passwords and user IDs are used, making these identifications less reliable.

B.   Chain of Custody

Digital forensic evidence comes in a wide range of forms from a wide range of sources. For example, in a recent terrorism case a computer asserted to be from a defendant was provided to the FBI by someone who purchased the computer at a swap meet. These are generally outdoor small vendor sales of used equipment of all sorts — from old guns to old electronic equipment — sold over folding tables and from the backs of cars. Some of it is stolen, some of it is resold by people who bought new versions, some is wholesale, some are damaged goods, and some is made by those who sell them. This computer was asserted to contain evidence, but establishing a chain of custody was a very difficult proposition, especially considering that the defendant claimed to never have had such a computer.

C.   How the Evidence Was Created

The information that becomes evidence may be generated for various purposes, most of which are not for the purpose of presentation in court. Although the business records exception to the hearsay rule applies to normal business records, many other sorts of records may not be allowed in, depending on how they are created, collected, maintained, and presented and by whom. In most cases when information is gathered from systems as they operate, the systems under scrutiny are altered during the gathering process. Although this does not necessarily taint the evidence, it provides an opportunity for tainting that should not be overlooked if there is a reason to believe that tainting may have taken place.

D.   Typical Audit Trails

Typical audit trails include the date and time of creation, last use, and/or modification as well as identification information such as program names, function performed, user names, owners, groups, IP addresses, port numbers, protocol types, portions or all of the content, and protection settings. If this sort of information exists, it should be consistent to a reasonable extent across different elements of the system under scrutiny.

E.   Consistency of Evidence

For example, if a program is asserted to generate a file that was not otherwise altered, then the program must have been running at the time the file was created, must have had the necessary permissions to create the file, must have the capacity to create such a file in such a format, and must have been invoked by a user or the system using another program capable of invoking it. There is a lot of information that should all link together cleanly, and if it doesn't, there are reasons to question it.

This is not to say that all of these records always exist in the proper order on all systems. For various reasons, some records get lost, others end up out of order, and times fluctuate to some extent; however, these are all within some reasonable tolerance, and substantial deviations are often detectable. Such deviations are indicators that things are not what they seem, and in such cases alternative explanations are available and should be pursued.

F. Proper Handling during Collection

In most police-driven investigations normal evidence-handling requirements are used for digital forensic evidence, with a few enhancements and exceptions. Photographs and labels are commonly used, and an inventory sheet is typically made of all seized evidence. Suspects and others at the location under investigation are interviewed, passwords and similar information are retrieved, and in some cases this is used on-site to gain access to computer systems. If proper procedures are not followed, then the evidence arising from this process may be invalidated. For example, if a suspect is arrested and not Mirandaized and asked for a password to a computer system, then all of the evidence from that system may become unavailable for prosecution if the password is used to gain access.

G. Selective Collection and Presentation

In some cases, prosecution teams have opted to not do a thorough job of collecting or presenting evidence. They prefer to seek out anything that makes the defendant look guilty and stop as soon as they reach a threshold required to bring the case to court. Many prosecution teams try to prevent the defense from getting the evidence, provide only paper copies of digital evidence, and so forth. In such cases the defense should vigorously challenge the courts to require that the prosecution present all of the evidence gathered in the same form as it was made available to them and for a similar amount of time. On the other hand, most defense teams fail to present evidence that would tend to convict their clients, and they certainly don't try to help the prosecution find more evidence against their clients.

A good example of such an attempt involved the prosecution providing a printout listing the files on a disk. The printout was hundreds of pages long, contained no useful information, and could not be processed automatically. The defense in this case brought forth arguments that this was unfair and that the evidence should not be admitted at all unless the defense had adequate access to it. The issue of best evidence was also brought up. A paper copy of an extract from original electronic media is not best evidence and should not be allowed to be used when the original and more accurate copies are available and can be provided. This discussion is not intended to indicate that such behavior is limited to prosecution teams. Defense teams also do everything they can to limit discovery and make it as ineffective as possible for the other side. But because the prosecution is the predominant gatherer of digital forensic evidence in most criminal cases, it ends up being the prosecution that conceals and the defense that tries to reveal.

H.   Forensic Imaging

In order to address decay and corruption of original evidence, common practice is to image the contents of digital evidence and work with the image instead of the original. Imaging must be done in such a way as to accurately reflect the original content, and there are now studies done by the United States National Institute of Standards and Technology (NIST) to understand the limitations of imaging hardware and software, as well as standards for forensic imaging. If these standards are not met, there may be a challenge to the evidence; however, such challenges can often be defeated if proper experts are properly applied.

In at least one case, a disk dump (dd) image of a disk was thrown out because some versions of the dd program operating on some disks fail to capture the last sector of the disk. This is rare, and in the particular case no finding was made to indicate that this had happened, yet the people who were trying to get the evidence excluded won, presumably because of the incompetence of the side trying to get the evidence in. Here are just some of the counterarguments.

The original evidence disk is normally seized and retained. If it is still there, it can be reimaged and the full content examined. The image with dd is only inaccurate on disks of certain sizes, and because the disk in this case has not been shown to be such a disk, the image can be shown to be accurate. The image taken with dd is accurate except for that last sector, so all of the evidence provided using it is still accurate. If the other side wants to assert that there is some evidence in the last sector that makes a difference, they can feel free to, but nothing there invalidates the evidence that does exist.

In many cases it can be demonstrated that the last sector of a disk does not have any relevant evidence because many operating systems use it for redundant copies of other data, in which case the contents can be accurately reconstructed. It turns out that every current imaging product has been shown to have similar flaws under some circumstances. None of them are more accurate than dd according to NIST, so unless all such evidence is to be ignored, this evidence must be allowed. But in this case it seems clear that justice was not served, and the process failed.

Proper technique in forensic imaging starts with a clean palate for the results of the image. Typically, to assure that no evidence is left over from previous content of the media, the media is first cleared of data through a forensically sound erasure process. This is often not done. After clearing of the information, it is common to put a known pattern that is unlikely to appear in normal evidence on the media to later detect failures to properly image the media. After verifying this content is correct, the image is then taken. The original media is cryptographically checksummed, either in parts or as a whole, the image is made, then the result is verified with the cryptographic checksums. The result can be tested for the presence of the identifiable cleared content, and the start and end of the evidence can be clearly verified by these patterns.

Although failure to do any of these steps does not invalidate the image, they do bring into question the potential for contamination. Similarly, cryptographic checksums can be questioned as can the validity of the mechanisms for extracting and storing data on the media, but these challenges are rarely likely to succeed against a competent forensic imaging expert because the processes are so effective and hard to refute. Perhaps the most promising area for technical challenges in cases where proper technique was used lies in the potential for disk content as reflected at the normal interface to fail to reflect accurately the content of the physical media. This is because of the electronics that mediates between the interface and the media. Such challenges have never been made and would require a very high degree of expertise and great expense; however, it is a potential that has not yet been explored.

I.   Nonstored Transient Information

The collection of nonstored transient evidence typically involves a technical collection mechanism and often requires minimization in a law enforcement context. In the case of analog telephony, tape recorders and special electronics are used; whereas, in the case of digital traffic, the typical tool is a packet sniffer. Most packet sniffers have limitations in the form of collection rates, storage capacity, and ability to capture all packets. These limitations may be the basis for challenges involving missed information. Created data is far more difficult to deal with in a packet-sniffing technology. These technologies typically record what is sent through the media, but attribution to a source is more problematic.

Typical Ethernet interfaces use MAC addresses associated with packets to identify the hardware device associated with a transmission. Although these are manufacturer-specified serial numbers that are unique to a physical device, they can also be forged with special software. If the environment was not examined for the presence of such software and if other hardware is present, it is a reasonable challenge to assert that the data may not have come from the identified computer. In the absence of corroborating evidence, tying traffic to a computer is not directly evident.

In order to assert that such data is legitimate as evidence, there is a requirement that the manner in which it was gathered be demonstrated to be reliable. In cases involving communications media, there may also be requirements to follow wiretap laws as opposed to other laws, but other examples such as radar and infrared imaging, tape recording, and so forth may all involve digital forensic evidence.

This sort of evidence is also stored by the collection mechanisms in media with specific formats and characteristics and can be altered. Again, the evidence has many characteristics that allow it to be examined by experts to determine whether any obvious alteration has taken place. Many examples of this sort of content now exist because of the ready availability of computers with image and sound manipulation programs. In some cases people alter voices by combining recordings or reordering portions of them; pictures can be easily merged or altered to create false backgrounds and contexts; so-called morphing can be used to make characteristics seem similar; and digital artists can be quite skilled at creating digital renderings. Tools exist for creating shadows and similar realistic patterns and are relatively easy to use and inexpensive.

J. Secret Science and Countermeasures

This is another similar line of pursuit that has been used to prevent criminal defense teams from gaining access to key evidence and methods of gathering and analyzing evidence. In essence, the prosecution says that they have an expert who used a secret technique to determine that the defendant typed this or that. The defense asks for access to the means and detailed evidence so that they can try to refute the evidence, and the prosecution claims that this information is a government secret, classified at a level so that the defense team cannot see it. In addition, because of the way classifications work and because of a concerted effort by those who represent the government, anyone who works for a defendant is prevented from access to many of the people and techniques used by prosecution teams. Secret science presented by secret scientists is presented as objective fact that cannot be challenged. Even worse, some trial judges have let such evidence in.

There are some methods for countering such abuses, and they should be pursued with great vigor. One method is to have a digital forensic evidence expert on your team that has security clearances. This may be hard to do because very few such experts exist; however, there are some available. With such a person available, the secrecy argument can largely be eliminated from the process of examining the evidence, but the problem remains of how to try the case. Is the defense expert going to say that the prosecution expert is wrong and provide no details? This would seem ridiculous, and yet it may be the only alternative. Another alternative is to have this part of the case tried before the judge with a resulting stipulation. Yet another alternative is to ask revealing questions that don't violate the secrecy requirements while still getting at the fundamental issues in the case.

For example, a lawyer might go through each of the known technologies for gathering and analyzing the evidence and ask whether each of them was used. Even if there is no response, each can be pursued for its potential flaws with questions that the expert may or may not be able to answer. The opposing expert can then address the flaws associated with the technologies and indicate whether any of them may have been present in this matter without revealing which ones are relevant and thus without revealing the secrets. The best course would be to have the evidence thrown out for any of the following reasons: (1) It is not best evidence; (2) it is hearsay; (3) it is highly prejudicial; (4) it was not made available to the defense, thus preventing the defendant from a fair trial; (5) its scientific validity has not been established; (6) the expert has not been shown to be an expert in the particular type of evidence under scrutiny; and (7) the defense has been denied the right to challenge the scientific evidence. If the case can be made that it is more prejudicial than probative, the case stands a chance — if not in court, then on appeal.

IV. Seizure Errors

The evidence seizure process has the potential of producing a wide range of errors that may lead to challenges. Search and seizure laws may mandate Title 3 searches for live capture of digital data passing through telecommunications channels; permission for searches may be removed at any time during a permission search, and continued searching at that time may violate rules of evidence; search warrants must be adequately specific to avoid becoming fishing expeditions; and the searches must be limited to meet the requirements of the warrant if a warrant exists. Hot pursuit laws rarely apply to digital evidence, but the laws regarding plain sight are far more complex. There have been cases that have gone both ways in searches of digital media for the purpose of seizure.

A.   Warrant Scope Excess

In one case a warrant for a search for pornographic images was found to be exceeded when the officer making the search looked in directories with names that were indicative of other legitimate use. Of course, this is patently ridiculous because plenty of criminals have been found to store pornographic images under false names, in hidden files, in directories that hold legitimate images, and so forth, but the challenge worked because the judge was convinced. This is the combined result of a poorly written search warrant and a poorly educated judiciary, and this case was one of the earliest ones in this area, so such errors are likely on all sides.

There are legitimate cases on both sides, not all judges will rule the same way on the same information, and not all experts do the same things on the same cases. This sort of variation is in the nature of the work and is to be expected. Challenges should be undertaken when the evidence search and seizure process used in a nonpermission search fails to meet the reasonable requirements, when search warrant bounds are exceeded, when minimization is not adequately applied, and whenever evidence is found in a search that does not meet the original warrant and the search is not immediately stopped pending a new search warrant or the new sorts of information. In permission searches there is normally a scope of permission, and, unless it is unlimited, it may have the same problems as a warrant search in terms of admissibility.

B.   Acting for Law Enforcement

Similar limitations exist for situations in which a non–law enforcement person is acting on behalf of law enforcement or the government. In most cases when a private individual undertakes a search of their own volition and reports results to law enforcement, there is no problem associated with illegal search and seizure, although the purity of the evidence may of course come into question. But in cases where there was a preexisting relationship with law enforcement, when the specific case was under discussion between law enforcement and the person doing the search, or when the search was ordered by someone who was in touch with law enforcement on the matter, there may be an issue of admissibility under this provision.

C.   Wiretap Limitations and Title 3

In some cases where a wiretap or network tap is used, there may also be issues associated with the legality of such a wiretap. There are many states in which all parties to a communication must give permission for a recording. Without such permission, the recording may be inadmissible, and the person doing the recording may be legally liable for a criminal act. The laws on real-time collection are not very clear, and inadequate case law exists at this time; however, this makes an ideal situation for attempting to challenge evidence. The expertise of the person gathering the evidence is important to examine. In addition, if minimization is done, then an argument can sometimes be made that the exculpatory evidence was excluded in the gathering phase. This depends heavily on the specifics of the situation.

D.   Detecting Alteration

Detecting alteration is very similar to the field of questioned documents, except that in this case the documents are digital rather than analog. There is a lot of tradecraft involved in trying to figure out whether there are forgeries and what is real and fake in such digital images of real-world events. For example, the locations of light sources and their makeup generate complex patterns of shadows that can often be traced to specifics. Specific imaging technologies leave specific headers and other indicators in the image files that result from their use. Aliasing properties of digitizers, start and stop transients, scratches on lenses, frequency characteristics of pickups, and similar information often yields forgeries and digital alterations readily detectable by sufficiently skilled experts. As in other forms of digital forensic evidence, the cases where this sort of examination is relevant to the matter at hand are rare, but there are times when such analysis yields a valid challenge.

This particular sort of challenge has a tendency to appear more often in civil suits than in criminal cases because it is rare to find an instance where a member of the prosecution team creates such a forgery, and defense teams haven't the desire, time, or money to create such a forgery.

In civil matters, however, these sorts of situations are far more common. For example there are many cases in which a celebrity's head is placed on a naked body for the purposes of increased sales of pornographic material, and these forgeries tend to be readily detectable.

Another interesting example was the case of a digital image purported to be one of the airplanes photographed from the top of one of the World Trade Center towers as it was about to hit the building. This was asserted to be evidence that the Masaad (the Israeli secret service) was a co-conspirator in the September 11, 2001, attacks. The forgery was rapidly detected by an examiner who found many errors in the rendering, including wrong light direction for the time of day, improper scaling for the angle and distance, shadowing errors, edge line aliasing errors, and so forth.

E.   Collection Limits

Because all collection methods are physical, there are inherent physical limits in the collection of digital evidence. The digitization process further introduces sources of low-level errors because of the rounding effects associated with clocks relative to time bases and voltages or currents with respect to bit values. The challenge evidence collected based on signals approaching these limits is typically based on the inability of the mechanism used to gather the evidence to accurately represent and collect the underlying reality it is intended to reflect. Error-correction mechanisms often imply changes to underlying physical data to regain consistency, and they produce a probabilistic and increasing chance of error as the physical signals approach these limits.

F.   Good Practice

It is good practice to secure the scene and move people away from computers and power. This is a basic safety issue and assures that the people, investigators, and equipment are protected. Failure to do so is not likely to produce any false evidence, but it may result in the loss of otherwise valid evidence.

The investigator should not turn on the computer if it is off, not touch the keyboard if the computer is on, and not take advice from its owner or user. Clearly, a computer that is not turned on should not be turned on because this is very likely to produce alterations to the computer that may destroy its evidentiary value. Not touching the keyboard is somewhat more problematic. For example, many systems use a screen saver to lock out users after inactivity, but in the vast majority of cases, it is better to leave the keyboard and mouse alone. In terms of taking advice from the owner, more care may be necessary. Many systems are interconnected via the Internet, and if the user asserts some potential for harm associated with actions and that harm takes place, liability may be accrued. Still, such information should be passed through an experienced investigator and not taken out of hand. This is a place where good judgment may be important, and, of course, judgments are always within the realm of being challenged.

The screen should be photographed or its content noted, the printer or similar output processes should be allowed to finish, and the equipment should be powered off by pulling out all plugs. Taking a photograph or making notes of what is on the screen is certainly a reasonable step and cannot reasonably be expected to destroy or create evidence. Indeed it is likely to assure purity and consistency. Allowing output to finish may leave time for other undesirable alterations to the system. However, it may also provide additional evidence. If the system is networked, this becomes a more complex issue. For example, a remote user might alter the system after finding out that the normal user is not there, or even observe what is happening via an electronic video link. Powering off systems may also create problems, particularly if these systems act as part of the infrastructure of an enterprise. For example, this could cause all Internet access to many domains to fail or cause loss of substantial amounts of data. In some data centers with large numbers of computers, this is simply infeasible or so destructive as to be imprudent.

The investigator should label and photograph or videotape all components; remove and label all connection cables; remove all equipment, label, and record details; and note serial numbers and other identifying information associated with each component. The area should be searched for diaries, notebooks, papers, and for passwords or other similar notes. The user should be asked for any passwords, and these should be recorded. This process is clearly prudent and, to the extent that something is not photographed or labeled, it may lead to challenges. Wrong serial numbers, missing serial numbers, and similar errors may destroy the chain of evidence or lead to challenges about what was really present. At a minimum, these sorts of misses create unnecessary problems later in the case.

G.   Fault Type Review

Faults in collection are most commonly misses of content, process failures or inaccuracies, missed opportunities caused by inadequate collection technology or skill, missed relationships, missed timing information, missed location information, missed locations containing information, missed corroborating content, and missed consistencies.

V.   Transport of Evidence

When digital evidence is taken into custody, appropriate measures should be taken to assure that it is not damaged or destroyed, that it is properly labeled and kept together, and that it is not mixed up or otherwise tainted. If these precautions are not taken, the results can be effectively challenged.

A.   Possession and Chain of Custody

It is common practice in some venues to videotape the evidence collection process, and this has been invaluable in meeting subsequent challenges in many cases. In one example, a challenge was made based on the presence of a floppy disk in a floppy disk drive; however, the videotape clearly showed that no floppy disk was present, and this defeated the assertion.

B.   Packaging for Transport

Packaging for transport of digital forensic evidence has requirements similar to those of other evidence. The evidence should be transported in a timely fashion to a facility where it can be logged into an evidence locker. Chain-of-custody requirements must be met throughout the process, and the evidence has to be kept in a suitable environment to the preservation of its contents.

   If a claim of evidence tampering is to be made, this will have to be shown to have taken place when it was in the custody of the person who is asserted to have taken this action. In one case we were able to show that the amount of time available to an individual accused of tampering was inadequate to have planted the evidence asserted to have been planted. Tampering is not an easy thing to do without detection. Because of all of the inherent redundancy associated with digital forensic evidence, as described earlier, tampering can often be detected by a detailed enough examination.

C.   Due Care Takes Time

Based on the requirement for a speedy trial and high workloads in most forensic laboratories, time constraints are often placed on storage and analysis of evidence. A job done quickly normally translates into a job done less thoroughly than it might otherwise have been done. The more time spent, the more detailed an examination can be made and the more of the overall mosaic will be pieced together. In practice, most cases are made with a minimum of time and effort on such evidence, and this opens the opportunity for errors and the resulting opportunity for challenges.

D.   Good Practice

Transportation should be done with the following good practice elements. Handle everything with care; keep it away from magnetic sources such as loudspeakers, heated seats, and radios; place boards and disks in antistatic bags; transport monitors face down buckled into seats; place organizers and palmtops in envelopes; and place keyboards, leads, mouse, and modems in aerated bags.

VI.   Storage of Evidence

Evidence must be stored in a safe, secure environment to assure that it is safe from alteration. Access must be controlled and logged in most cases. But this is not enough for most digital evidence. Special precautions are needed to protect this evidence, just as special precautions are needed for some sorts of biological and chemical evidence.

A.   Decay with Time

All media decays with time. Decay of media produces errors. Typically, tapes, CDs, and disks last 1 to 3 years if kept well but can fail in minutes from excessive heat (e.g., in a car on a sunny day, on a radiator, or in a fire). Electromagnetic effects can cause damage in seconds, as can high impulses or overwriting of content. Non-acid paper can last for hundreds of years but can also fail in minutes from excessive heat or in seconds from shredding or being eaten. An audit trail is another thing that tends to decay with time.

Some are never stored, whereas others last minutes, hours, days, weeks, months, or years.

B.   Evidence of Integrity

Evidence of integrity is normally used to assert that digital forensic evidence is what it should be. This is generally assured by using a combination of notes taken while the data was extracted; using a well-understood and well-tested process of collection; being able to reproduce results, which is a scientific validity requirement in any case; using chain-of-custody records and procedures; and applying proper imaging techniques associated with the specific media under examination.

The establishment of purity of evidence is generally better if established earlier in the process. The media being imaged or analyzed should be write-protected so that accidental overwrite cannot happen. A cryptographic checksum should be taken as soon as feasible to allow content to be verified as free from alteration at a later date. It may also be wise to do cryptographic checksums on a block-by-block and file-by-file basis to assure that even if part of the evidence becomes corrupt or loses integrity with time, the specific evidence is covered by additional codes. This allows us to assure the freedom from alteration of portions of a large media even if the overall media becomes corrupt. Keeping the original pure by only using it to generate an initial image and working only from images from then on is a wise move when feasible. Validating purity over time also helps to assure that time is not wasted and that no alteration occurs in the analytical process.

Nobody knows for certain that any evidence is completely pure and free from alteration, and likely nobody ever will. But this does not mean that all evidence can be successfully challenged or should be. Just because people are not perfect, that doesn't mean they are not good enough. Just because evidence is not perfect, that doesn't mean it is not good enough.

C.   Principles of Best Practices

Principle 1: No action should change data held on a computer or other media.

Principle 2: In exceptional circumstances where examination of original evidence is required, the examiner must be competent to examine it and explain its relevance and implications.

Principle 3: Audit records or other records of all processes applied to digital evidence should be created and preserved. An independent third party should be able to reproduce those actions with similar results.

Principle 4: Some individual person should be responsible for adhering to these principles.

VII. Evidence Analysis

Evidence analysis is perhaps the most complex and error-prone aspect of digital evidence. It is also the most subjectively applied in many cases. But in almost all cases it should not and need not be subjective. It is subjective largely because of the failure of those undertaking analysis to spend the time and effort to be careful in what they do.

A.   Content

Making content typically involves processing errors. For example, an unclean palate is used in the analysis process, and the analysis finds evidence that was left over from a previous case. This was addressed under imaging, discussed earlier. The challenge to this can come in many forms, and if original evidence or cryptographic checksums are not used, such challenges have a good chance of success because of the inability to independently verify results. If originals are present and checksums can be shown to match, then such challenges will only succeed in the presence of actual and material error because the validity of the evidence can be properly established.

Missing content typically results from limited time or excessive focus of attention. Limited time is almost always an issue because there is usually an enormous amount of evidence present, most of which can only be peripherally examined with simple tools. Examining every bit pattern from every possible perspective is simply too time-consuming to be feasible and is almost never necessary to get to the heart of the evidence. Excessive focus, on the other hand, is easier to avoid. By simply taking an open view of what could be meaningful evidence and being thorough in the evaluation process, such misses are avoidable. The challenge is simple. Did you look at everything? Is there any exculpatory evidence? Where did you look? Why did you not look in the other places? What technique did you use? Why did you not use a more definitive technique? Is there a more definitive technique? The questions can be nearly endless.

B.   Contextual Information

Information has meaning only in context. Analysis can make context by making assumptions that are invalid or cannot be demonstrated. Context is missed when assumptions that are valid and can be demonstrated are not made. The challenge to context that has been made starts with questioning the basis for assumptions. If assumptions cannot be adequately demonstrated, the context becomes dubious, the assumptions fall away, and the conclusions are not demonstrable. If an alternative context can be demonstrated with the same or better basis, that context can be substituted and the interpretation of the evidence altered. Missed context can be challenged with the introduction of alternative contexts. It then becomes the challenge of the other side to disprove these contexts.

An excellent example of this was a case in England where the defense challenged the validity of the evidence by introducing the potential that an attack on the computer system being examined caused the illicit effects rather than the user at the console. In the end, the prosecution could not convincingly demonstrate the validity of its assumption that the user who owned the computer carried out the behavior in question, and the case was dismissed. Although many computer security experts assert that there was no evidence of the presence of such an attack, the lack of a demonstration of its presence by the defense is not the same as the demonstration of its absence by the prosecution.

C.   Meaning

The meaning of things that are found is obviously the basis for interpretation. Meaning that is missed leads to a failure to interpret, and meaning that is made is an interpretation without adequate support.

For example, the presence of a file with a name associated with a particular program might indicate that the program was present at some time in the past, but not necessarily. The filename could be a coincidence or it could have been placed there by other means, such as part of a backup or restoration process. In most cases there are a variety of different meanings that can be applied to content, and determining the most likely meaning typically involves reviewing the different possible meanings relative to the rest of the environment. The same applies to the context, presence or absence of files, directories, packets, or any other things found in material under examination.

D.   Process Elements

Content does not come to exist through magic. It comes to exist through a process. The notion that a sequence of bits appears on a system without the notion of how that sequence came to exist there makes for a very weak case. If the bits were created within the system, the means for their creation should be there unless it was somehow removed. If the bits were obtained from somewhere else, the process by which they got there should be identified. If there are alternative explanations for the arrival of the bit sequence, why is one interpretation better than the other?

Processes normally generate audit records of some sort somewhere. Files have times associated with them in most file systems. If a file was retrieved from a network, audit records from the location it came from and the connection to the network may be recorded. If some image was deleted and the residual information from it is gone, there must be some process by which that event sequence occurred. Without evidence of the process, alternative explanations may be offered with as much credibility as the explanation preferred by one side. The plausibility of these explanations is key to the meaning of the content they refer to.

E.   Relationships

Just as sequences of events produce content, relationships between event sequences and content produce content. The presence or absence of related content causes differences in the content generated by related processes. The presence or absence of a directory prior to running a program that uses or creates it produces a difference in the time associated with the creation of the directory. Similarly, the placement of the directory in the linked lists associated with the file system relative to the placement of files within that directory may indicate the differences in these relationships. There are many such relationships within systems, and those relationships can be explored to challenge the assertions of those who make claims about them.

F.   Ordering or Timing

Sequences are a special case of orderings. More generally, orderings can involve things that cannot be differentiated from being simultaneous, whereas sequences are completely ordered. Timing often cannot be established with perfection, but partial orderings can be derived. The possible orders of events can make an enormous difference in some cases. One obvious reason for this is that ordering is a precondition for cause and effect. To assert that one thing caused another, it must be demonstrable that the cause preceded the effect. If this cannot be established by timing, there is the potential to challenge based on the lack of a causal basis.

Although this may seem like a highly theoretical argument, many cases have been made or broken by the ability to show time sequences. If an accusation of theft and disclosure of trade secret information is made and it cannot be shown that the theft preceded the disclosure, then the basis for the claim is invalid. If an attacker was supposed to be present at a computer to commit a crime at a particular time and they can show that at that time they were not present at that computer, then the alibi will refute the claim. If the time is uncertain in a computer system, the entire process becomes suspect because computers usually keep time very well. If ordering or timing is missed, the lack of the ordering or timing information leads to challenges. If timing assumptions are made and not validated, they can be questioned.

The most common challenge to compute-related times stems from the potential difference between a computer clock and the real-world time. Even accounting for time zone variations, this is an all too common problem that has to be addressed in the forensic process. If the time reference for the computer is not established at the time the evidence is collected, timing can sometimes be obtained by relating the timing of events within the computer to externally timed network events. Missed time can sometimes be made up for by correlation with outside events, whereas made time can often be demonstrated wrong by similar correlation. The lack of correlating information represents sloppiness in the collection and analysis process that may itself lead to the inability to determine timing.

A less used challenge stems from the ability to determine ordering of events in the absence of other timing information. For example, there are cases when times and exact sequences could not be determined but orderings could because of overwrite patterns on disks. In one such case it was shown that a file transfer happened before an erasure was done, because the area of the disk where the file would have existed had the erasure happened first was covered with the pattern associated with the erasure. What happened between these events and the precise times they occurred could not be determined, but the ordering could be, and it was one of the pieces in a larger puzzle that determined the outcome of the case.

G.   Location

Everything that happens in computers has physicality despite any efforts to portray it as somehow ephemeral. Physicality tends to leave forensic evidence in one form or another. For example, when a person uses a keyboard, particles from hair and skin fall into the keyboard and tend to get stuck there. In a similar fashion, data in computers tends to be placed on the disk and tends to get stuck there. Computer systems have physical characteristics as well, and sometimes they are dead giveaways to location.

In one example of a missed and made location, an attack against a government computer system had an Internet protocol (IP) address associated with a location in Russia. But when observing the traffic patterns shown in log files, it was determined that the jitter associated with packet arrival times was very small. Packet arrival-time jitter tends to occur when packets are mixed in delivery queues across infrastructure. More infrastructure tends to lead to more jitter. The lack of jitter meant that the arriving packets were not being mixed much with other packets and that the computer responsible was, therefore, physically close to the observation point. The attack was traced to a point only a few network links away from the surveillance point. Evidence such as this can make a compelling case, and it's easy to miss the real location and make a false location when such analysis is not thoroughly undertaken.

H.   Inadequate Expertise

We also face many low-quality experts and people with an axe to grind who are put up as experts. An excellent example of this was a case involving copyright infringement in which a court-appointed special master made claims including (1) the accuser may have altered data, (2) date and time information was unreliable, (3) the system never worked when returned to its owner after it was forensically investigated, (4) programs were destroyed, and (5) preexisting data was no longer present. In this case, all of these claims were refuted by a better expert who used recorded statements, a videotape of the return process, some details of the physics of writing to disks that dismissed the possibility of forgery, and correlation with other records. It is important to note that, under some circumstances, all of the things asserted by this special master could have been true, so the claims were not outrageous in the general sense. It is only that they were not in fact true in this case.

I.   Unreliable Sources

There are a lot of unreliable sources of digital content. For example, the Internet is full of the widest possible range of different content, only a small portion of which is really accurate and a significant portion of which is just plain false. There is a tendency for people to believe some of these things, and once these things are believed, the belief transcends the original source. For example, when looking up information about the function of a hardware device or software program, at a detailed level, much of the information on the Internet is not accurate. It might reflect a different version; it might reflect a mistake by the author; it might reflect a simplification by the author for reader convenience; and it might be an intentional or malicious misstatement by a disgruntled ex-employee. Although this information may be convenient or readily available and useful in many circumstances, it is not generally suited to the level of trust required for digital forensic evidence purposes.

As a good example, the question sometimes comes up of the list of all circumstances under which a file access date and time will be altered by a Windows operating system under normal use. It turns out that this is not an easy question to answer. The answer varies on different versions of Windows, different applications may use different system calls for the same outcome with different side effects, and programs that deal with forensic processes typically do things differently than other operating system programs. Even such simple questions do not have easy answers, and the Internet answers are not consistent or accurate in many cases.

J.   Simulated Reconstruction

In some recent court cases, computer-based reconstructions of physical events have been used in presentations to juries. In some sense this is no different than the use of storyboards to show how a crime is purported to have happened, but in another sense it can be too realistic in that it can give the appearance of certainty about many things that there is no certainty about. In such a case there are a number of approaches to reducing the impact of such fabricated evidence.

One of the keys to countering this sort of evidence is to use the terms *fabricated, fabrication,* and *fabricating*. When referring to this evidence, it should always be identified as a fabrication. Underlying this question is the issue of the prejudicial value as opposed to the probative value. The question is one of differentiating the part of the fabrication that is more probative than prejudicial from the part that is not. Is the use of continuous video more probative or prejudicial than a set of storyboards? The enhancement generated by motion is, in almost all cases, more prejudicial than probative because the intervening fabrication of motion is highly specific while the real knowledge of the details is almost always very limited. Did the perpetrator use their right or left hand? Did they really bend their elbow like that? Did they trip over an obstruction on the floor? Did their shirt really wrinkle like that?

If the information provided by the fabrication is not demonstrably accurate, it is not relevant and provided without a proper foundation. If the coloring of the face is similar to that of a defendant, this is prejudicial and, unless there is evidence as to the coloring of the face of the perpetrator, green might be a better choice. It is valid to zoom in on the parts of the presentation and ask whether the information at that detailed level is accurate. If the depicted gun is a different sort than the one used in the crime, the gun type should be shown to the finder of fact, and the question should be asked about whether this is evidence that the defendant did not do this crime. The answer will be no, and this gives the opportunity to again point out the fabricated nature of the display and its gross inaccuracy as to the facts. What in fact is real about this fabrication? Can you tell us whether the colors in this fabrication are real? How about the shadows? Is the time on the fabricated clock real? Are the footfalls real? Does this fabrication show any trace evidence being left on the site? What evidence do you have of the height of the person in this fabrication?

K.   Reconstructing Elements of Digital Crime Scenes

Digital crime scenes can also be reconstructed, and this is a critical area for scientific evidence. Although experts may assert any number of things about what might be within a computer, the ultimate test can often be made through a reconstruction. But even reconstruction of a digital crime scene has its limits. Although similar circumstances can be created, identical ones often cannot. As a rule of thumb, simple questions can often be answered by digital reconstructions, but complex sequences of events are far harder to confirm or refute.

A simple example where reconstruction is very effective is determining whether or not a file is created by an application in the normal course of operation. To test this, it is a simple matter to install the application on a system, operate it normally, and see whether this file is created. It is far harder to make this determination through reconstruction in abnormal operation. An excellent case example of a reconstruction that refuted evidence was a case in which the prosecution asserted that a particular program could be used to extract deleted file content from a floppy disk. The prosecution knew that a utility program by a particular name was present and that this program was commonly used for this sort of operation. The defense did a simple reconstruction. They took the actual program on the defendant's system and tried to do what the prosecution claimed could be done. This failed. It turned out that the particular version of this utility program on the defendant's computer did not have the capability the prosecution claimed it had. Earlier and later versions had this capability, but not the one on the defendant's system. Case dismissed.

Digital reconstruction can be a powerful tool, but it cuts both ways. There are plenty of cases in which reconstruction confirms rather than refutes the evidence. Indeed, this is one of the great values of doing reconstruction. It tends to get at the truth. The problems with such reconstructions come when they are interpreted too generally or when they are used to try to make claims about complex situations. A good example of the limitations of such reconstructions is any case where many possible sequences of events could have taken place, and these events involve complex interactions between components. The larger the number of possible sequences, the more reconstruction runs are necessary to exhaust the space of possibilities. In cases where exhaustion is not feasible, statistical samples can be taken, but the nature of digital systems makes such statistics highly questionable. The more intertwined the elements are, the more complex the potential sequences become.

In a simple case where the ability of a program to perform a function through the normal user interface is at question, reconstruction is simple and effective. Simply install the specific software on the specific system in question and try to use the interface to generate the desired results. In some cases complex sequences are required in order to generate specific outputs, but manufacturers and manuals are usually adequate to generate things that are meant to be generated.

If the goal is to prove that a program could have generated an output, it may be far more complex, depending on the specifics. Whereas some outputs are generated often or predictably, other outputs may be very situation-specific and may involve complex interactions with the environment. Creating the entire environment may be problematic if it involves such things as network events that are usually out of the control of those doing reconstruction. There are forensic technologies that can largely accomplish these sorts of reconstructions, but they are rarely used and difficult to properly implement.

If the goal is to show that it was impossible for a perpetrator to have entered a computer and performed a function without leaving any evidence, the task may be very difficult. More generally, proving an assertion about something with unlimited numbers of possibilities or disproving something under the assumption of the perfect opponent is very hard and sometimes impossible. But in almost all such cases a demonstration can be constructed to show some subset of the scenarios. If this is done, the challenge can be made on the basis that the space was inadequately covered.

L.   Good Practice in Analysis

It turns out that nobody has yet compiled a widely accepted collection of good practices for analysis of digital evidence. In fact, parts of this book and the references provided may be considered as close to such a compilation as you are likely to find.

As a result, all analysis is subject to expert interpretation and challenges of all sorts, and each case will be judged on its merits without appeal to some standard, regardless of how tentative it is. But there are some time-tested analysis techniques that should be covered despite the lack of any widely published good practices.

1.   The Process of Elimination

It is generally considered good practice to use the process of elimination. In this process, a list of the possibilities is made and items on the list are eliminated one at a time or in groups for specific reasons that can be backed up by facts. The challenges to the process of elimination start with the initial list. Is the list comprehensive? How do you know it is comprehensive? If I find one thing missing, does this invalidate the list as being comprehensive? What if I find two? Are there implicit assumptions in the list? What are they? Are they demonstrably true? What if they are wrong? The next challenge comes in the application of the process. Was the test of each item on the list definitive? Was it properly done? What are the cases in which this test would fail to be revealing? Does a positive or negative result in your test environment represent the same result as what would happen in the real environment? In other words, what are the possible differences between the real world and the test environment? And finally, almost all such tests make assumptions about the independence of the items on the list or the elements within the computer systems involved. Suppose these things are not independent, would that invalidate this test? In many cases these assumptions can be demonstrated to be incorrect under certain circumstances.

2.   *The Scientific Method*

The basis of the scientific method is that the truth can be verified by the failure of experiments that attempt to disprove an assertion. But even one refutation implies that the hypothesis under test or the testing method was incorrect in some respect.

3.   *The Daubert Guidelines*

Case law in the United States has led to the Daubert Guidelines for the admissibility and validity of scientific evidence. These almost always apply to digital forensic analysis issues. The tests of scientific evidence in this case include four basic issues: (1) Has the procedure or technique been published? (2) Is the procedure generally accepted? (3) Can and has the procedure been tested? (4) What is the error rate of the procedure?

Most digital forensic analysis methods in use today have not been widely published. Those that are published are rarely published in referenced scientific journals. There are several books on this subject and more such books are being written. In addition to these publications, there are manuals from products and books on special purpose topics. Finally, hardware and software design and source code information is often available to those properly trained to understand it. These then form the literature in this area. The lack of published material leads to many challenges to the admissibility or validity of this evidence. Perhaps most importantly, most of the forensic examination and analysis tools that are made for sale include trade secrets and unpublished content that form the intellectual property basis that creates competitive advantages and barriers to entry in the market. As a result, the most commonly used tools do not include the information required to determine what precisely they do. Their use and their results can be strongly challenged on this basis. Similarly, file formats, hardware device operations, and similar functions of components are not known at the most detailed level, and their operation is not published.

In terms of being generally accepted, there are few generally accepted analysis techniques for digital forensic evidence. In some sense, without publication, general acceptance is impossible, but on a more general basis, almost any presentation of analysis of digital forensic evidence is challengeable on this basis. For example, if a forensic analyst asserts that a file contains some specific data and was created at some particular date and time, in addition to the technical limitations of this assertion, the methods used to derive this information can be questioned in great detail to try to shake confidence in the validity of the technique undertaken. The problem with such a challenge is that it risks alienating the finder of fact and is likely to come down to things that users do every day but that are not documented as forensic processes. This approach is more applicable in cases where the technique is believed to have produced wrong results. In such cases, wrong results are usually easily demonstrated by following the specific steps taken by the examiner.

Public testing of analysis techniques has not been done to date. Although the United States NIST is undertaking tests of forensic imaging processes, analysis techniques are essentially only tested today by the individuals doing work in this area. The tests undertaken can usually be described by the forensic examiner, but they are likely to be very limited. It is reasonable in most cases to challenge the tests done to validate the technique used by the examiner, but the import of this depends heavily on the evidence being presented. If the person presenting the evidence has not tested their own tools, they will probably be hard-pressed to show that it has been tested elsewhere, and the credibility of the technique and the person applying it can be challenged.

The error rate of forensic analysis tools is even harder to attest to, because in almost all commercial products no error rate can be established without independent tests. As a result, although error rates for such things as cryptographic checksums on forensic images can be estimated, error rates on disk searches and depictions of images based on file content are far harder to ascertain. The problem with this approach to challenging evidence is that the underlying digital technology is very good at nearly error-free operation. Although there are almost always errors in the programs implementing any digital forensic process, these errors are not apparent, and similar processes can be undertaken with independent software to mitigate against these challenges. Again, challenges here should be made only in cases where there is a good reason to believe that the resulting facts are in error.

4.   *Digital Data Is Only a Part of the Overall Picture*

Almost every analysis of digital forensic evidence ultimately involves ties to the real world. In order for analysis to produce meaningful results, it must tie those results to the matter at hand. The analysis process as a technical matter can often be resolved, and some set of resulting bit sequences with some time sequencing can be revealed to the finder of fact without significant disagreement. In fact, this is often done by stipulation, subject to an adequate presentation. However, the interpretation of those results is subject to far more variation than the setting of the bits.

The attribution of actions to actors is often hard to pin down. Although there are cases in which there are films of people using their computers and typing the material of interest to a legal matter, this is certainly the exception rather than the rule. Attribution has been and continues to be studied, and there are many indications that behavioral and biometric indicators can be used to attribute actions to actors. However, the amount of scientific study in this area to date is limited, and the results are far from definitive. Furthermore, the characteristics used in attribution are usually tied to time sequences and interaction sequences. For example, different keyboards produce different error rates and error types for typists with different training and experience, but if all we have is a spell-corrected end document with no data-entry sequences, these errors will not appear in the analysis. This is often a basis for challenge, and in some cases it is highly successful.

Physical evidence can often be tied to digital evidence. For example, an online credit card theft may be challenged, but if the credit cards stolen resulted in purchases delivered to the defendant's address, and the defendant did not question these items, try to return them, and is using them, the computer evidence of the theft may be hard to discredit. On the other hand, the lack of a nexus with real-world events should lead to a serious question about validity. Just because someone wrote about a credit card fraud scheme does not mean they perpetrated one. Even if their computer was involved in one that is similar to their writings, the lack of a physical nexus is a potentially fatal flaw.

Means, motive, and opportunity apply to the digital world as well as the analog one. If the evidence shows a level of expertise in developing and hatching a scheme, and the individual on trial does not have the necessary expertise, the means does not exist. Digital systems are complex, and a great deal about the knowledge of individuals is often revealed by the audit records and software present on the system under examination. Opportunity in computers does not always require presence. Because of the potential for telepresence in a networked computer, an analysis of events in a computer do not always tie the individual to the events or the events to the presence of any individual. Making or missing these times is commonplace.

5.   *Just Because a Computer Says So Doesn't Make It So*

This is perhaps my favorite basis for challenging the analysis of digital forensic evidence. The seeming infallibility of computers leads many to believe that, if a computer says, so it must be so. People are increasingly realizing that this is not true, but the point still must be made in many cases. The sources of errors in computers are wide-ranging. From computer viruses that leave pornographic content in computers, to remote control via Trojan horses that allow external users to take over a computer from over the Internet, to just plain lies typed in by human beings, computers are full of wrong information. In some studies of data-entry errors, rates on the order of 10% to 20% are common. That is, 1-in-5 to 1-in-10 data entries in a typical commercial database are not complete, accurate, and reflective of reality.

VIII. Overall Summary

The number of ways that digital forensic evidence can be challenged is stag-
gering, and many of these challenges can be successful in the proper circumstances. But a competent digital forensics process and examiner can avoid all
of these challenges by diligent efforts and thorough consideration of the
issues.

Avoiding all faults is impossible, but almost all failures can be avoided
by prudent efforts. When faults occur, they may or may not produce failures.
And some failures are recoverable, whereas others are not. At steps in the
process where faults lead to failures that are not recoverable, special care
should be taken to avoid these faults.

Limits of budget, training, tools, and simple human errors have many
effects on the challenges to digital forensic evidence, and those who wish to
use this evidence should take note of the need for overcoming these limits
within their organizations.

Those who seek to challenge such evidence have an equally daunting task
because of the widespread perception of computers as perfect, which leads
to excessive belief in the content within them. But as more and more people
have identities stolen, computerized records create financial problems, computer failures cause missed flights, and fraudulent spam e-mails sent to them,
this will change. Planting the seeds of distrust in computers and computer
evidence is the basis of any challenge, and these seeds exist for those who
seek to find them.

When those engaged in the forensic process miss or make, through
accident or intent, it is the job of those who see these faults to point them
out and act to correct any failures that may result. A healthy forensic process
seeks to poke holes in its own system in order to improve it and seeks ways
to compensate for holes it identifies. Hopefully these challenges will be met
by those in the digital forensics community so that these challenges never
have to rear their ugly heads again.

Strategic Aspects in International Forensics

8

DARIO FORTE, CFE, CISM

I.   The Current Problem of Coordinated Attacks

In this chapter we will discuss investigations of hacking incidents. The most recent hacker-oriented police operations have highlighted resurgence in the trend. Crimes involving extortion, sabotage, and fraud are on the rise, as well as information theft and leaks in the industrial espionage theater. The following provide an explanation of some basic concepts:

- *Extortion attacks* are deployed in two basic ways: the first involves stealing information from the target and then asking a ransom to get it back or else laying out demands that must be met to stop the attacker from releasing the information to an undesired audience. The payment is usually made into a bank account outside the country where the target and the extortionists reside in order to hamper investigations on the part of law enforcement agencies. The preference is for offshore entities, whose banking system makes retracing the perpetrators much more difficult. The second method involves rooting out an architectural vulnerability in someone's system that may be exploited with serious impact. The attackers then leave a note in the compromised architecture so that the target owner, once contacted, can verify that the criminals do indeed pose a threat. And we are talking about having a bona fide security advisor verify this, because what happens after the extortionists notify the target owner of the existence of the vulnerability is that they propose a security consultation to resolve the problem. The target's obvious fear is that, if he or she refuses, the news of his vulnerability might be put into circulation.

- *Information theft* may take place for a variety of reasons, ranging from underhanded competition to full-scale industrial espionage and terrorism. The violations are carried out both by insiders and outsiders using a variety of techniques of varying sophistication. When you hear the term *coordinated attacks*, it means that the hackers are waging their attacks from a number of sources, forcing investigators to seek traces that are spread out across multiple physical and virtual locations.
- *Damage to information* can be accomplished by a number of factors, from malicious code to illicit intrusions.
- Data availability criterion violation

When people talk about coordinated attacks, they mean attacks waged from multiple locations, agents, and intermediary points (known as stepping stones) that route communications and/or criminal activities. As a result, an investigator's job immediately takes on an international scope, and he or she will have to deal with a series of international coordination factors that will be described later in the chapter.

II.   The New Antibacktracing and Antiforensics Tools, and Onion Routing

Numerous tools are coming out whose objectives are to complicate and hinder digital forensics. We will concentrate on some of the tools and their modi operandi that represent a potential threat for the future.

A.   Using Covert Channels to Elude Traffic Analysis: NCovert

During the Black Hat conference 2003 in Las Vegas, a program called NCovert was presented. It uses spoofing techniques to hide the source of communications and the data that travels over the network — a potential boon to both privacy advocates and hackers, according to Mark Lovelace (a.k.a. Simple Nomad), senior security researcher for BindView, who unveiled the program.

The technique essentially creates a covert channel for communications by hiding four characters of data in the header's initial sequence number (ISN) field. The header is the part of data packets that tells network hardware and servers how to handle the information. The header also includes source and destination Internet protocol (IP) addresses. Those addresses are used to add anonymity to the communications.

B.   Difficulties in Backtracing Onion Router Traffic

1.   *The Goal: Protection from Traffic Analysis*

Traffic analysis is used in part to identify the addresses that a given IP address seeks to contact. This technique may have various purposes, from simple statistical analysis to illegal interception. In response to this, researchers from the U.S. Naval Research Laboratory conceived a system, dubbed *Onion Routing*.

2.   *Onion Routing: What It Is*

The objective of Onion Routing is to make it completely impossible for third parties to perform traffic analysis. This goal is achieved by applying crypto-graphic techniques to networking. The packets transiting the chain of onion routers thus appear anonymous. Yes, we are talking about a chain. Practically speaking, there is a group of Onion Routers distributed around the public network, each of which has the task of encrypting the socket connections and to act in turn as a proxy. Experiments with Onion Routing have already been carried out on Sun Solaris 2.4 using proxies for HTTP (www), or hypertext transfer protocol, and RLOGIN. At the moment, proxy operations are planned for e-mail (simple mail transfer protocol, or SMTP), file transfer protocol (FTP), and a slew of other protocols.

Let's imagine we have to make an HTTP transaction. Here's how it works:

1. The application does not connect directly to the destination Web server but rather to a socket connection with an Onion Routing proxy.
2. The Onion Routing proxy establishes a direct anonymous connection with its nearest sister. To guarantee the impossibility of interceptions, the first Onion Routing proxy makes another connection with others of its ilk to complete the chain. To avoid hijacking and man-in-the-middle phenomena, the communication between onion routers is forced. Practically speaking, each Onion Router is only able to identify and dialog with its adjacent kin included in the route. Each packet can currently make a maximum of 11 hops, and then it has to reach its destination.
3. Each time an Onion Router handles a transaction, it strips away a layer of encryption with respect to the preceding hop. This means that at the end of the route the packet arrives in clear text. This is one of the first problems an investigator may encounter. Because of the encryption and because at each hop the link to the preceding routing point is literally stripped away, backtrace becomes impossible. The only way to carry out an effective investigation is to implement a logging function at the proxy level, as we will describe in greater detail later in this chapter.

Onion Routing: simple flow example

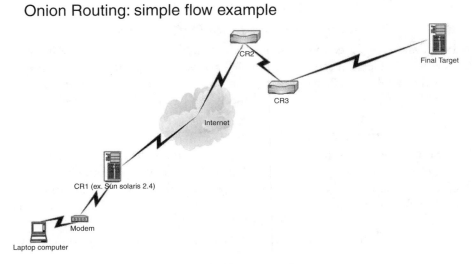

Figure 8.1   Onion Routing: simple flow example.

4. The encryption and transmission of data through the links of the chain is carried out randomly in such a way as to render impossible any sort of sequence prediction. Furthermore, whenever the connection is interrupted, for any reason, all information relating to a given transaction is deleted from the rest of the chain. It is basically a sort of no-cache system.

It is also possible to use Onion Routing together with the Windows 95/NT NRaD redirector, acting at the TCP/IP (transmission control protocol/Internet protocol) network protocol stack level and forcing the connection routing through the Onion Routing network. The only practical limitation is that the NRaD redirector cannot be freely distributed because of licensing restrictions.

Figure 8.1 provides a graphic representation of Onion Routing packet flow.

Of course, such a routing can also be implemented by using multiple stepping stones. In both cases, the investigator's work will be very difficult, all the more so because the deployment is on an international scale. The version using multiple stepping stones is illustrated in Figure 8.2.

3.   *The Differences with the Other Anonymizers*

According to the official project documents (http://www.onion-router.net), Onion Routing differs from other anonymity services in three ways: Communication is real-time and bidirectional; the anonymous connections are application-independent (as opposed to services like anonymizer.com and

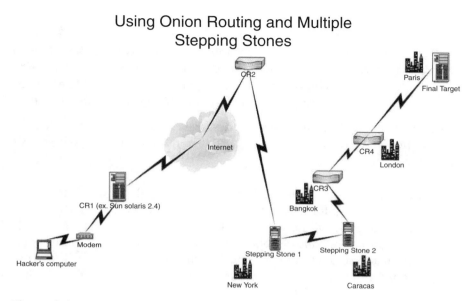

Figure 8.2   Onion Routing and multiple stepping stones.

its ilk); and there is no centralized component. Applications may choose whether to identify their users over an anonymous connection. However, the use of a switched public network should not automatically reveal who is talking to whom. This is the traffic analysis that Onion Routing complicates.

4.   The Onion Routing Roadmap

The Onion Routing (OR) concept was introduced in early 1996. The basic idea achieved proof of concept with the implementation of the Onion Router I project comprising five OR devices, wholly managed by the U.S. Naval Research Laboratory. The project has recently undergone further developments and now includes 50 core Onion Routers composing the second generation of the chain and having the hop randomization characteristics described earlier. The interesting aspect with respect to the first generation is that ORtNG (Onion Routing the Next Generation) has a series of added features, many of which constitute improvements of the cryptosystem with particular reference to transaction speed. This thus resolves the potential overhead penalty of the earlier project, which was eventually performance limiting, even with the use of accelerators.

5.   A Glossary of Project Terms

Mix: According to the original project documents, a Mix is a store-and-forward device that accepts a number of fixed-length messages from numerous sources, performs cryptographic transformations on the messages, and then forwards the messages to the next destination in an order that cannot be predicted on the basis of the order of inputs. A single Mix renders difficult tracking of a particular message either by specific bit-pattern, size, or ordering with respect to other messages. Routing through numerous Mixes in the network makes determining who is talking to whom even more difficult.

Cell: In the context of OR, the term describes fixed-sized entities that the router moves across a connection. ORtNG can be split into seven basic modules:

a. Database Engine (DB) — The DB is responsible for distributing and maintaining information about the entire network. It learns the public certificates for all nodes, the link state of the entire network graph, the exit access control policies for each node, and the current operational state of each node. This information is critical for the application proxy (see next entry) to be able to create an effective route through the network.

b. Application Proxy (AP) — This is the application-specific proxy that handles interfacing into the OR network. For the reader's information, after version 1 of the project, OR has worked with proxy-aware and several non-proxy-aware applications without modifying the applications. This description of the AP might seem to contradict what we said earlier regarding application independence in the OR system. Actually, in this case, the independence is to be attributed to the fact that there are no technological limits to the type of proxy that can be implemented within the chain, in spite of the fact, as we will see later, that currently only certain protocols are supported. Hence, the main difference with conventional anonymizers is that these latter only work with HTTP protocols. It is the application proxy that contains the database engine (DE) because the AP now does route planning and Onion creation (formerly done by the first Core; the trust for generating the Onions has been moved closer to the user). When we talk about Onion creation in this case we mean the first step in the routing decision-making process evidently taken by the AP. Because the DE contains the AP, its crucial importance to the whole architectural structure appears clear. The team is currently planning APs for HTTP/1.1-HTML/4.0, SMTP, FTP, RLOGIN, TELNET, NNTP, talk, finger, whois, gopher, WAIS, dns, nfs, RAW sockets, Virtual LANs, and SOCKS5.

c. Core (C) — The Core is the heart of OR. It moves cells along anonymous connections throughout the OR network. Currently it is the only element that contains a Chaum Mix, but other elements, for example, input funnel, AP, or output funnel, could also have them added.

d. Crypto Processor (CP) — The CP is responsible for processing Onions at each C. The CP performs the necessary public-key decryption and prepares the Onion for the next hop, returning the result back to the C. This unit is critical to prevent processing burps at Cs during costly public-key operations.

Figure 8.3 is a diagram of the Onion Router's output side, without optional components.

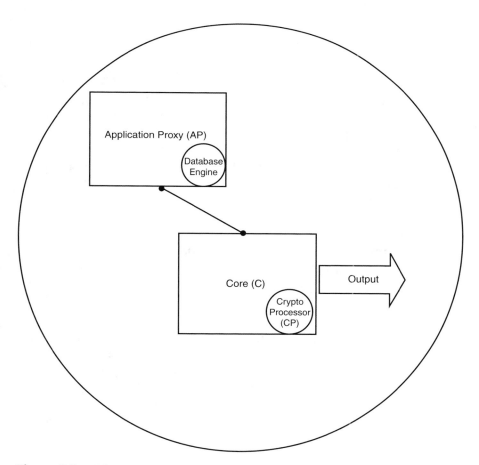

Figure 8.3   The Onion Router's output side.

The input management side is composed of:

5. Responder Proxy (RP) — The RPs interpret the material transmitted
    by the application proxy. There are a number of different types of
    RPs that deal with different types of circuits:
    a. Short-Lived (RPSL) — Short-lived connections are things such as
        HTTP.
    b. Long-Lived (RPLL) — Long-lived connection are things such as
        RLOGIN or TELNET.
    c. Reply Onion (RPRO) — Any connection utilizing a Reply Onion
        must route through here or else all crypto activity will fail for that
        circuit.
    d. Virtual LAN (RPVL) — Specialized RP to handle virtual local area
        networks (VLANs).

There are also a couple of optional components:

6. Input Funnel (IF) — This is an optional unit used to multiplex more
    APs into one C, or to span a firewall without having to reveal the
    network topology on the secure side of the firewall. IFs can be stacked
    as deep as necessary (no limit) between the AP and the C. Ultimately,
    IFs will be able to load-balance between multiple Cs.
7. Output Funnel (OF) — The OF is responsible for de-multiplexing
    the circuits from the C to the RPs. Because there are multiple types
    of RPs, the OF must peek initially into the stream to determine which
    RP is most appropriate for a new circuit;

6.   *The Potential Dangers of Onion Routers*

Although, on the one hand Onion Routers mean that user privacy can be
definitively protected, the adoption of these chaining systems represents a
potential means of limiting backtrace. Here are the main reasons:

1. Within the encryption done by the Onion Router, another crypto-
    graphic operation may be encapsulated that is completely transparent
    to the former. This means a doubling of packet payload masking
    operations. During the lecture associated with this chapter, made at
    DFRWS (Digital Forensic Research Workshop) 2002, one of the re-
    searchers said that even within non-OR architectures, encryption of
    payloads is often performed on the client application side. It is diffi-
    cult enough for investigators to analyze these payloads without having
    also to worry about the routing information being encrypted. This is

true, but it is sometimes possible, with proper preparation, to carry out a coordinated approach based on the interception of data flows (e.g., on an Internet service provider, or ISP, or at a specific point in the normal path of a packet) and on the forensic investigation carried out on the computer of the suspected person. The use of an OR-based system can introduce significant complications into this process, which cannot always guarantee success even when unhindered.

2. At the moment, the system is able to generate access control policies (ACP) regarding who can access the service and from what ingress, what types of protocols can be used, who manages the pertinent public-key infrastructures, and so on. On this point let us remind you that there is no centralized body for administrating architectural design credentials. Law enforcers and investigators, in general, have to contend with nonstandard approaches and distributed management. This increases the time it takes to perform the needed analysis.

3. The following protocols and services are currently supported: HTTP, SMTP, FTP, RLOGIN, TELNET, NNTP, talk, finger, whois, gopher, WAIS, DNS, NFS, VLANs, RAW connections (NRaD redirector), and SOCKS5. The designers do not exclude a rapid updating of the list, which is potentially limitless, even if, as stated on the official OR Web site, the project source code may one day be released. Because there are no limits to the types of protocols supported, the difficulty in managing investigations and reconstructing transactions is quite great. And besides, the possibility of using RAW connections may mean, in practical terms, being able to manipulate the stack just about any way one pleases.

4. And last but not least, a further thought. As is now known, without the possibility to intercept the traffic or the payload, the only way to successfully complete a backtrace is to make a correlation among packets. Not being able to monitor the flow of packets, partially because of the complete lack of control over hop randomization and over the no-cache setup of ORs, it may become impossible to conduct an investigation.

7.   *Onion Routers in the Real World: The Dual Use of Dual Use*

How can malicious hackers use Onion Routers? Basically, there are two ways. The first is that if they own the chain, they can obviously set it up so there will be no activity logging at the proxy level and perhaps set up the ACP with some user restrictions, but certainly not regarding the protocols that can be used. This ultimately means it is almost impossible to backtrace the evildoer who used the chain for illicit purposes. The second possibility that might raise its ugly head is if an attacker uses an OR chain and attempts to compromise a router or wages a denial of service (DoS) before or after a specific attack. Here the routers are hit both with DoS and with a bona fide attack against a specifically targeted vulnerability. In the given context, it would seem more sensible from the attacker's point of view to opt for the second alternative, given that in terms of economy of attack the following are possible:

- Control, at least partially, the management of the components. This means also being able to influence Chaum Mix (and therefore traffic management) and the packet's next hop. Mix management is already per se a problem for investigators as pointed out earlier.
- Carry out a sort of interference in the management of the digital certificates related to the various routers. This means potentially being able to insert one's own router into the chain. It may be true that such an operation is complicated in that, in addition to generating a DoS against one of the routers in the chain to silence it, the attacker would then have to be capable of compromising another one in order to get on with the actions described above. Anyway, because of OR's architectural design, even man-in-the-middle/hijacking should be difficult to generate.

If the features so far described might seem marginal, there are significant problems in the realm of logging. Practically speaking, it is not clear who, in this period of cyberterrorist threat, has to keep the transaction logs necessary for backtracing alleged attacks. This means, first of all, that it is almost impossible to generate correlations among events. In addition to the lack of certainty as to the existence of a time stamp, this makes it virtually impossible to sustain an accusation in court. The problem is that, as opposed to the U.S. Navy's Onion Router I project, the second generation of Onion Routers can be independently managed by different groups and distributed anywhere in the world. Who handles the cryptography? How? Is it possible in all cases to get back to clear text?

III. Planning an International Backtracing Procedure: Technical and Operational Aspects

Whether one is operating in the private, academic, or law enforcement sphere, handling a backtracing operation on the international level requires adherence to several technical and operational parameters that cannot be ignored. Here are some examples:

- *Reconstructing the chain of attack.* The chain may be composed of several dozen stepping stones, and its reproduction is one of the most complex operations in that it involves a number of target owners that is directly proportional to the number of machine locations. In most cases, the direct proportionality is also related to the number of police departments involved in the case and their associated courts and legal systems. Although this *may* represent a problem from the legislative and economic viewpoints (*formal* difficulty in coordination among various police departments and excessive costs) it is an obstacle that can be overcome if a contact list of operators potentially able to speed up the information-gathering process can be drawn up beforehand. Normally the creation of this contact list is done with the help of the electronic crime task forces, which, relatively unhindered by bureaucratic stumbling blocks, are able to coordinate contacts among investigators both in the private and public sectors to facilitate a swift exchange of preliminary investigative information. The following are some recommendations for the strategies of individual investigators:
  - *Research the existing worldwide task forces.* Starting with your all-important personal network of contacts and with the help of a search engine, you can come up with a general overview of the different task forces operating throughout the world. The foremost task forces currently in operation are
    1. NYECTF — New York Electronic Crime Task Force, located in New York City
    2. EECTF — European Electronic Crime Task Force, located at the U.S. Secret Service (USSS) office in Milan, Italy
    3. MECTF — Manila Electronic Crime Task Force, covering Asia, located in Manila
    4. HTCC — High Tech Crime Cops, listserv located in the United States
    5. HTCIA — High Technology Crime Investigation Association, located in various states within the United States.
  - *Apply for admittance to one of the task forces.* The task forces are not open to everyone. The aspiring member (be it an office, company, or single investigator) first of all has to find a contact who can describe the activity of the candidate's target group and who will then vouch for the new member. The task force generally carries out some screening process to check the credentials of the candidate and then approves or rejects the application.
  - *Actively participate in task force work.* Participate both via listserv and in the periodical meetings. The latter provides an irreplaceable opportunity to consolidate interpersonal contacts.

- *Respond to all calls and requests for help put out by a member of the force.* This is assuming, of course, that some minimum of help toward reaching a solution to the given problem can be provided.
- *Use discretion when submitting an investigative need.* When you have a technical and/or investigative need to submit to the group, avoid naming names, giving details, or publishing IP addresses of compromised machines. Very often the task force's frequently asked questions list will provide indications in this regard.
- *Research foreign legal systems.* In the case of international operations, once the contact has been established with your counterpart in the public or private sector, do some research into the legal system of the foreign country with which you will interact. Similarly, communicate to your counterpart any Web resources that might be useful to them for doing the same.

- *Normalizing inputs in electronic format.* Another aspect in international operations is the need to *normalize* inputs in electronic format. We are obviously talking about log files (in network forensics*) and image formats (for digital forensics in the strictest sense). We will discuss several of these aspects later in this chapter. Information regarding normalization of input emerged recently from the Digital Forensic Research Workshop held in Cleveland, Ohio. Requests came in from several fronts to normalize image formats to avoid operational discrepancies among forensic examiners. According to the author of one of the submitted papers**, a raw image format such as that created by disk dump (dd) clearly makes the most sense. It is a true and accurate copy of the original with no embedded information. An image file created by dd compared to the original media will match sector by sector. *Whatever the case may be, the common log and digital forensics image formats must be decided beforehand.* Regarding log files, the formats of the following tools are generally used: TcpDump, Snort, Shadow, and JID (governmental). Also keep in mind that all the libpcap-compatible formats are read by many of the network forensic analysis tools, which can also operate offline. Obviously, the syslog-like format is much used, but in this case it will be necessary to correlate this type of information source with other log outputs, especially if the syslogs reside on the potentially compromised machine, that is, the so-called log delegation was not planned.

- *Coordinating with foreign colleagues.* Once the colleagues from around the world who can provide help in the investigation have been

---

* And you must remember to check the time zones of the various log files that are acquired.
** Thomas Rude, "The Need for a Standard Image Format," CISSP, DFRWS 2003. Proceedings online at: http://www.dfrws.org.

tracked down, you must gain knowledge of the various legal systems involved and identify the representatives of the various judicial offices who will approve the formal paperwork once the investigation is formally opened. To this end, it is advisable to obtain beforehand the telephone numbers and points of contact of those handling the international coordination of the *formal* investigation, as well as those of the representatives who will handle international rogatory affairs in the judicial offices.

A.   Some Commonly Used Tools in Digital and Network Forensics

This chapter will not mention commercially available tools in the context of digital and network forensics but rather several open source/GPL tools that can be freely used and that are compliant with the standards that have been referred to. Further details may be found in Chapter 4, "Investigative Strategy and Utilities," by R. Mayfield.

1.   *Why Use Freeware and Open Source for Digital Forensics?*

Some time ago, I was invited as a representative of an Italian governmental office to give a speech on new issues in security management in a forum organized by an important American ISV (commercial, obviously). The only condition I put on it was to be able to speak of the positive aspects of the freeware and open source movement with respect to the ISV-oriented one, with particular reference to security.

My attention was focused particularly on the fundamental principle that there are full-spectrum security tools that are truly valid, and the nice thing about them, apart from the availability of the source code, is the complete lack of licensing costs.

Every system administrator and forensic examiner has a favorite toolkit. He or she runs it from a central console (where possible) and, especially in small-to-medium networks, tries to keep an orientation toward public domain tools. Personally, I use a Linux-based environment made up of the tools I am going to describe here.

In the December 2000 issue of *;login:*, the magazine of the USENIX Association, I wrote about Trinux, a light distribution of Linux, which shares a broader realm with other mini-Unixes, such as tomsrtbt, LEM, PicoBSD, and others. Even if Trinux (http://www.trinux.org) is not updated as before, it's still a very interesting model to follow.

Trinux is booted from a single floppy; loads the rest of its modules from a FAT/Ext2 partition, from other floppy disks, or from an HTTP/FTP server; and runs completely in RAM. One of the most important features is that

Trinux contains a series of precompiled versions of security tools such as nmap, tcpdump, iptraf, and ntop. Furthermore, this distribution works by default with DHCP.

2.   *Tcpdump*

Trinux includes a precompiled version of tcpdump, which was created as a network diagnostics tool for Unix but has gone on to be used in a great variety of ways. The transactions that this tool intercepts are, practically speaking, all the IP, TCP, UDP, and ICMP packets. Without getting too deeply into this topic (check out http://www.tcpdump.org), we could say that it is a continuously evolving tool that has its sniffer aimed at an increasingly large number of protocols. For this very reason, the amount of packets intercepted is very often so high that only external tools can sift out data and information that are truly interesting from the security point of view.

Network forensic examiners could use tcpdump in various cases; for example, when they suspect that any machine is compromised by an LKM (loadable kernel module). In this case, putting a box with tcpdump installed could be useful (the logs generated could indicate what is happening at layer-3 level).

The following is an example of tcpdump log (as used by Shadow IDS):

```
Timestamp Source.port Dest.port flags Beginning_seq_#
: Ending_Seq_#(bytes) options
```

Example:

```
08:14:47.158382 cc644109-a.hwrd1.md.home.com.sunrpc >
mylinuxgw.homeoffice.net.sunrpc: SF 2002853141:
2002853141(0) win 1028
```

The ">" and/or "<" symbols are the direction of the traffic. Depending on the tool configuration and the presence of a valid DNS, tcpdump can try to resolve the domain as well as the service associated with a specific port number.

3.   *Sanitize*

Sanitize is one of the data-sifting tools that can be used with tcpdump. It is a collection of five Bourne shell scripts for reducing tcpdump traces in order to address security and privacy concerns by renumbering hosts and stripping out packet contents. Each script takes as input a tcpdump trace file and generates a reduced, ASCII file in fixed-column format to stdout.

Here is a list of the scripts:

sanitize-tcp has the task of reducing all TCP packets
sanitize-syn-fin does the same reducing on TCP SYN/FIN/RST packets

sanitize-udp reduces UDP packets
sanitize-encap reduces encapsulated IP packets (usually MBone)
sanitize-other reduces any other type of packet

What is important to emphasize is that the performance of Sanitize (http://ita.ee.lbl.gov/html/contrib/sanitize.html) depends on the type of traffic it is handling. For example, reduced TCP traffic retains the packet size (amount of user data), whereas other reduced traffic does not. In addition to Bourne shell, the scripts were written using tcpdump, and the common Unix utilities sed and awk. Regarding the latter, it is a good idea to use the most recent versions.

Unfortunately, Sanitize also has its limits, albeit fewer than its brethren. For example, the contents of the sniffed packets are stripped out, while their size is revealed only for TCP traffic. For encapsulated IP traffic (usually MBone) and for non-TCP, non-UDP, non-encapsulated-IP traffic, only timestamps are generated. The script for reducing TCP SYN/FIN/RST packets is separate from the one for reducing all TCP packets, so the host renumbering performed by each will be independent.

a. Sanitize in Detail.   The five scripts carry out a renumbering of hosts and the extrapolation of the packet contents. The sanitize-tcp script works on TCP traffic and generates output in six columns:

1. Timestamp of packet arrival
2. (Renumbered) source host
3. (Renumbered) destination host
4. Source TCP port
5. Destination TCP port
6. [sixth column] Non-TCP, non-UDP, non-encapsulated traffic timestamp

Timestamp of packet arrival. For the first packet in the trace, this is the raw tcpdump timestamp. For the remaining packets, this is the offset from the integer part of that first timestamp. There is a difference between what this script does and what sanitize-syn-fin does. The latter uses as its base time the arrival of the first TCP packet in the file rather than the first TCP SYN/FIN/RST packet (this helps when comparing sanitize-syn-fin times with those produced by sanitize-tcp).

(Renumbered) source host and (renumbered) destination host. When you use this product, you will realize that this renumbering process causes the loss of all the other network information.

Source TCP port and destination TCP port. These are the number of data
bytes in the packet, or 0 if none (this can happen for packets that only lack
data sent by the other side).

The sanitize-syn-fin script reduces TCP SYN/FIN/RST traffic for analysis.
Its output is eight columns. The first five correspond to the same columns
as for sanitize-tcp, using the same host renumbering. The remaining three
columns are these:

- TCP flags (e.g., FP for a packet with FIN and PSH set)
- Sequence number
- Acknowledgement sequence number

For the initial SYN sent to set up a connection, this will be zero. Experience has shown that you should not trust the sequence numbers used in
RST packets.

The sanitize-udp script reduces UDP traffic. Output comprises five columns, corresponding to the first five columns for sanitize-tcp (i.e., packet
size is not reported).

The sanitize-encap script reduces encapsulated IP packets (these usually are
Mbone packets). Output is a single column that gives the arrival timestamps.

Finally, sanitize-other analyzes all non-TCP, non-UDP, nonencapsulated
traffic. Only a timestamp is reported.

As you can see, there are not a lot of scripts but they are good ones.
Thanks to its extreme granularity, tcpdump contains a great deal of information, but it is not always easy to organize. Sanitize may thus be an excellent aid.

4.   A Series of Questions

Can Trinux contain all the tools we have talked about? This is one of the
most recurrent questions, partially driven by the fact that the community of
Trinux users is rapidly growing. In an e-mail exchange with the maintainer
of the project, Matthew Franz, it was concluded that there should not be
problems here, especially in light of the heft (5 Kb) of the Sanitize package.
Nevertheless, whether the sed/grep in BusyBox supports everything in the
scripts and whether it will be necessary to add egrep and awk still needs to
be seen. Another question concerns the compatibility of Sanitize with the
various versions of tcpdump. According to Vern Paxon, Sanitize's creator, it
should be compatible, except perhaps for very old versions of tcpdump (or
unofficial releases that have altered its output format).

5.   More Tools

The following are other tools that could be used with tcpdump. Obviously,
such tools have their limits, which is why I suggest using them together.

- Tracelook is a Tcl/Tk program for graphically viewing the contents of trace files created using the -w argument to tcpdump. Its latest release is from 1995.
- TCP-Reduce is a collection of Bourne shell scripts for reducing tcp-dump traces to one-line summaries of each TCP connection present in the trace. This tool was also written by Vern Paxon, but it is less powerful than Sanitize (as I see it, of course).
- Tcpdpriv is a program for eliminating confidential information from packets collected on a network interface (or from trace files created using the -w argument to tcpdump).

6.   *Snort*

Snort is another interesting tool, which, of course, is known for its intrusion detection capabilities. I refer you to the Web site http://www.snort.org for any details about this very famous IDS. However, here we have a Snort log example for you to read just to gain some additional understanding of the possible use of this tool in your network forensic environment.

First of all, let's look at a general Snort log structure. Note the port legend as follows:

```
Port Legend:

0 - 1023 -> Well Known Ports

1024 - 49151 -> Registered Ports

49152 - 65535 -> Dynamic Ports
```

Usually a log file from Snort contains the following information:

```
Num. Date Time Attack Source IP Addr. Source Port
Target IP Addr. Target Port
```

Where:

- "Num." is the entry number.
- "Date Time" is related to the event (please do not forget the time zone when you analyze the logs).
- "Attack" is the type of attack recognized by the IDS. Please note that some attacks might be identified thanks to the rule written by the IDS admin, so do not forget to gather that information as well.
- "Source Port" is the data related to the source IP address and the inherent port number.
- "Target Port" is the same data, but related to the destination of the attack.

For example, the following entry is an attempt to get access to an FTP server via anonymous login:

```
43 06/15 14:07:17.505022 [1:553:4] POLICY FTP anony-
mous login attempt 129.100.12.230 65308 192.168.0.2 21
```

Another good tool to use is WinSnort2Html by Chris Koutras. It is based on the Perl script snort2html by Dan Swan. You can find more info at http://www.snort.org.*

B.   The CLF Paradigm (Common Log Format)**

Most logging stuff is based on common log format (CLF). The CLF file contains a separate line for each request. A line is composed of several tokens separated by spaces:

```
host ident authuser date request status bytes
```

If a token does not have a value, then it is represented by a hyphen (-). The meanings and values of these tokens are as follows:

> host — The fully qualified domain name of the client, or its IP number if the name is not available.
> ident — This is the identity information reported by the client. Not active, so we will see a hyphen (-).
> authuser — If the request was for a password-protected document, then this is the userid used in the request.
> date — The date and time of the request, in the following format:
> date = [day/month/year:hour:minute:second zone]
> day = 2*digit
> month = 3*letter
> year = 4*digit
> hour = 2*digit
> minute = 2*digit
> second = 2*digit
> zone = (`+' | `-') 4*digit
> request — The request line from the client, enclosed in double quotation marks (" ").
> status — The three digit status codes returned to the client.
> bytes — The number of bytes in the object returned to the client, not including any headers.

---

* Another interesting tool is Microsoft's LogParser. You can understand log file forensics for IIS using SQL queries with Microsoft's LogParser tool by reading the article at http://www.securityfocus.com/infocus/1712.
** For more info about CLF, check the page http://weboffice-old.web.cern.ch/WebOffice.

Investigators must be familiar with all this information and record it on their investigative documentation each time an investigation starts.

1.   *Where the Logging Information Could Be Found*

In a classic distributed-attack scheme, or more generally an attack based on stepping stones, we have the following machine roles:

1. Master: The machine that, in a DDoS, presses the virtual red button or directs the group of attackers. It usually represents one of the first two points in the chain of hacking. In 90% of the cases, the master machine belongs to the hacker, and it may be very complicated to come up with traces during the preliminary investigation phase.

2. Handler: Intermediate machines that are compromised and then used as stepping stones to handle subordinate machines (agents). Handlers, often used in DDoS attacks, may be *unknowing* or may belong to people who are in on things. The former may be found on the basis of reports from internal attack detection tools and/or from those belonging to other infected entities who report the circumstances to the agent indicated in the whois record. Here is how it usually takes place:

    a. The owner of a compromised agent in network A performs an analysis of his machine. The examination reveals a series of connections to a certain IP address. The whois of that address leads to network B.

    b. The two owners contact each other to coordinate the investigation of the event.

    c. Depending on the type of attack and the hierarchy of compromised machines, it is possible that one of the two will have to provide logging information to the other.

    d. Usually the machines that contain the unknowing handlers can supply useful information on the basis of an examination of any root kits they may contain. If the machine is turned on, it is advisable to perform an analysis (with associated memory dump) in order, in part, to limit the operation of any LKM-based root kits.

    e. The *knowing* handler machines, on the other hand, are those that are often placed at the disposal of the crew by hackers who have access (or shells) within very large organizations, such as ISPs, universities, or big corporations. If it should be ascertained that the handler is aware of his role, it will be very useful to coordinate efforts in preparing an inquiry into the overall scheme of compromised machines. A lot of information can be found on these machines. It is recommended that you start with any firewall configuration files or those indicating a trust relationship with other machines up or down the hierarchy.

3. *Agent*: These are usually machines that have been compromised, perhaps via automatic means, whose owners are unaware of the status and, therefore, remain unchanged for a long time. The average duration of the compromised state of such a machine is about 90 days. I have personally seen one-shot compromising (machines that are compromised and used for a single attack) and others lasting up to 200 days. It may be very difficult to reconstruct a scheme of this type. Usually one is alerted to the dialog between the agent and its superior (e.g., handler) when the IDS of the agent's network notes anomalous outgoing traffic (usually encrypted). In this case it is clear that a check using tcpdump may not provide much useful information. Thus, it may be necessary to carry out a more in-depth examination* of the compromised machine.

4. Final Target: To be honest, it has become difficult to declare a machine as a final target unless the attack is a DoS or a Defacement. In these two cases various types of information may be gathered. However, in the case of a DoS, without a bit of luck and correlated log files, this information may not provide a definitive result. It must be kept in mind that in 80% of current cases a compromised machine used as a stepping stone is also defined as a target.

A DDoS scheme is illustrated in Figure 8.4 that uses all the functions so far mentioned.

A distributed scheme may also be used in the initial information gathering phase, as illustrated in Figure 8.5.

IV. Preventive Methods: Information Sharing and Honeynets

A. Deploying Honeynet: Background and Implications

1. Low- and High-Interaction Honeypots

Another weapon available to investigators is technical information sharing with the objective of a behavioral analysis of the attacker's activities. Each type of incident has its own management process. Some are publicly discussed, whereas others are highly reserved, partially because of the public relations policies of the infected targets. In incident prevention and response

---

* Also known as a *liturgical examination*.

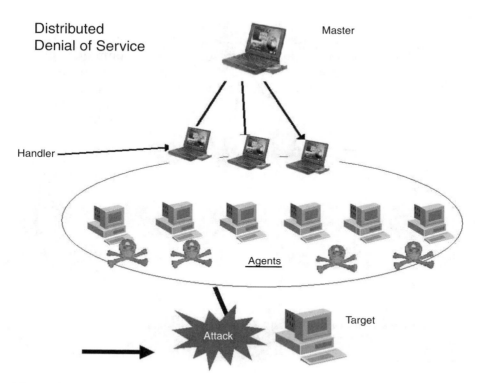

Figure 8.4   A DDoS scheme.

we are beginning to see the first examples of systems that monitor the behavior of malicious hackers within specific real or simulated realms: honeynets.

A *honeynet* is a modular system composed of *honeypots*. Each honeypot can simulate one or more environments (e.g., operating systems, deamons, and services) and operate on different platforms. The module is there to be compromised, but only in order to allow the honeypot owner to monitor the hacker's actions and perform a detailed *behavioral analysis.*

A honeypot will require varying amounts of RAM and CPU capacity depending on the type of simulation and number of services and active processes. It is a little more thrifty on Linux (no graphics required), but Windows-based products are also available.

The real value in this type of solution is that you can limit the number of false positives much more effectively than with a conventional IDS. This is known in the jargon as *noise reduction,* and it means lower consumption of logging resources. That translates into less analysis time because there are many fewer events to evaluate.

But this sort of tool is not without risks. As opposed to distributed intrusion detection systems (DIDS), indicated for distributed capture of

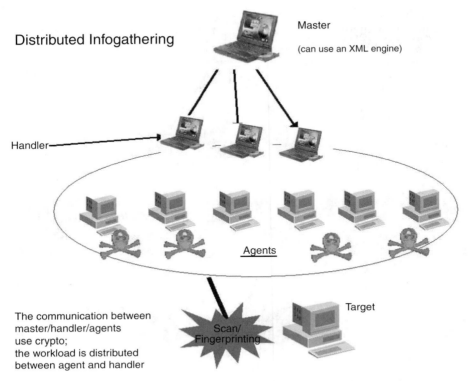

Figure 8.5   A distributed scheme used for information gathering.

suspect packets and patterns across the entire network segment, honeypots are mainly host-based and only pick up activity directed against the machine on which they are installed. Hence a more articulated and granular deployment is needed to achieve the same results as a DIDS, with which the honeypots interface in 80% of the cases.

Another risk is the use of honeypots by attackers as stepping stones to attack third systems. This could be a problem in certain legislative contexts, such as Italy, and even in the United States there appear to be legal complications, as we will see later in this chapter. Whatever the case may be, this type of preventive countermeasure is represented by an extremely granular monitoring system that allows fast handling of advanced or stable attacks.

There are, however, many pluses of honeypot systems, ranging from the ability to handle new-generation IP traffic, such as IPV6, which is not always recognized by IDSs, to the ability to accumulate and aggregate information on ongoing attacks in a much simpler way than an IDS can. No special algorithms are required, and the flexibility of these tools significantly reduces the problem of false alarms and false positives.

There are different kinds of honeypots. They differ as to the level of interaction with the rest of the public network, whether they are free or commercial, and what type of simulation is carried out. Generally speaking, a honeypot can operate at a low or high level of interaction. It all depends on the level of activity granted to attackers once the machine has been compromised.

Low-interaction honeypots, for example, handle single operating systems and/or single services. This means that once an FTP server is called up, the only commands allowed an attacker are those related to that service. It is clear that this type of honeypot is useful only for basic investigative operations, involving low risk. The main disadvantage in this case is that only a part of the attacker's activities is logged. If the attacker is skilled, he or she may be able to figure out the origin of the apparent anomaly and abandon the target. This type of setup would seem to be justified for a broad deployment or a basic setup to allow users to get a grasp on how such a behavioral analysis tool works.

Thus, it is preferable to flank this type of honeypot with high-interaction services, which are more complex and fundamentally without emulation. This means that the attacker has a complete target at his or her disposal and there is a greater possibility of monitoring his or her actions, including those that are totally new.

2.   *Two Types: More Risks*

At the recent RSA Conference in San Francisco a Department of Justice (DOJ) attorney advanced the hypothesis of a violation of the Electronic Privacy Act by a honeynet setup when it monitors the conversations of an intruder and uses the information against him or her in court.

The basic entreaty is to not abuse these tools to track down and report attackers. In Italy there are various juridical organs that might look askance at such behavior. This does not mean that the implementation of a honeynet is illegal. Rather, you just have to decide the investigative or research objectives ahead of time. Put simply, project contents, security rules, and support documentation have to be available and examined in advance.

3.   *Honeypots in Detail: The Variations*

As we said before, there are different types of honeypots; they vary in terms of management method and who does the monitoring. Most honeypots installed on complex architectures and having complex functions are based on high-interaction systems. One of these is Symantec's Decoy Server, which fakes e-mail traffic to fool attackers. Its defenses include automatic shutdown of the entire honeynet in the event of a sudden increase in attacker activity, in a technique known as *frequency-based policies*.

Earlier in the chapter, I mentioned the importance of traffic monitoring. The new generation of high-interaction honeypots provides accurate reporting that can be used by both management and technicians. The purpose is to prioritize events to proactively resolve potential stepping stone issues.

Furthermore, the first examples of stealth monitoring and containment are emerging in the technology market, as well as real-time attack analysis. The main objective here is to have both host-based and network-based intrusion detection without tipping off the attacker to the surveillance. And with the need to centralize management and consolidate reporting functions, the graphic interface greatly facilitates use of the product even by nonexperts.

There are also low-interaction honeypots, which are useful when the maintainers are not able to guarantee that the process will be excluded from the rest of the network activity during an attack. Put simply, low interaction is recommended for nonexperts who do not want to risk being used as a launchpad.

One of the most frequently used low-interaction examples is Honeyed. It is an open source daemon mainly for Unix systems, although its porting for Windows was recently announced. At the latest meeting of EECTF (European Electronic Crime Task Force), the Italian technical study group involving members of the public and representatives from the world's foremost enterprises (e.g., Warren Kruse II, Lucent investigations manager) characterized the functioning of Honeyed as being both extremely simple and flexible. The principle behind Honeyed is the monitoring of unused IP space. It intercepts calls to IP addresses not related to machines located in a specific subnetwork and begins to simulate traffic (as if it were a truly functioning target). The tool can also simulate individual services and ports. This may be useful for observing the behavior of an attacker during and immediately after the illicit access phase.

Another interesting aspect is the ability of some honeypots to simulate operating systems, as well as single services. There are emulators for Windows XP, Linux, and Cisco IOS. At any rate, what determines the quality of a honeypot is the *spoofare*, a special operating system stack. A well-crafted honeypot can emulate not only the individual services but also fake the operating system, whereas others might raise suspicions during the targeted scanning phase. A practical example is the fake daemon httpd that runs on Windows.

We have explained that a honeynet is an architecture, often complex, made up of various types of honeypots. Generally, one opts for a honeynet comprising high- and low-interaction honeypots in order to guarantee an attacker a certain operating autonomy without being tipped off.

Another important concept is what is known as a *honey wall*. This is a gateway through which all the connections to and from the honeynet are routed. Generally, a high percentage of inbound and a limited amount of outbound traffic are allowed, especially when the outgoing packets have a negative payload, that is, serving the attacker's purposes.

There is a wide range of applications of honeypots. Although their intrinsic value as a research tool into new attack patterns is not yet fully determined, one of the most effective practical examples regards protection from automated attacks (e.g., ones based on worms) that may use complex scanning techniques. There is what is known as *sticky* honeypots that slow an attack via a series of TCP-based techniques, such as the use of Windows Zero Size (check tcpdump logs for this particular field). Sticky honeypots fall into the category often called *no-interaction* honeypots, which extinguish or slow the attack to the point that it is rendered innocuous. Because the input is generated by an automated tool, there is no risk that the attacker will catch on to what is happening.

Another example of a low-interaction honeypot is the Deception Toolkit. This tool deviates, right from the active fingerprinting phase, an attacker who uses mixed social engineering and information-gathering techniques.

4.   *How Investigators Can Use Honeynets*

Honeynet implementations provide solutions for almost any need. The software is highly modular and permits step-by-step implementation both in the architectural and the administration and monitoring phases. The management of the type of composite architecture described here requires four full-time people, who also have to coordinate with the worldwide Project Honeynet, which has very rigorous access parameters. Obviously, such an implementation does not necessarily have to be inserted into a worldwide context. Nevertheless, what is recommended is total compliance with the technical and architectural parameters described in the literature, so as not to risk working in vain. One thing is for sure: Once you start your own honeynet, you will achieve the best results by sharing the information with your peers worldwide.*

V.   An Example of International Cooperation: Operation Root Kit

In August 2002, the Nucleo Regionale di Polizia Tributaria of Lombardia of the Guardia di Finanza (Italian Financial Police), directed by the Turin, Italy, assistant prosecutor, Mr. Cesare Parodi, discovered and neutralized two dangerous hacking groups that were responsible for thousands of intrusions into

* More info can be found on http://www.tracking-hackers.com.

public and private computer networks on several different continents. Of the compromised systems, some of the major ones were NASA, the U.S. Army, the U.S. Navy, and a famous American company that produces firewalls (i.e., a security system designed to protect a computer system from intrusions). Attacks were conducted in European countries, Asia, and South America, especially against universities and aerospace and thermonuclear research facilities.

The investigation began in October 2001 based on information received from U.S. authorities (USSS Milan office) who reported intrusion attacks, originating in Italy, against U.S. government and military sites. The files stolen from the sites were strategically important files, later recovered by the Italian Guardia di Finanza. The agents of the USSS Milan office later provided the Milan Guardia di Finanza with the information required to conduct the investigation.

The investigation, with the collaboration of the U.S. Army CID and the U.S. Navy, allowed us to locate the two hacking groups, Mentor and Reservoir Dogs, based throughout Italy (Lombardy, Piedmont, Liguria, Veneto, Calabria, Sicily, Campania, and Emilia-Romagna) and communicating constantly across the Internet.

Among the 14 people indicted, including four minors, one was the security manager of an important Italian provider, one was the network security manager of a well-known computer consulting company, and several of the accused were consultants in the field of information security. In some cases the accused had been using the computers of their unsuspecting clients, used as a stepping stone. In certain circumstances the security system installed in the private company's network was actually hiding a back door that allowed the hackers to conduct their attacks.

The members of the hacking groups came from many different backgrounds, including people with close ties to different protester groups. The objectives of the intrusions were varied, for example, the cloning of credit cards, later used to purchase expensive items, and the cracking of the satellite encryption system. In other circumstances, some of the accused were rewriting copyrighted software and selling it to their clients as their own. During the execution of the search warrants several hundred counterfeit movie DVDs were seized, some of which were still being shown in theaters. The hackers were storing the files of the movies on university computers that acted as remote storage sites. When they received an order for a particular movie, they would simply download and burn a DVD for their customer. The same procedure was used to store the group's hacking tools (programs used to break into computer networks) created by the hackers themselves, on the FTP site of an Italian provider.

VI. Conclusions

The investigation discussed in the previous section was the first EECTF-managed operation. In addition, Operation Root Kit has demonstrated that international cooperation between agencies (five different ones in this particular case) is the only possible solution to such complex cases. Actually, the case was difficult to manage only in terms of its bureaucratic component.

- Almost all of the investigators were speaking the same technical language. The rest were very quick to get into sync with the others.
- Thanks to the task force, the investigators were able to produce the paperwork faster than usual.
- Logs, tools, forensic investigations, and correlation techniques were determined before the investigation began. Hence, the use of a common language, the establishment of a proper and secure communication channel, and knowledge of the tools and techniques used by the hackers all accelerated the investigative process, including the paperwork!

I personally believe that any international forensic and incident response strategy must be based upon the preceding three points. Believe me, hackers do the same.

References

UNIX Forensic. Dario Forte. Chapter of "The Handbook of Information Security", Dr. Hossein Bidgoli, Ed., Wiley, to be published in Nov 2005.

The file Hierarchy Standard, Version 2.3 http://www.pathname.com/fhs/

[Carrier02] A Hardware Based Memory Acquisition Procedure for Digital Investigations — Carrier and Grand, Digital Investigation Journal, Feb 2004, Elsevier Science, U.K.

[DoE01] http://www.linuxsecurity.com/resource_files/documentation/firstres.pdf.

RFC 2350 Expectations for Computer Security Incident Response. N. Brownlee, E. guttman, June 1998. (Format: TXT=86545 bytes) (Also BCP0021).

RFC 3227 Guidelines for Evidence Collection and Archiving. D. Brezinski, T. Killalea. February 2002. (Format: TXT=18468 bytes) (Also BCP0055).

Forte, Dario. Analyzing the Difficulties in Backtracing Onion Router Traffic. *The International Journal of Digital Evidence,* Utica College, United States. www.idje.org JDE 2002 1:3.

Mark Reith, Clint Carr, Gregg Gunsch. An Examination of Digital Forensic Models. *The International Journal of Digital Evidence,* Utica College, United States. www.idje.org JDE 2002 1:

Dittrich, Dave. Basic Steps in Forensic Analysis of Unix Systems, University of Washington, http://staff.washington.edu/dittrich/misc/forensics/.

Carrier, Brian and Eugene Spafford. *Digital Crime Scene Event Reconstruction.* The American Academy of Forensic Sciences (AAFS). 56th Annual Meeting.

Brian Carrier and Eugene H. Spafford. Getting Physical with the Digital Investigation Process. *International Journal of Digital Evidence.* Fall 2003.

The Computer Forensics Tool Testing (CFT). Nist, collection of papers. http://www.cftt.nist.gov/.

Cyber Terrorism 9

THOMAS A. JOHNSON

The National Strategy for Homeland Security identified information systems as one of the important elements we must address as we secure our nation from terrorists. Because information is fundamental to every government, and because it is the foundation for our security efforts in preventing cyber terrorism, we must take extraordinary care to improve our nation's information systems.

Although American information technology is the most advanced in the world, our country's information systems have not adequately supported the homeland security mission. Today, there is no single agency or computer network that integrates all homeland security information nationwide, nor is it likely that there ever will be. Instead, much of the information exists in disparate databases scattered among federal, state, and local entities. In many cases, these computer systems cannot share information — either "horizontally" (across the same level of government) or "vertically" (between federal, state, and local governments). Databases used for law enforcement, immigration, intelligence, and public health surveillance have not been connected in ways that allow us to recognize information gaps or redundancies. As a result, government agencies storing terrorist information, such as terrorist "watch lists," have not been able to systemically share that information with other agencies (National Strategy for Homeland Security 2002a, 55).

The president's National Strategy for Homeland Security also observed that, despite spending some $50 billion on information technology per year, two fundamental problems have prevented the federal government from building an efficient government-wide information system. First, government acquisition of information systems has not been routinely coordinated. Second, many new information systems have been acquired to address specific agency requirements. However, agencies have not pursued compatibility across their respective governmental domains, with the resulting impact of the creation of silos of technology.

This silo phenomenon has not only precluded coordination among federal agencies, it has all but made it impossible for any coherent program plan between the federal system and state and local agencies. To remedy these problems, the Homeland Security office identified five important principles that would guide our nation's approach to developing information systems for Homeland Security:

1. Balance our homeland security requirements with citizen's privacy.
2. View the federal, state, and local government as one entity.
3. Information will be captured once at the source and used many times to support multiple requirements.
4. Create databases of record that will be trusted sources of information.
5. Homeland security architecture will be a dynamic tool, recognizing that the use of information technology to combat terrorism will continue to evolve to stay ahead of the ability of terrorists to exploit our systems (National Strategy for Homeland Security 2002a, 56).

One of the principal reasons for creating the Department of Homeland Security (DHS) was to fully integrate and coordinate disparate agencies that share the mission of protecting the homeland. The creation of DHS brought together 22 agencies and more than 180,000 employees into an organization that inherited as many as 8,000 information technology applications. One hundred of these are considered major, such as systems for threat identification and management, incident response, law enforcement, and warning and alert communications. In essence, using information technology and building communications infrastructure is critical to fulfilling DHS's mission (America at Risk 2004, 1).

Although the United States has not suffered a terrorist attack since September 11, 2001, the number of potential targets in the United States is nearly endless. For example, there are more than 7,000 U.S. chemical facilities where a toxic release could kill or injure over 10,000 people; an accident at any one of more than 120 of those facilities could threaten over one million people. The massive blackouts in the United States in August 2003, although not terrorism-related, demonstrated serious vulnerabilities in our electricity infrastructure. Transport systems of all sorts are particularly vulnerable to terrorist attack. The millions of rail and truck cars carrying toxic and combustible chemicals around the country daily are potential bombs on wheels. Every day, millions of citizens are potential targets at concentrated travel points such as subway systems, train stations, bridges, and tunnels. Citizens are also vulnerable at concentrated public settings such as large buildings and public entertainment venues. Intelligence officials have warned of threats to water supplies and dams and of airplane attacks against nuclear facilities. Incidences of foot-and-mouth disease point out risks in the agricultural sector, and our ever-growing reliance on computers heightens the risk of cyber attacks.

The scope of the challenges confronting all levels of government, as well as the private sector, can be seen by the sheer numbers of assets we must protect throughout our nation, as shown in Table 9.1.

Our nation cannot ignore these challenges, because we have already experienced attacks on our infrastructure, and it was only a few years ago that a computer hacker gained control of a telephone system and disabled the control tower of the Worcester, Massachusetts, airport, shutting down the airport for more than 6 hours. Others have penetrated the computer systems of the California Independent System Operator, the nonprofit corporation that controls the distribution of 75% of the state's electricity, and the Roosevelt Dam in Arizona. In the latter case, it is believed that the intruder gained command of the system that controlled the dam's floodgates and 400 trillion gallons of water. If he had released the flood gates, there would have been widespread loss of life and damage to the towns downstream of the dam. Some communities and infrastructures, in addition to our economy, have already suffered from cyber attacks. For example, an individual gained access to a utility company computer in Australia in 2000, releasing millions of gallons of raw sewage into a Queensland community's waterways (America at Risk 2004, 1).

Table 9.1 National Assets to Protect from Terrorist Attacks

Selected Infrastructure or Key Assets	Asset Details
Agriculture and food	87,000 food processing plants
Water	1,800 federal reservoirs; 1,600 municipal wastewater facilities
Public health	5,800 hospitals
Telecommunications	2 billion miles of cable
Energy	2,800 power plants; 300,000 oil and natural gas-producing sites; 2 million miles of pipelines
Transportation	120,000 miles of major railroads; 590,000 highway bridges; 500 major urban public transit operators; 5,000 public airports; 300 inland/coastal ports
Chemicals and hazardous materials	66,000 chemical plants, of which 12,000 are highly toxic and could put large numbers of Americans at risk in the event of terrorist-caused release
Nuclear power plants	104 commercial nuclear power plants
Dams	80,000 dams
Large high-volume structures	460 skyscrapers; 250 major arenas and stadiums

(Source: America at Risk 2004, 1–2)

I.   Policy Issues Regarding Cyber Terrorism

The astounding progress society has made through the use of computer systems and modern technology has permitted the use of the Internet and cyberspace to become an unregulated frontier capable of both excellent opportunities and colossal vulnerabilities. Brian Jenkins correctly notes in his monograph "Terrorism: Current and Long Term Effects," that cybercrime has evolved rapidly with the growth of the Internet, and that cyber terrorism and cyber war are still in their infancy, with potential attacks likely to follow (Jenkins 2001).

Jenkins frames one of the more significant policy issues our nation must face as we confront the potential of cyber terrorism. Quite succinctly, how are we as a democratic nation going to defend ourselves while protecting individual civil rights so that we remain a democratic society? This policy issue has already become a major point of concern for our policy makers, government officials, and those charged with protecting our nation.

One of our difficulties from a policy point of war is that not everyone subscribes to the belief that cyber terrorists will attack our nation. In fact, some security experts maintain that we have overreacted to the perceived risk to our critical infrastructure by cyber terrorists, and that if anything this medium may be more effective for both seeking legitimacy within certain societies and also recruiting new members to their respective organization or causes.

Clay Wilson reports that some observers believe that terrorists will avoid launching a cyber attack because it would not have such a dramatic impact as a bombing or planes flying into the World Trade Center. Unless a cyber terror event can be designed to attract as much media attention as a physical terror event, the Internet may be better utilized by terrorist organizations as a tool for surveillance and espionage as opposed to cyber terrorism (Wilson 2003, 8).

Wilson summarizes his report to Congress by stating, "Currently no evidence exists that terrorist organizations are actively planning to use computers as a means of attack, and there is disagreement among some observers about whether critical infrastructure computers offer an effective target for furthering terrorist goals" (Wilson 2003, 1).

There exists an agreement among security experts that terrorist organizations do use the Internet to communicate and possibly plan future attacks or send "go" signals for an attack.

Michael Vatis directed a report titled "Cyber Attacks during the War on Terrorism: A Predictive Analysis" in which is outlined four case studies of political conflicts that have escalated and resulted in attacks on cyber systems. This important piece of research clearly contradicts assertions made by several security experts that claim little empirical evidence exists to document the existence of cyber terrorism. Due to the importance of this study, each of the four case studies analyzed will be presented.

Case Study #1

Afghanistan's Neighbors: The Pakistan/India Conflict

The tension between India and Pakistan over Kashmir, the disputed territory bordering both countries has resulted in military confrontations, as well as cyber attacks. Sympathizers on both sides of the Kashmir conflict have used cyber tactics to disrupt each other's information systems and disseminate propaganda. Pro-Pakistan hackers eager to raise global awareness about the conflict have hit Indian sites especially hard... In the case of the Bhabha Atomic Research Center, five megabytes of possible sensitive nuclear research or other information was reportedly downloaded. Another pro-Pakistan hacker group, the Pakistan Hackerz Club, has also targeted U.S. sites in the past, defacing sites belonging to the Department of Energy and the U.S. Air Force. This conflict illustrates the vulnerability of critical infrastructure systems to cyber attacks and the increasing willingness of groups to target sensitive systems during political conflicts (Vatis 2001, 5).

Case Study #2

The Israeli/Palestinian Conflict

Paralleling the Middle East's most violent conflict, the ongoing cyber battle between Israelis and Palestinians has escalated over the past few years. This cycle of attack and counter attack reveals the breadth of cyber targets, attack methodologies, and the vulnerability of electronic infrastructures. Cyber attackers have perpetrated significant web site defacements, engineered coordinated Distributed Denial of Service (DDoS) attacks and system penetrations, and utilized worms and Trojan horses in their efforts.

- The current bout of cyber attacks was spurred in part by the kidnapping of three Israeli soldiers on October 6, 2000. In response, pro-Israeli hackers launched sustained DDoS attacks against sites of the Palestinian Authority, as well as those of Hezbollah and Hamas.
- Pro-Palestinian hackers retaliated by taking down sites belonging to the Israeli Parliament (Knesset), the Israeli Defense

Forces, the Foreign Ministry, the Bank of Israel, the Tel Aviv Stock Exchange, and others.

- The Palestinian attacks, which have been dubbed a "cyber jihad," are following a strategy of phased escalation. According to one of the participating groups, UNITY: Phase 1 targeted Israeli government sites; Phase 2 directed attacks against Israeli economic services, such as the Bank of Israel; Phase 3 involved hitting the communications infrastructure, such as Israel's main Internet service provider (ISP), Net Vision; and Phase 4 calls for a further escalation, including foreign targets.

(Vatis 2001, 6–7)

Case Study #3

The Former Republic of Yugoslavia (FRY)/NATO Conflict in Kosovo

Cyber attacks were also directed against North Atlantic Treaty Organization (NATO) infrastructures as allied air strikes hit Former Republic Yugoslavia (FRY) targets in Kosovo and Serbia during the spring of 2000.

- During the bombing campaign, NATO web servers were subjected to sustained attacks by what NATO sources suspected to be hackers in the employ of the FRY military. All NATO's approximately 100 servers, hosting NATO's international website and e-mail traffic, were reportedly subjected to "ping saturation" DDoS assaults and bombarded with thousands of e-mails, many containing damaging viruses. The attacks periodically brought NATO servers to a standstill over a number of days.

(Vatis 2001, 7–8)

Case Study #4

U.S.–China Spy Plane Incident

The repercussions of the mid-air collision between an American surveillance plane and a Chinese fighter aircraft on April 1, 2001, also offer insight into how political tensions increasingly find expression in cyber attacks. The ensuing political conflict between the two major powers was accompanied by an online campaign of mutual cyber attacks and website defacements, with both sides receiving significant support from hackers around the globe (Vatis 2001, 8–9).

In discussing recent trends in cyber attacks, and despite the four case studies, the report also notes that it is unclear whether Osama bin Laden's international Al Qaeda organization or other terrorist groups have developed cyber warfare capabilities, or how extensive these capabilities may be. To date, few terrorist groups have used cyber attacks as a weapon. However, terrorists are known to be extensively using information technology and the Internet to formulate plans, raise funds, spread propaganda, and communicate securely. For instance, the convicted terrorist, Ramzi Yousef, who was responsible for planning the first World Trade Center bombing in 1993, had details of future terrorist plots (including the planned bombing of 12 airliners in the Pacific) stored on encrypted files on his laptop computer. At the same time, the September 11, 2001, attacks on the World Trade Center and Pentagon and previous terrorist targets, such as the British security forces discovery that the Irish Republican Army (IRA) planned to destroy power stations around London, demonstrate an increasing desire by terrorist groups to attack critical infrastructure targets (Vatis 2001, 12).

The final section of this report discusses the potential targets of cyber terrorist attacks and identifies very serious potential attacks as Web defacements; domain name service attacks; and router attacks.

Web Defacements

The most serious consequences of web defacements would involve "semantic" attacks. Such attacks entail changing the content of a web page subtly, thus disseminating false information. A semantic attack on a news site or government agency site, causing its web servers to provide false information at a critical juncture in the war on terrorism, could have a significant impact on the American population (Vatis 2001, 14).

Domain Name Service (DNS) Attacks

Computers connected to the Internet communicate with one another using numerical IP addresses. Domain name servers (DNS) are the "Yellow Pages" that computers consult in order to obtain the mapping between the name of a system (or website) and the numerical address of that system. For example, when a user wants to connect to the CNN web site (cnn.com), the user's system queries a DNS server for the numerical address of the system on which the CNN web server runs (64.12.50.153). In this example, if the DNS server provided an incorrect numerical address for the CNN web site, the user's system would connect to the incorrect server. Making matters worse, this counterfeit connection would likely be completed without arousing the user's suspicion. The result would be that the user is presented a web page that he believes is on the CNN web server but, in reality, is on the attacker's server. An attacker could disseminate false information with a successful attack on a select DNS server (or group of servers), by passing the need to break into the actual web servers themselves. Moreover, a DNS attack would prevent access to the original web site, depriving the site of traffic (Vatis 2001, 14).

Routing Vulnerabilities

Routers are the "air traffic controllers" of the Internet, ensuring that information, in the form of packets, gets from source to destination. Routing operations have not yet seen deliberate disruption from malicious activity, but the lack of diversity in router operating systems leaves open the possibility for a massive routing attack. For example, the vast majority of routers on the Internet use Cisco's Internet work Operating System (IOS), and vulnerabilities in the Cisco IOS have been uncovered in recent months. While routers are less vulnerable than most computers due to the fact that they offer fewer services, there is the possibility that a current or as yet undiscovered vulnerability could be used to gain control of a number of backbone routers. If an attacker could find a common vulnerability, the ensuing attack on routing operations would bring the Internet to a halt. One example is possibly attacking the border gateway protocol (BGP), which routers use to make decisions about where to send traffic on the Internet. This protocol is vulnerable to information poisoning that could corrupt routing tables. The result of this action would be a very effective Internet "black hole" where large volumes of information headed for destinations all over the world would be lost (Vatis 2001, 16–17).

II. Cyber Terror Policy Issues Linking Congress and Executive Branch of Government

National Security Presidential Directive 16 issued in July 2002, clarified the circumstances as to when an information warfare attack by our Department of Defense would be justified in response to a cyber attack by a terrorist organization or a nation state responsible for such an attack. By February 2003, the National Strategy to Secure Cyberspace was released, and it articulated that if we are attacked by a computer assault, we reserve the right to respond in an appropriate manner. Furthermore, this response could involve the use of U.S. cyber weapons, or malicious code designed to attack and disrupt the targeted compuster and electronic systems of those who chose to attack the United States (Wilson 2003, 15).

The delicate sense in which policy, strategic, tactical, and operating plans would be formulated as national-level guidance for determining when and how the United States would launch a computer attack against an adversary would require congressional support as well as legal scrutiny. Among the multitude of issues confronting policy makers is the concern that it is possible to spoof a terrorist site making it appear the attack came from one group when in fact it originated from another cyber attacker all together. Another policy issue and concern centers on the use of cyber weapons that may have effects that are widespread and beyond the limited pin point precision of some weapon system resulting in serious cascading effects not fully anticipated (Wilson 2003, 15).

A.   Protection of Critical Infrastructure Sectors

One of the important policy decisions made by the executive branch of government and supported by congressional effort was the protection of our critical infrastructure sectors. This effort became a central part of our national strategy for homeland security, and our leaders recognized the importance of our critical infrastructure system by expressing their concern that any attack that would incapacitate or destroy parts of our infrastructure would result in a debilitating impact on both our economy and national security. It is one thing to recognize the importance of our critical infrastructure, but quite another to devise a systematic and coherent plan to protect it.

Agriculture	Information and telecommunications
Food	Energy
Water	Transportation
Public health	Banking and finance
Emergency services	Chemical Industry
Government	Postal and shipping
Defense industrial base	

B.   Securing Cyberspace

Every day, somewhere in America, an individual company or a home computer user suffers what for them are significantly damaging or catastrophic losses from cyber attacks. On a national level, we find that our business community, as well as all levels of our government, confronts the same potential vulnerabilities and losses to such cyber attacks. Those who have the intention of launching cyber attacks know they can utilize attack scripts available on the Internet and target the computer systems of our critical infrastructure sectors. In cyberspace, a single act can inflict damage in multiple locations simultaneously without the attacker ever having physically entered the United States (National Strategy for Homeland Security 2002b, 34).

The DHS would also unify the responsibility for coordinating cyber and physical infrastructure protection efforts. Currently, the federal government divides responsibility for cyber and physical infrastructure, and key cyber security activities are scattered in multiple departments. Although securing cyberspace poses unique challenges and issues, requiring unique tools and solutions, our physical and cyber infrastructures are interconnected. The devices that control our physical systems, including our electrical distribution system, transportation systems, dams, and other important infrastructure, are increasingly connected to the Internet. Thus, the consequences of an attack on our cyber infrastructure can cascade across many sectors. Moreover, the number, virulence, and maliciousness of cyber attacks have increased dramatically in recent years. Accordingly, under the president's proposal, the DHS will place an especially high priority on protecting our cyber infrastructure (National Strategy for Homeland Security 2002b, 31).

Our society has become increasingly dependent on our critical infrastructure sectors, and it is so ubiquitous that we do not recognize how interdependent these sectors have become one to the other. For example, our nation's transportation systems are dependent on the oil and gas storage and delivery sector, the telecommunications sector, and electric grid system. Furthermore, our banking and finance sector, as well as our water and emergency service systems, are also critical to the efficient operation of this one sector — our transportation infrastructure.

The attacks on our transportation sector, as was the case in the September 11 attack in New York City, and now the situation confronting Madrid, Spain, by the attack against people on their railroad system has three very fundamental consequences in addition to the death and destruction created by these terrorist attacks:

1. Erodes confidence in critical services and harms public welfare
2. Damages the economic system
3. Attacks the national security of a nation, thus reducing their ability to act in their citizens' best interests

The merging of both physical structures, as well as cyberspace for attacks to occur make this problem more difficult than most. For example, in the case of our transportation sector's vulnerabilities to physical structure attacks, we also recognize how a cyber attack on its computer systems could also be most devastating. In the past, we have experienced cyber attacks against Federal Aviation Administration (FAA) tower systems that monitor air flight controls.

The new arsenal of cyber attack tools includes the following:

- Trojan horses
- Viruses
- Denial-of-service attacks
- Data theft
- Data modification
- Web spoofing
- E-mail attacks

An example of a data modification attack that could have profound impact on our pharmaceutical firms would be an alteration in the formulas for drug manufacture. Such an alteration would pose an enormous health risk to the public, while exposing the pharmaceutical firm to both financial loss and legal exposure to countless lawsuits.

This new arsenal of cyber weapons provides the tools that can be invoked to launch a cyber attack against individuals, businesses, governments, or any target the terrorist would be inclined to exploit. Indeed, the skill sets required to mount a cyber attack can be minimal, because there already exist such tools freely available on the Internet and easily launched by following minimal steps and easy directions.

It is important to note how the threat spectrum, outlined in Table 9.2, involving cyber attacks has progressed from the recreational hacker who engaged in this behavior as proof of accomplishment and acquisition of skill sets in which the thrill or the challenge was the only goal. The emergence of the institutional hacker has created a great number of problems both for the private sector and the government. The motivation for the institutional hacker also included the challenge but frequently went beyond the goals of the recreational hacker, as we now encounter in social statements or monetary enrichment in some cases. The institutional hacker and the recreational hacker operate well beyond the local level they once began their escapades in, and now function freely within both a national and global environment.

Organized crime has found cyberspace to be an enormously profitable venue for its activities in pornography. Industrial or corporate espionage has

Table 9.2   Threat Spectrum

National Security Threats	Info warrior	Reduced U.S. decision space, strategic advantage, chaos, target damage
	National intelligence	Information for political, military, economic advantage
Shared Threats	Terrorist	Visibility, publicity, chaos, political change
	Industrial espionage	Competitive advantage Intimidation
	Organized crime	Revenge, retribution, financial gain, institutional change
Local Threats	Institutional hacker	Monetary gain, social statements, thrill, challenge, prestige
	Recreational hacker	Thrill, challenge

(Source: Giovagnoni 1997)

profited on trade secrets and the obtaining of intellectual property documents, formulas, and other similar corporate assets. The terrorist has utilized computers in a variety of ways ranging from creating Web sites, such as the FARC (Revolutionary Army of Columbia), as a means to both seek out new members, to secure legitimacy by posting their message for the world to view it, and to see pictures of their leaders attempting to acquire international status by visits of their delegation to other nations. Another terrorist organization, HAMAS, keeps their Web site updated by tracking the number of Israeli soldiers they wound or kill each quarter. This terrorist organization also uses streaming video to show the shooting and assassination of their captives.

The emergence of information warriors began as an outgrowth of the collection of intelligence information. As nations realized the major paradigm change in electronic warfare, we saw the emergence of the information warrior. Today, there are several nations that have committed resources, training, and personnel to assigned duties as cyber warriors.

III.   Information Warriors

Information warfare has emerged as a result of the development of computer technology and vast number of computer networks. The ability to capture information, process it, and provide decision makers with the data on which they base their decisions has refined the manner in which information is collected, analyzed, and introduced into command and control decision loops.

The guiding vision for information warfare can be simply stated: information superiority through the availability and use of the right information, at the right place, at the right time, to all decision makers, while denying that information to the enemy. Information superiority is achieved through the development of core capabilities such as knowledge management, joint surveillance, information warfare, and information technology.

The conceptual framework for information warfare is aptly described by Fred Cohen, who observes that to fully appreciate what information warfare brings to strategic analysis one must examine three new matrices:

1. The Target Matrix will assist in the classification problem of the different classes of targets that information warfare focuses on.
2. The Weapons Matrix will focus on the new arsenal that is needed to wage an information war.
3. The Information Warfare Strategy and Planning Matrix is based on possible targets and types of weapons needs to be developed. This matrix will be used as part of the strategic planning process (Cohen 2002).

The information revolution coupled with the rather sophisticated digital environment we now live within has transformed not only society but also our warfare. Furthermore, we now live in a global information environment in which information warfare has become an entirely new type of weapon. In the Persian Gulf War, the United States applied an incredible display of information warfare by totally blinding the Iraqi command staff from the information they required in their command and central systems. Our ability to utilize satellites, electronic targeting and weapons systems, databases, sophisticated computer systems, and our global information infrastructure saved many lives and shortened what otherwise could have been a lengthy engagement.

> The United States is the most advanced nation in the world in cyber space, but the dilemma for the Pentagon is that it may also be the nation most vulnerable to attacks in that arena. Take the military itself. Nearly everything it does — from designing weapons and guiding missiles to paying, training, equipping and mobilizing soldiers — depends on computer-driven civilian information networks. About 95 percent of military communications travel over the same phone networks used to fax a contract or to talk with a friend in another state. American military bases are powered by the national electric power grid. Pentagon purchases are paid for via the federal banking network. Soldiers are transported under

the guidance of civilian rail and air traffic control systems. Each of these information nodes represents a substantial vulnerability for the military in times of crisis (Molander 1995).

Our reliance on information technology has grown much faster than our grasp of the vulnerabilities inherent in the networks, systems, and core technologies that knit the nation together. This reliance continues to be a driving force that only in the past few years has resulted in a concentrated effort to improve information system security. For example, the original design of the Internet was never intended for worldwide use, and principally was utilized by scientists, researchers, and operation entities within our university communities, as well as governmental entities. Security was never a major driving factor in the network original design. The idea was to provide a mechanism to enhance communication capabilities among these users. Once the Internet became such a useful environment for the business community, focus was placed on encouraging ease of use and not creating barriers by creating security mechanisms. Indeed, to this day, most software applications and operating systems are provided to the user with the security features defaulted, as opposed to being ready for immediate use.

Even more disturbing has been the pattern of the corporate community viewing information security and computer security as a cost center, thus minimizing their support for securing the very systems they are becoming more reliant on to do business both locally and on a national and global level.

Our government has been limited in what it can do to enhance information systems security, because there is no regulatory role they have been able to marshal in this area. In fact, the Internet functions in a totally open environment with no control over it.

IV. Net War and Cyber War

John J. Arquilla and David F. Renfeldt discuss the concept of information warfare from an interesting perspective in which they compare Internet, or Net war to cyber war, and the distinction they draw on is that Net war is a society-level conflict in which they foresee information-related conflict between nations or societies. They describe this as a process in which some nation or group is trying to disrupt or damage what a target population knows or believes about itself. Therefore, a Net war focuses on public opinion and may involve psychological campaigns and propaganda, political subversion, deception, infiltration of computer networks, and creation of databases to promote dissident or opposition movements across computer networks (Arquilla and Ronfeldt 1995).

Cyber War refers to conducting military operations according to information-related principles. It means disrupting or destroying information and communications systems. It means trying to know everything about an adversary while keeping the adversary from knowing much about oneself. It means turning the "balance of information and knowledge" in one's favor, especially if the balance of forces is not. It means using knowledge so that less capital and labor may have to be expended. . . . This form of warfare may involve diverse technologies, notably for command and control, for intelligence collection, processing and distribution, for tactical communications, positioning, identifying friend-or-foe, and for "smart" weapons systems, to give but a few examples. It may also involve electronically blinding, jamming, deceiving, overloading and intruding into an adversary's information and communications circuits. . . .Cyber War may also imply developing new doctrines about the kinds of forces needed, where and how to deploy them, and how to strike the enemy. How and where to position what kinds of computers, sensors, networks and databases may become as important as the question once was for the deployment of bombers and their support functions (Arquilla and Ronfeldt 1993, 141–165).

Roger Molander provides a very concise and useful characterization as to what his research has shown about cyber war, where he enumerates four basic findings:

1. Waging information war is relatively cheap. Unlike traditional weapon technologies, acquiring information weapons does not require vast financial resources or state sponsorship. Computer expertise and access to major networks may be the only prerequisites.

2. Boundaries are blurred in cyberspace. Traditional distinctions — public versus private interests, warlike versus criminal behavior, geographic boundaries, such as those between nations — tend to get lost in the chaotic and rapidly expanding world of cyberspace.

3. Opportunities abound to manipulate perception in cyberspace. Political action groups and other non-government organizations can utilize the Internet to galvanize political support, as the Chiapas of Mexico was able to do. Further, the possibility arises that the very "facts" of an event can be manipulated via multimedia techniques and widely disseminated.

4. Information war has no front line. Potential battlefields are
   anywhere networked systems allow access. Current trends suggest that the U.S. economy will increasingly rely on complex,
   interconnected network control systems for such necessities as
   oil and gas pipelines, electric grids, etc. The vulnerability of these
   systems is currently poorly understood. In addition, the means
   of deterrence and retaliation are uncertain and may rely on
   traditional military instruments in addition to Cyber War
   threats (Molander 1995).

V.   Cyber Intelligence or Cyber Terrorism

One of the most informative and provocative studies of cyber terrorism to
date was completed by the Naval Postgraduate School (NPS) in March 2000.
This study provided an overview of the issues underlying realistic assessment
of cyber terrorism risks and showed the fundamental flaw in vulnerabil-
ity-based assessments used to make claims about terrorist potentials. The
flaw is that most studies lack detailed analysis of threats and consequences.
Other authors have pointed out that it is the combination of threats, vulnerabilities, and consequences that conspire to produce risk, but, in the context
of cyber terrorism, recent assessments have lacked this rigor.

In an attempt to get at these issues, the NPS study identified several
classes of cyber terrorist threats: religious, single-issue "new age,"
ethno-nationalist, separatist, revolutionary, and far-right extremist (Arquilla,
Tucker, et al. 1999, 1). Although this study represented an exceptional roll-up
of the issues surrounding cyber terrorism and formed a rich model that is
useful in looking at these issues, the report also leaves several large gaps that
need to be explored in order to confirm or refute its assumptions, model,
and conclusions.

Based upon a review of over 110 reported computer and information
system attacks included in the Georgetown Universities Terrorism Research
Center's Information Warfare Database, Philip Osborn's paper "Terrorist
Threat," and other related articles, it seems clear that the media may have
exaggerated the potential for cyber terrorist attacks (Osborn 2000).

Clearly, there exists a potential for cyber terrorism, but as the NPS study
suggests, cyber terrorism may be more of a challenge for the future than a
dire national priority. I believe the potential for cyber terrorism is within the
reach of terrorist organizations, and that many of these terrorist organizations
are only now becoming aware of the potential for use of information technologies in furthering their objectives. This should not be a surprise, because
our world's leading educational institutions have only recently embarked on
a concentrated effort to adapt these technologies to distribute their respective

mission via distance education strategies. If institutions of higher education are still discovering potentials for information technologies in having effects at a distance, there is no reason to believe that terrorist organizations, which are not well-known for scientific innovation, would have made this discovery much earlier. Even more importantly, there is even less reason to suspect they are now on the threshold of materially refocusing their modus operandi and attack structures.

As these groups are examined, experts should focus on how each terrorist group either uses or anticipates the use of information systems. They should explore the extent, if any, to which these groups use information systems to recruit other individuals into their cause. Some experts hypothesize that terrorist organizations will use information systems to seek greater legitimacy within their society, while at the same time enhancing their opportunity to recruit more participants and members to their cause. The use of information systems to more efficiently market their message and their cause may well confuse many people who otherwise would remain in more established opposition to the terrorist group. Experts are also interested in exploring if and how these terrorist groups attempt to more surgically disrupt their targets through the use of information technologies.

It is believed that terrorist organizations may be drawn to the use of information technologies because of the opportunity for repeat attacks, which will have the cumulative effect of not only causing greater disruption and loss but also will induce greater psychological distress to those members of the society attacked. The more traditional terrorist attack modality, which results in bodily injury or death, results in society focusing great consensus against the attacking terrorist organization. On the other hand, the terrorist group that utilizes a more economically disruptive attack focused more on the critical infrastructure of a society may not encounter such total societal rejection. This permits a greater opportunity to mold public opinion toward their objectives. If combined with appealing arguments designed to market and sell their belief system, such a terrorist group might require a totally different response on the part of authorities.

Given the global nature of the Internet and its easy use and availability to terrorist organizations, coupled with the high profile given to cyber terrorism, one must inquire as to why cyber terrorist attacks are not more frequent than those reported. One theory suggests that terrorist organizations are committed more to destruction than disruption. The devastating planes flying into the World Trade Center or the bombing of a Madrid railway focuses more immediate attention as to the terrorist strategy. Also, the terrorist organizations are relying on the use of the Internet for intelligence acquisition activities, as well as recruiting new members and using this medium to conduct their command and control activity. Currently there is no definite answer to this dilemma, although it is clear that terrorist organizations are utilizing more sophisticated strategies to plan and conduct their attacks. Research will be necessary to focus this issue on all identified terrorist organizations, to enable a detailed profile to emerge on the use of technologies and cyberspace by the terrorist community.

VI. Research Issues in Cyber Terrorism

Of course, there are numerous models and approaches to researching the subject of cyber terrorism. One useful approach is to select terrorist organizations that have been defined as such and appear on the United States Department of State listing of declared terrorist organizations. By focusing on the specific terrorist organization designated for research, you can begin a rich inquiry into open source information that may be obtained from a variety of venues, and specifically through Internet sources. This would entail a substantial formulization with the targeted terrorist group by reviewing both printed and online information about the terrorist group. The research into the history of the terrorist group and its background, as well as its leadership structure, stated goals, and mission would be key items for further development and refinement. In performing what amounts to this intelligence assessment, you are probing for the strategy and tactics of the terrorist group and how their doctrine has enabled them to become effective and recruit members to their organization. To what degree has their doctrine permitted stability of their organization, and how has it shaped their operational methods? In fact, assessments as to the terrorist groups command and central structures must be analyzed, because this will become important for preparing counterintelligence operations as well.

In acquiring information on the selected terrorist organizations, you will obviously focus on their use of information systems and how they have used cyber systems. Also, you will want to assess and develop a profile of the terrorist group's cyber capabilities and the manner in which they are most likely to invoke these skills.

Around this framework, a number of basic intelligence issues would be worthy of acquisition and analysis. One useful methodology would entail the following areas of inquiry:

1. **Group history:** Identify and trace the origin and emergence of the terrorist organization. What was the rationale and driving force that created this terrorist group?
2. **Membership:** What are the characteristics of the known members? What are their educational levels and technology skill capabilities?

What languages are spoken? How large is the group, and where do their members originate from?

3. **Their views of themselves:** What can you learn about them from their media, Web site, or other open source statements?

4. **What others say about them:** What is the prevailing view of media sources on this group? Also, what do other governments say about them?

5. **How and who do they recruit:** Do they use the Internet to recruit? How do existing members recruit new members, and what is the driving force for joining the group?

6. **How they communicate:** Do they use typical communications media, or do they use the Internet or a combination of methods? How do they communicate their message to the media? Whom do they communicate through, and who speaks for them? What language do they use?

7. **How and where they operate:** Are they a local, regional, or global terrorist organization? What are the types of activities they perform, and where do they do these activities? What is their command and control structure?

8. **How they are organized:** Do they use a cell structure, small units? What is their leadership structure? What is their financial structure, and how do they feed, house, and pay their members?

9. **Personality traits of known members:** Can you identify any personality traits of leaders or members by the things they do and say, or by their behavior and how they function?

10. **Skills, experience, and capabilities:** Do the members of the terrorist group demonstrate any special skills? Do they have any computer or information network skills? What identifiable capabilities do they possess?

11. **Funding:** What is the source of funds? How much money? From where and how is the money spent?

12. **Reason to exist:** What is the terrorist group's rationale and motive?

13. **Method of operation:** What are the things they do? How do they go about doing these things?

14. **Sponsorship:** Who supports and funds the terrorist members, and are there multiple sponsors? What are the parameters of the financial support they receive?

15. **Known information technology capabilities:** Do they have a Web site? Who hosts the site? Who maintains the site, and who runs it? Does their site use multiple languages? Are they using streaming video? Are they using the site for recruitment and sending attack signals?

VII. Summary

Although there is little consensus among computer security experts that cyber terrorism exists, there, nevertheless, is research that has documented cyber attacks throughout the world. Clearly, terrorists have at their disposal an incredible utility in the existence of the Internet, and many terrorists are utilizing this as a resource to further their own goals and objectives. There are examples of some terrorist organizations that clearly have begun to use this medium as a weapon, and it is our responsibility to launch efforts to protect our nation from this phenomenon. Accordingly, our government is engaged in developing plans and programs to reduce our national vulnerability to cyber attacks. As programs are developed to prevent cyber attacks on our critical infrastructure, we also must be realistic to the development of programs that will permit rapid recovery from those cyber attacks that do successfully occur.

Our nation is currently preparing a cyber security response system, which will concentrate on reducing the vulnerabilities that have been identified through carefully analyzing our nation's computing resources and dependencies. Fundamental to our immediate and long-term success will be an investment in our educational system, so that our nation will continue to produce the professionals who will be responsible for directing and leading our cyber security response system. The research and development that must occur to assure for our nation's protection from cyber attacks and cyber terrorism will be a continuing challenge that our country's universities must address more systematically and coherently.

References

America at Risk: Closing the Security Gap. 2004. Protecting America with Information Technology. Democratic Member of the House Select Committee on Homeland Security, March 2004.

Arquilla, John, David Tucker, Bill Nelson, Rodney Choi, Michael Iacobucci, Mark Mitchell, and Greg Gagnon. 1999. Cyberterror: Prospects and Implications. Paper for Naval Post Graduate School, Department of Defense, U.S. Government, October 1999.

Arquilla, John J., and David F. Ronfeldt. 1993. Cyber War and Net War: New Modes, Old Concepts, of Conflict. In *Comparative Strategy*, vol. 12, 141–165. Online at: http://www.rand.org/publications/randreview/issues/RRR.fall95.cyber/CyberWar.html.

Cohen, Fred. Information Superiority. 2002. Online at: http://www.fc@all.net/books/iw/iwframe/iw.html.

Giovagnoni, Robert. 1997. Critical Foundations: Protecting America's Infrastructures. The Report of the President's Commission on Critical Infrastructure Protection. Washington, D.C.: U.S. Government Printing Office, October 1997.

Jenkins, Brian. 2001. Terrorism: Current and Long Term Threats. Rand Testimony Series, CT — 187, November 2001.

Molander, Roger C. 1995. Information Warfare: A Two Edged Sword. On the RAND Web site, Fall 1995, vol. XIX, no. 2. Online at: http://www.rand.org/publications/randreview/issues/RRR.fall95.cyber/infor_war.html.

National Strategy for Homeland Security. 2002a. Information Sharing and Systems. U.S. Government Printing Office.

National Strategy for Homeland Security. 2002b. Protecting Critical Infrastructure and Key Assets. U.S. Government Printing Office.

Osborn, Phillip. 2000. An Examination of Terrorist Groups and the Threat to the National Information Infrastructure. And also Terrorism Research Center, "Information Warfare Database," Georgetown University, 2000.

Vatis, Michael A. 2001. Cyber Attacks during the War on Terrorism: A Predictive Analysis. Institute for Security Technology Studies at Dartmouth College, September 22, 2001.

Wilson, Clay. 2003. Computer Attack and Cyber Terrorism: Vulnerabilities and Policy Issues for Congress. Congressional Research Service Report for Congress, Library of Congress, October 17, 2003.

Future Perspectives  10

THOMAS A. JOHNSON

In preparing this text on *Forensic Computer Crime Investigation*, the authors outlined the challenges our law enforcement and legal community confronted in developing the skills and knowledge required to address this growing problem of computer crime within our nation. The procedures required to process an electronic crime scene, as well as the staffing of a computer crime unit, were also analyzed. Training strategies and the use of forensic utilities were explored, as were challenges to digital forensic evidence. The emergence of Internet Crimes Against Children (ICAC) units and child exploitation issues were discussed against the background of criminal investigative analysis and behavioral characteristics of computer criminals. The international aspects of cybercrime and the issues involved in cyber intelligence and cyber terrorism were also described in terms of contemporary challenges facing not only our nation but societies throughout the world. In short, the global nature of computer crime and the digital environment, which has eclipsed the ability of any one department, state, or nation to individually manage this new paradigm change in crime, now requires more skilled and educated personnel.

The provision of these new skilled and educated employees, not only for our forensic computer investigation units but also for a range of subdisciplines within the emerging body of knowledge — sometimes referred to as computer forensics, information assurance, computer security, and software security — will have to come from our nation's universities.

Candidly, our nation has been ineffective in producing the scholars, creating the academic discipline, and developing the research necessary to provide us with the security requisite to our dependence on these computer systems that are the engines that permit our critical infrastructure and society to function so effectively.

Thus, one of our nation's most important challenges for the future is to create and to support the emergence of an academic discipline that will produce the next generation of faculty, university researchers, industry professionals, and national security experts. These are the professionals who will all work to ensure the integrity of our computer and information systems. This effort will require an investment of an immediate nature because so many of the academicians who are capable in this area are now in an age cohort close to retirement, with few standing ready to replace them.

Despite this paradox, our nation continues to rely on our computer systems to operate our financial institutions, our electric and power grid systems, our water, our food production systems, and almost all of our critical infrastructures that have made our nation one of the richest in the history of the world. Yet, the computer systems and networks connecting our interdependent economy are so vulnerable to attack.

I.   Network Infrastructure: Security Concerns

Government, industry, and all institutions that have created computer networks to operate within their respective spheres of operation have confronted the problem of securing their computer information systems. The task of providing access control through the use of passwords, tokens, biometrics, or public-key encryption is designed to authenticate the user of the computer system. The need for creating a firewall system of both hardware and software to create a safe boundary for the operation of the information resources is an additional and necessary responsibility for securing our resources. Unfortunately, these efforts in and of themselves are not enough; we must also apply intrusion detection systems to identify and send an alert if someone is attempting to gain unauthorized access to the computer system. Intrustion detection systems must be designed to protect against an ever-growing range of attacks. The virus scanners, which are designed to capture malicious code and detect and isolate worms, Trojans, and viruses, require constant monitoring and updating to further protect our information resources. Finally, in some cases, it is even necessary to rely on encryption algorithms to protect data packets in transit so as to assure for the security of the information being processed by our computer systems.

The requirement for securing our computer systems adds an immense cost to our production systems, because we must not only acquire this hardware and software but also educate and train our personnel to design and use the systems.

II. The Role of Education and Training

Bill Spernow has articulated the differences between education and training with his compelling chart, which clearly delineates the continuum in functional responsibilities between knowledge and skills; abstraction and application; developing tools and using tools; establishing procedures and applying procedures; developing theory and implementing a practice based on this theory (Spernow 2004).

Table 10.1   The Education Training Matrix

Functional Responsibilities Differentiating Each Area	
Education	Training
Knowledge	Skills
Abstraction	Application
Developing Tools	Using Tools
Establishing Procedures	Applying Procedures
Theory	Practice

This Education Training Matrix (see Table 10.1) reveals the symbiotic relationship that exists between education and training. Clearly, the roles and functional responsibilities of trainers are dependent on their knowledge and information derived from theoretical constructs developed within the educational environment. On the other hand, pure theory and application of abstract concepts is improved by the need for training and trainers abilities to implement theory into meaningful professional practice in which there is an application of concepts to best practices and standards of the professional practitioner.

We expect our universities to produce graduates with the requisite knowledge to visualize the need for new and secure software and to advance both theory and knowledge resulting in an enlightened individual capable of improving society's access to effective and secure computer and information systems. More specifically, in the field of computer forensics, we expect our graduates to assume critical roles in teaching, research, and guiding our nation in securing our critical infrastructure by producing the next generation of practitioners and professionals who will assume important roles within our homeland security enterprise. Furthermore, we believe our graduates must understand and appreciate our legal systems, fully embracing our Fourth Amendment rules of criminal procedure, laws of evidence, and search and seizure. At the same time, we expect our graduates to possess a rich understanding of computer science and to have attained competencies in the following areas:

- Knowledge of computer operating systems, such as Windows, UNIX, and LINUX
- Knowledge in disk structure and file systems
- Use of forensic utilities, such as image acquisition tools
- Knowledge of network hardware and software topology
- Knowledge of network security concepts, intrusion detection systems, and firewall boundary methodologies
- Knowledge of network packet sniffers and the ability to capture and analyze data packet traffic to detect network anomalies
- Knowledge of static and dynamic routing tables and TCP/IP (transmission control protocol/Internet protocol)
- Knowledge of configuration and management of domain name servers, e-mail, and Web servers
- Capable of writing windows and Perl scripts for analyzing audit logs for various exploits
- Knowledge of routing protocols as they relate to traffic flow on the Internet over access provided by common carriers
- Knowledge and capability of identifying and acquiring evidence from production servers without disrupting the ongoing business process
- Knowledge of computer viruses and malicious code, and the ability to create a new virus in a controlled laboratory experiment to appreciate how to defend and implement intrustion detection software
- Knowledge of secure enterprise computing and, in a laboratory setting, the construction, deployment, and testing of a firewall against common Internet-based attack methods
- Knowledge of audit-based computer forensics and techniques for tracking attackers across the Internet and capturing forensic information from computer systems
- Knowledge of cryptographic and stenographic systems and the major types of cryptosystems and cryptanalytic techniques and how they operate (Spernow 2004)

In addition to the knowledge and proficiency in both our legal system and computer systems, we expect our graduates to fully understand our forensic investigation process and to not only be capable of implementing it but also to contribute to its advancements in both science and technology.

III. The Emergence of a New Academic Discipline

Academia's role in providing our nation with graduates capable of producing secure software and secure information systems has never been more important than the present. Educational support grants and research funding at universities in this area have been inadequate to sustain both full-time faculty and the production of new graduates. Compared to areas such as computer graphics, analysis of algorithms, and distributed computing paradigms, the budgets related to computer security and software security are, and have always been, minuscule. Computer science departments have focused on so many subdisciplines within their area of study, with the resulting impact of little to no emphasis on information assurance and computer security. In fact, with few academic courses and little research in this area, the production of scholars who might be inclined to pursue computer security as a career path is severely constrained. Furthermore, the design and emergence of a new academic discipline in this important area is even less feasible without the academicians who dedicate their academic career to this subject matter. It should hardly be a surprise, then, to learn that little progress has been made in this area and that academia has not sustained information protection as a discipline.

Although our recommendations provide some ways in which limited short-term improvements can be made through education, the quick-fix approach to information protection has been shown time and again to lead to the very situation we are in today. This is to suggest that paying billions of dollars per year for patching software and operating systems that remain insecure even after they are patched is not a viable long-term solution. The increased use of less-skilled and less-trusted people to build increasingly critical systems with higher consequences for their failure is also an unacceptable option, despite its financial attractions of outsourcing strategies to nations where computing costs are less than in the United States. Similarly, if a training approach is used to mitigate immediate challenges, the result will be no different than the situation as it stands today. Although training is certainly a necessary component of a national strategy, it will fail to accomplish the objectives of increased software security unless an educational effort is undertaken to combine the advancement of knowledge with the creation of expertise. We cannot rely on training strategies to relieve a problem we have historically ignored within our educational institutions, and the time for action is critical.

If educational institutions are to be successfully engaged in meeting the national needs, the way they operate must be understood. Unlike training academies, industry, and government, which all have a more or less hierarchical structure, institutions of higher education are run by the faculty. The faculty in higher education is responsible for the lion's share of the decision making: They create and implement the curriculum; they lead the research efforts; they propose the grants; and they lead the educational efforts. Academic accreditation of academic institutions is done by faculty from other comparable institutions that send their faculty to observe the programs and assure that they meet the standards set forth by national groups of faculty.

Advanced degrees involve personal interactions between experienced faculty and advanced students in a mentoring relationship over periods of years. Although a master's degree in some institutions can be earned in as little as a year of full-time effort, most master's students take 2 years or more to achieve their degree, and in-service students often take 3 or 4 years. A doctorate typically takes several years of full-time effort after a master's degree is completed. Even the smartest people take years of concerted effort to reach a level where they even qualify for an entry-level position as an assistant professor. Although it can be argued that the number of people required to possess the knowledge levels associated with advanced degrees for implementing secure software is limited, creating a curriculum, teaching it in universities, producing research results that will advance the state of the art, writing textbooks, and similar activities cannot be done effectively by people with less expertise.

The tenure process that assures academic freedom for faculty to pursue their areas of research normally comes only after approval by existing tenured faculty. This process typically requires a long-term commitment to academic excellence, publishing work in refereed professional journals, teaching classes at suitable levels within the curriculum, and obtaining successful research funding and performing that funded research. After the 4 years of undergraduate education, 2 years of master's study, 3 to 5 years of doctoral-level study, and the 7-year tenure process, faculty members typically begin to pursue the most advanced work of their career. If they are exceptional, they gain stature over time and are granted full professorships. These professors are then considered the most influential of the faculty members and leaders within their departments, are recognized around the world for their excellence, become members of accreditation boards, and are considered in the prime of their academic careers. This is the career path for the best in academia, and these are the people that the nation requires in order to bring about the changes required in information protection.

In order to engage faculty in universities in an area such as information assurance and computer security, there must be a discipline and a career path that will last them throughout their career. There is a very large body of knowledge that has to be understood in order to achieve excellence. It requires in-depth understanding of many different subfields of computer science and computer engineering, as well as substantial knowledge about a wide range of other fields from forensic investigation and law.

Although a doctoral-level mathematician with expertise in number theory can do some limited work in theoretical cryptography and protocol analysis, and a person with a doctorate in computer engineering with a specialization in computer architecture can design new structures to support operating system enhancements, these and many other subspecialties are required for the systems-level understanding required to meet requirements for high-security systems. To be successful, a collaborative effort among many experts is required. No single person can be expected to have all of the necessary expertise to do all of these things well. Thus, there is a need for a national community of professors with the combined understanding of these issues and a collaborative structure to produce the next generation of prac-titioners and scholars who will be responsible for building the high-security systems required for the future security of the United States (Cohen 2004b).

IV. Our Nation's Investment in Cyber Security Research

The costs associated with computer software security lapses are estimated to be in the tens of billions of dollars per year. The GAO estimates the U.S. losses to be about $38 billion, and Microsoft's tracking of virus incidents alone run in the range of $80 billion per year worldwide. Another way to look at this issue is to compare the funding levels for research in information protection to funding levels in other areas. The NSF budget, for example, has about $18 million in information protection research funding. This funds about 15 projects per year as well as a small number of graduate students. Of this work, software security research is only covered in two or three of these projects. So the nation has a $38 billion problem, and we are spending $3 million to research ways to solve it, or about 1/10 of one cent per dollar of loss. Human-computer interaction and information management gets funded at $44 million. Almost $25 million goes to software design, but none of that involves high-security software research. Almost $35 million goes to software for improving education, but none of it is related to information protection. Advanced computational infrastructure gets more than $71 million, but none of it is associated with making that infrastructure meet security requirements. Roughly $50 million goes to intelligent systems — intelligent perhaps, but not secure (Cohen 2004a).

There can be little doubt that without a very substantial amount of long-term funding to support academic research in information protection, the situation will continue to deteriorate. The only real question is when it will deteriorate to the point of total collapse.

V.   Recommendations

The main problem we face is generating the capacity necessary to do the appropriate research and education to move this field forward. The capacity to do this does not exist today, and it will never exist without the necessary backing of government and industry. Without the people with state-of-the-art knowledge, research support, and educational commitment, we will not create secured computing systems and secured software systems and infrastructures that meet the national security requirements of the United States (Cohen 2003). The following are some recommendations for how to support research and development of secured computing and software systems:

1. Fund long-term fellowships in universities to support their research and educational efforts. These positions should be at the full professor level and should be provided to qualified individuals with substantial industry expertise, adequate publications, and academic credentials to meet the challenges of research and education in information protection. The funding and qualifications should be designed to assure that high-quality mid-career and late-career individuals can spend the rest of their careers working on these issues and to assure that they have adequate funding to support both a rigorous ongoing research program and a strong teaching and graduate education component.

2. Create a computer security education/training summer session to educate the instructors in intensive sessions. This recommendation will support summer education of instructors from junior colleges, community colleges, and other undergraduate institutions so that these educators will have the knowledge necessary to infuse information protection into their courses and to teach specialty courses in these areas to their students. Over time, this will produce a national momentum and change the undergraduate curriculum to bring information protection into line with other elements taught in our computer science departments. During these programs, these professors will participate in research, attend graduate programs with other faculty, and gain access to teaching materials and the knowledge required to effectively use them.

3. Develop educational material and capabilities that can be used across the nation to educate new students and assist properly trained educators in teaching the most critical material in this area. These materials will include a range of items such as texts, collections of classic articles in the field, standards, technical examples, worked examples of problem sets, and online simulations.

4. Faculty should engage in research that demonstrates a process to monitor outcomes, validate results, and refine methodologies for change to the content over time. This includes a strict requirement for experimental validation of results in keeping with the scientific

method and the development of repeatable tests with metrics to measure the efficacy of results.

5. Progress will be measured in the number of fellowships developed, in curriculum development, in institutional accreditations, in the production of graduates at each level; and, finally, in research results.

VI. Conclusion

The need for academic institutions to refocus their limited resources and develop curricula and research agendas that will substantially improve the production of scholars and graduates interested and focused in computer security and information protection will be of invaluable assistance to our nation. As we focus more effort on developing interdisciplinary academic programs that embrace and include computer science, engineering, law forensic investigation, and national security, we will be in a position to meet the challenges of the next decade.

In essence, we as a nation need to develop academic programs that will permit research and education across major academic disciplines that will enhance the protection of our information assets and the security of our nation's computing resources and systems. Our nation requires additional capacity in designing and building defensible information system security architecture, and this will require not only multidisciplinary academic programs but also the emergence of new academic disciplines. Our university community will and properly should assume the leadership role in addressing this imperative need of our nation. The commitment of our academic community will be a major step forward in enhancing our national capability for improved research, education, training, and analysis that will provide strategic benefits for many years to come. With a renewed focus on computer security and information protection and assurance, a multidisciplinary structure that provides a fusion of critical academic core disciplines will enlighten and enhance those who have the responsibilities for protecting our nation's critical infrastructure and computing resource.

References

Cohen, Fred. 2004a. Cyber Security Task Force Education Subgroup, February, 13, 2004.

Cohen, Fred. 2004b. Personal conversation discussing the challenges confronting higher education in computer security, February 10, 2004.

Cohen, Fred. 2003. Discussions regarding improvements in computer security education, November 2003.

Spernow, Bill. 2004. Cyber Cop Training, Southeast Cyber Crime Summit, Data Forensics Track, March 2–5, 2004.

Concluding Remarks 11

THOMAS A. JOHNSON

This book has brought together a group of contributing authors who have been among the first wave of experts to assist our nation in confronting this new paradigm of criminal activity. Each author has played a pivotal role in the operation of computer crime units, and collectively they also participated in the education and training of more than 4,000 federal, state, and local law enforcement officers. In addition, over the past decade, these authors have participated in the graduate and undergraduate education of many outstanding university students. The overarching purpose of this text was to provide an introduction to the forensic computer crime investigation process. We hope this modest effort will encourage an interest in the student and officer of tomorrow to pursue this subject matter and to acquire the expertise to function as effectively as possible.

In our view, the subject of forensic computer investigation intersects at three important academic disciplines: computer science, law, and forensic investigation. The importance of each of these disciplines requires a respect and inclusion of other principles and concepts so that a body of knowledge will continue to emerge and grow with a richness that can only be attained by their interdisciplinary inclusion.

There have been many excellent contributions by authors throughout the world who have offered their unique insights. Also, there have as well, been many timely and influential books that have shaped the emergence of this field of study. There is one book that merits our praise for the role it played in moving our nation forward in this important area. This book, *Computers at Risk: Safe Computing in the Information Age*, by the National Research Council and under the leadership of Dr. David D. Clark, was prepared in response to a 1988 request from the Defense Advanced Research

Projects Agency (DARPA). The focus was to create a national research, engineering, and policy agenda to assist our nation in achieving a more trustworthy computing technology by the end of the century. This important effort sought to achieve an understanding of the nature of computer security as expressed in terms of vulnerability, threat, and countermeasure. This was the first comprehensive effort to analyze the concepts of information security; to examine them in terms of confidentiality, integrity, and availability; and to discuss technology in terms of achieving secure computer systems. The criteria to evaluate computer and network security as well as agenda for pursuing research to enhance our nation's computer systems was a valuable and insightful contribution. If the National Research Council's text served as one of the important benchmarks in our past, we feel the addition of the four appendices to this text will focus the reader on several important works that will guide our future. Accordingly, we have provided the executive summaries of three important national studies and a useful appendix on sample language for search warrants and accompanying affidavits to search and seizure computers, from the United States Department of Justice Computer Crime and Intellectual Property Section, Manual on Electronic Search and Seizure.

Appendix A, the Executive Summary of the *National Strategy to Secure Cyberspace*, reviews our nation's strategic objectives that are consistent with our national strategy for homeland security. The role of government in securing cyberspace as well as critical priorities for cyberspace security and a national cyberspace security response system is presented as the first major national effort since the landmark *Computers at Risk* study was completed almost 15 years earlier. In addition, this report recommended a national cyberspace security threat and vulnerability reduction program as well as a national security cyberspace awareness and training program. The securing of our nation's cyberspace was not the sole focus; recommendations were also made to develop an international cyberspace program in cooperation with our nation's efforts.

Appendix B, which is the Executive Summary of *National Strategy for the Physical Protection of Critical Infrastructures and Key Assets*, discusses the need for a national policy and guiding principles to protect our nation's critical infrastructure sectors. This report discusses both governmental and private sector responsibilities and provides a strategy for both planning and resource allocation. The report provides a strategy and identifies major initiatives that we as a nation must implement to protect our key assets. Because cyber attacks could be focused on any one of these key and critical infrastructure assets, it is important that the reader direct attention to this important resource document.

Appendix C is the Executive Summary of the National Institute of Standards and Technology report *Computer Security Incident Handling Guide*, as well as its recommendations. This report is noteworthy for its insight in terms of organizing a computer security incident response capability, as well as recommending establishment of incident response policies and procedures. Also useful was the structure of the incident response team and the description of a number of incidents one is likely to encounter.

Appendix D, the excellent document titled *Sample Language for Search Warrants and Accompanying Affidavits to Search and Seize Computers*, as prepared by the United States Department of Justice, Computer Crime and Intellectual Property section, provides excellent guidelines for law enforcement agencies to review as they create their computer crime units.

In closing, we encourage the reader to carefully review these appendices because they offer great insight into the challenges the forensic computer investigator of the future will have to be prepared to meet.

APPENDIX A

Executive Summary

National Strategy to Secure Cyberspace Recommendations of the National Strategy for Homeland Security

Our Nation's critical infrastructures are composed of public and private institutions in the sectors of agriculture, food, water, public health, emergency services, government, defense industrial base, information and telecommunications, energy, transportation, banking and finance, chemicals and hazardous materials, and postal and shipping. Cyberspace is their nervous system — the control system of our country. Cyberspace is composed of hundreds of thousands of interconnected computers, servers, routers, switches, and fiber optic cables that allow our critical infrastructures to work. Thus, the healthy functioning of cyberspace is essential to our economy and our national security.

This *National Strategy to Secure Cyberspace* is part of our overall effort to protect the Nation. It is an implementing component of the *National Strategy for Homeland Security* and is complemented by a *National Strategy for the Physical Protection of Critical Infrastructures and Key Assets*. The purpose of this document is to engage and empower Americans to secure the portions of cyberspace that they own, operate, control, or with which they interact. Securing cyberspace is a difficult strategic challenge that requires coordinated and focused effort from our entire society — the federal government, state and local governments, the private sector, and the American people.

The *National Strategy to Secure Cyberspace* outlines an initial framework for both organizing and prioritizing efforts. It provides direction to the federal government departments and agencies that have roles in cyberspace security. It also identifies steps that state and local governments, private companies and organizations, and individual Americans can take to improve our collective cybersecurity. The *Strategy* highlights the role of public-private engagement. The document provides a framework for the contributions that we all can make to secure our parts of cyberspace. The dynamics of cyberspace will require adjustments and amendments to the *Strategy* over time.

The speed and anonymity of cyber attacks make distinguishing among the actions of terrorists, criminals, and nation states difficult, a task which often occurs only after the fact, if at all. Therefore, the *National Strategy to Secure Cyberspace* helps reduce our Nation's vulnerability to debilitating attacks against our critical information infrastructures or the physical assets that support them.

Strategic Objectives

Consistent with the National Strategy for Homeland Security, the strategic objectives of this National Strategy to Secure Cyberspace are to:

- Prevent cyber attacks against America's critical infrastructures;
- Reduce national vulnerability to cyber attacks; and
- Minimize damage and recovery time from cyber attacks that do occur.

Threat and Vulnerability

Our economy and national security are fully dependent upon information technology and the information infrastructure. At the core of the information infrastructure upon which we depend is the Internet, a system originally designed to share unclassified research among scientists who were assumed to be uninterested in abusing the network. It is that same Internet that today connects millions of other computer networks making most of the nation's essential services and infrastructures work. These computer networks also control physical objects such as electrical transformers, trains, pipeline pumps, chemical vats, radars, and stock markets, all of which exist beyond cyberspace.

A spectrum of malicious actors can and do conduct attacks against our critical information infrastructures. Of primary concern is the threat of organized cyber attacks capable of causing debilitating disruption to our Nation's critical infrastructures, economy, or national security. The required technical sophistication to carry out such an attack is high — and partially explains the lack of a debilitating attack to date. We should not, however, be too sanguine. There have been instances where organized attackers have exploited vulnerabilities that may be indicative of more destructive capabilities.

Uncertainties exist as to the intent and full technical capabilities of several observed attacks. Enhanced cyber threat analysis is needed to address long-term trends related to threats and vulnerabilities. What is known is that the attack tools and methodologies are becoming widely available, and the technical capability and sophistication of users bent on causing havoc or disruption is improving.

In peacetime America's enemies may conduct espionage on our Government, university research centers, and private companies. They may also seek to prepare for cyber strikes during a confrontation by mapping U.S. information systems, identifying key targets, and lacing our infrastructure with back doors and other means of access. In wartime or crisis, adversaries may seek to intimidate the Nation's political leaders by attacking critical infrastructures and key economic functions or eroding public confidence in information systems.

Cyber attacks on United States information networks can have serious consequences such as disrupting critical operations, causing loss of revenue and intellectual property, or loss of life. Countering such attacks requires the development of robust capabilities where they do not exist today if we are to reduce vulnerabilities and deter those with the capabilities and intent to harm our critical infrastructures.

The Government Role in Securing Cyberspace

In general, the private sector is best equipped and structured to respond to an evolving cyber threat. There are specific instances, however, where federal government response is most appropriate and justified. Looking inward, providing continuity of government requires ensuring the safety of its own cyber infrastructure and those assets required for supporting its essential missions and services. Externally, a government role in cybersecurity is warranted in cases where high transaction costs or legal barriers lead to significant coordination problems; cases in which governments operate in the absence of private sector forces; resolution of incentive problems that lead to under provisioning of critical shared resources; and raising awareness.

Public-private engagement is a key component of our Strategy to secure cyberspace. This is true for several reasons. Public-private partnerships can usefully confront coordination problems. They can significantly enhance information exchange and cooperation. Public-private engagement will take a variety of forms and will address awareness, training, technological improvements, vulnerability remediation, and recovery operations.

A federal role in these and other cases is only justified when the benefits of intervention outweigh the associated costs. This standard is especially important in cases where there are viable private sector solutions for addressing any potential threat or vulnerability. For each case, consideration should be given to the broad-based costs and impacts of a given government action, versus other alternative actions, versus non-action, taking into account any existing or future private solutions.

Federal actions to secure cyberspace are warranted for purposes including: forensics and attack attribution, protection of networks and systems critical to national security, indications and warnings, and protection against organized attacks capable of inflicting debilitating damage to the economy. Federal activities should also support research and technology development that will enable the private sector to better secure privately-owned portions of the Nation's critical infrastructure.

Department of Homeland Security and Cyberspace Security

On November 25, 2002, President Bush signed legislation creating the Department of Homeland Security (DHS). This new cabinet-level department will unite 22 federal entities for the common purpose of improving our homeland security. The Secretary of DHS will have important responsibilities in cyberspace security. These responsibilities include:

- Developing a comprehensive national plan for securing the key resources and critical infrastructure of the United States;
- Providing crisis management in response to attacks on critical information systems;
- Providing technical assistance to the private sector and other government entities with respect to emergency recovery plans for failures of critical information systems;
- Coordinating with other agencies of the federal government to provide specific warning information and advice about appropriate protective measures and countermeasures to state, local, and non-governmental organizations including the private sector, academia, and the public; and
- Performing and funding research and development along with other agencies that will lead to new scientific understanding and technologies in support of homeland security.

Consistent with these responsibilities, DHS will become a federal center of excellence for cybersecurity and provide a focal point for federal outreach to state, local, and nongovernmental organizations including the private sector, academia, and the public.

Critical Priorities for Cyberspace Security

The *National Strategy to Secure Cyberspace* articulates five national priorities including:

I. A National Cyberspace Security Response System;
II. A National Cyberspace Security Threat and Vulnerability Reduction Program;
III. A National Cyberspace Security Awareness and Training Program;
IV. Securing Governments' Cyberspace; and
V. National Security and International Cyberspace Security Cooperation.

The first priority focuses on improving our response to cyber incidents and reducing the potential damage from such events. The second, third, and fourth priorities aim to reduce threats from, and our vulnerabilities to, cyber attacks. The fifth priority is to prevent cyber attacks that could impact national security assets and to improve the international management of and response to such attacks.

Priority I: A National Cyberspace Security Response System

Rapid identification, information exchange, and remediation can often mitigate the damage caused by malicious cyberspace activity. For those activities to be effective at a national level, the United States needs a partnership between government and industry to perform analyses, issue warnings, and coordinate response efforts. Privacy and civil liberties must be protected in the process. Because no cybersecurity plan can be impervious to concerted and intelligent attack, information systems must be able to operate while under attack and have the resilience to restore full operations quickly.

The *National Strategy to Secure Cyberspace* identifies eight major actions and initiatives for cyberspace security response:

1. Establish a public-private architecture for responding to national-level cyber incidents;
2. Provide for the development of tactical and strategic analysis of cyber attacks and vulnerability assessments;

3. Encourage the development of a private sector capability to share a synoptic view of the health of cyberspace;
4. Expand the Cyber Warning and Information Network to support the role of DHS in coordinating crisis management for cyberspace security;
5. Improve national incident management;
6. Coordinate processes for voluntary participation in the development of national public-private continuity and contingency plans;
7. Exercise cybersecurity continuity plans for federal systems; and
8. Improve and enhance public-private information sharing involving cyber attacks, threats, and vulnerabilities.

Priority II: A National Cyberspace Security Threat and Vulnerability Reduction Program

By exploiting vulnerabilities in our cyber systems, an organized attack may endanger the security of our Nation's critical infrastructures. The vulnerabilities that most threaten cyberspace occur in the information assets of critical infrastructure enterprises themselves and their external supporting structures, such as the mechanisms of the Internet. Lesser-secured sites on the interconnected network of networks also present potentially significant exposures to cyber attacks. Vulnerabilities result from weaknesses in technology and because of improper implementation and oversight of technological products.

The *National Strategy to Secure Cyberspace* identifies eight major actions and initiatives to reduce threats and related vulnerabilities:

1. Enhance law enforcement's capabilities for preventing and prosecuting cyberspace attacks;
2. Create a process for national vulnerability assessments to better understand the potential consequences of threats and vulnerabilities;
3. Secure the mechanisms of the Internet by improving protocols and routing;
4. Foster the use of trusted digital control systems/supervisory control and data acquisition systems;
5. Reduce and remediate software vulnerabilities;
6. Understand infrastructure interdependencies and improve the physical security of cyber systems and telecommunications;
7. Prioritize federal cybersecurity research and development agendas; and
8. Assess and secure emerging systems.

Priority III: A National Cyberspace Security Awareness and Training Program

Many cyber vulnerabilities exist because of a lack of cybersecurity awareness on the part of computer users, systems administrators, technology developers, procurement officials, auditors, chief information officers (CIOs), chief executive officers, and corporate boards. Such awareness-based vulnerabilities present serious risks to critical infrastructures regardless of whether they exist within the infrastructure itself. A lack of trained personnel and the absence of widely accepted, multi-level certification programs for cybersecurity professionals complicate the task of addressing cyber vulnerabilities.

The *National Strategy to Secure Cyberspace* identifies four major actions and initiatives for awareness, education, and training:

1. Promote a comprehensive national awareness program to empower all Americans — businesses, the general workforce, and the general population — to secure their own parts of cyberspace;
2. Foster adequate training and education programs to support the Nation's cybersecurity needs;
3. Increase the efficiency of existing federal cybersecurity training programs; and
4. Promote private-sector support for well-coordinated, widely recognized professional cybersecurity certifications.

Priority IV: Securing Governments' Cyberspace

Although governments administer only a minority of the Nation's critical infrastructure computer systems, governments at all levels perform essential services in the agriculture, food, water, public health, emergency services, defense, social welfare, information and telecommunications, energy, transportation, banking and finance, chemicals, and postal and shipping sectors that depend upon cyberspace for their delivery. Governments can lead by example in cyberspace security, including fostering a marketplace for more secure technologies through their procurement.

The *National Strategy to Secure Cyberspace* identifies five major actions and initiatives for the securing of governments' cyberspace:

1. Continuously assess threats and vulnerabilities to federal cyber systems;
2. Authenticate and maintain authorized users of federal cyber systems;
3. Secure federal wireless local area networks;

4. Improve security in government outsourcing and procurement; and
5. Encourage state and local governments to consider establishing information technology security programs and participate in information sharing and analysis centers with similar governments.

Priority V: National Security and International Cyberspace Security Cooperation

America's cyberspace links the United States to the rest of the world. A network of networks spans the planet, allowing malicious actors on one continent to act on systems thousands of miles away. Cyber attacks cross borders at light speed, and discerning the source of malicious activity is difficult. America must be capable of safeguarding and defending its critical systems and networks. Enabling our ability to do so requires a system of international cooperation to facilitate information sharing, reduce vulnerabilities, and deter malicious actors.

The *National Strategy to Secure Cyberspace* identifies six major actions and initiatives to strengthen U.S. national security and international cooperation:

1. Strengthen cyber-related counterintelligence efforts;
2. Improve capabilities for attack attribution and response;
3. Improve coordination for responding to cyber attacks within the U.S. national security community;
4. Work with industry and through international organizations to facilitate dialogue and partnerships among international public and private sectors focused on protecting information infrastructures and promoting a global "culture of security;"
5. Foster the establishment of national and international watch-and-warning networks to detect and prevent cyber attacks as they emerge; and
6. Encourage other nations to accede to the Council of Europe Convention on Cybercrime, or to ensure that their laws and procedures are at least as comprehensive.

A National Effort

Protecting the widely distributed assets of cyberspace requires the efforts of many Americans. The federal government alone cannot sufficiently defend America's cyberspace. Our traditions of federalism and limited government require that organizations outside the federal government take the lead in many of these efforts. Every American who can contribute to securing part of cyberspace is encouraged to do so. The federal government invites the creation of, and participation in, public-private partnerships to raise cybersecurity awareness, train personnel, stimulate market forces, improve technology, identify and remediate vulnerabilities, exchange information, and plan recovery operations.

People and organizations across the United States have already taken steps to improve cyberspace security. On September 18, 2002, many private-sector entities released plans and strategies for securing their respective infrastructures. The Partnership for Critical Infrastructure Security has played a unique role in facilitating private-sector contributions to this Strategy. Inputs from the critical sector's themselves can be found at **http://www.pcis.org**.

These comprehensive infrastructure plans describe the strategic initiatives of various sectors, including:

- Banking and Finance;
- Insurance;
- Chemical;
- Oil and Gas;
- Electric;
- Law Enforcement;
- Higher Education;
- Transportation (Rail);
- Information Technology;
- Telecommunications; and
- Water.

As each of the critical infrastructure sectors implements these initiatives, threats and vulnerabilities to our infrastructures will be reduced.

For the foreseeable future two things will be true: America will rely upon cyberspace and the federal government will seek a continuing broad partnership with the private sector to develop, implement, and refine a *National Strategy to Secure Cyberspace*.

APPENDIX B

Executive Summary

National Strategy for the Physical Protection of Critical Infrastructures and Key Assets

This document defines the road ahead for a core mission area identified in the President's *National Strategy for Homeland Security* — reducing the Nation's vulnerability to acts of terrorism by protecting our critical infrastructures and key assets from physical attack.

This document, the *National Strategy for the Physical Protection of Critical Infrastructures and Key Assets*, the *Strategy*, identifies a clear set of national goals and objectives and outlines the guiding principles that will underpin our efforts to secure the infrastructures and assets vital to our national security, governance, public health and safety, economy, and public confidence. This *Strategy* also provides a unifying organization and identifies specific initiatives to drive our near-term national protection priorities and inform the resource allocation process. Most importantly, it establishes a foundation for building and fostering the cooperative environment in which government, industry, and private citizens can carry out their respective protection responsibilities more effectively and efficiently.

This *Strategy* recognizes the many important steps that public and private entities across the country have taken in response to the September 11, 2001, attacks to improve the security of their critical facilities, systems, and functions. Building upon these efforts, this document provides direction to the federal departments and agencies that have a role in critical infrastructure and key asset protection. It also suggests steps that state and local governments, private sector entities, and concerned citizens across America can take to enhance our collective infrastructure and asset security. In this light, this *Strategy* belongs and applies to the Nation as a whole, not just to the federal government or its constituent departments and agencies.

A New Mission

The September 11 attacks demonstrated our national-level physical vulnerability to the threat posed by a formidable enemy-focused, mass destruction terrorism. The events of that day also validated how determined, patient, and sophisticated — in both planning and execution — our terrorist enemies have become. The basic nature of our free society greatly enables terrorist operations and tactics, while, at the same time, hinders our ability to predict, prevent, or mitigate the effects of terrorist acts. Given these realities, it is imperative to develop a comprehensive national approach to physical protection.

Defining the End State: Strategic Objectives

The strategic objectives that underpin our national critical infrastructure and key asset protection effort include:

- Identifying and assuring the protection of those infrastructures and assets that we deem most critical in terms of national-level public health and safety, governance, economic and national security, and public confidence consequences;
- Providing timely warning and assuring the protection of those infrastructures and assets that face a specific, imminent threat; and
- Assuring the protection of other infrastructures and assets that may become terrorist targets over time by pursuing specific initiatives and enabling a collaborative environment in which federal, state, and local governments and the private sector can better protect the infrastructures and assets they control.

Homeland Security and Infrastructure Protection: A Shared Responsibility

Protecting America's critical infrastructures and key assets calls for a transition to a new national cooperative paradigm. The basic tenets of *homeland security* are fundamentally different from the historically defined tenets of national security. Traditionally, *national security* has been recognized largely as the responsibility of the federal government. *National security* is underpinned by the collective efforts of the military, foreign policy establishment, and intelligence community in the defense of our airspace and national borders, as well as operations overseas to protect our national interests.

Homeland security, particularly in the context of critical infrastructure and key asset protection, is a shared responsibility that cannot be accomplished by the federal government alone. It requires coordinated action on the part of federal, state, and local governments; the private sector; and concerned citizens across the country.[1]

The Case for Action

To build and implement a robust strategy to protect our critical infrastructures and key assets from further terrorist exploitation, we must understand the motivations of our enemies as well as their preferred tactics and targets. We must complement this understanding with a comprehensive assessment of the infrastructures and assets to be protected, their vulnerabilities, and the challenges associated with eliminating or mitigating those vulnerabilitiesóa task that will require the concerted efforts of our entire Nation.

The Importance of Critical Infrastructures

America's critical infrastructure sectors provide the foundation for our national security, governance, economic vitality, and way of life. Furthermore, their continued reliability, robustness, and resiliency create a sense of confidence and form an important part of our national identity and purpose. Critical infrastructures frame our daily lives and enable us to enjoy one of the highest overall standards of living in the world.

The facilities, systems, and functions that comprise our critical infrastructures are highly sophisticated and complex. They include human assets and physical and cyber systems that work together in processes that are highly interdependent. They also consist of key nodes that, in turn, are essential to the operation of the critical infrastructures in which they function.

The Importance of Key Assets

Key assets and high profile events are individual targets whose attack — in the worst-case scenarios — could result in not only large-scale human casualties and property destruction, but also profound damage to our national prestige, morale, and confidence.

Individually, key assets like nuclear power plants and dams may not be vital to the continuity of critical services at the national level. However, a successful strike against such targets may result in a significant loss of life and property in addition to long-term, adverse public health and safety consequences. Other key assets are symbolically equated with traditional

American values and institutions or U.S. political and economic power. Our national icons, monuments, and historical attractions preserve history, honor achievements, and represent the natural grandeur of our country. They celebrate our American ideals and way of life and present attractive targets for terrorists, particularly when coupled with high-profile events and celebratory activities that bring together significant numbers of people.

Understanding the Threat

Characteristics of Terrorism

The September 11 attacks on the World Trade Center and the Pentagon underscore the determination of our terrorist enemies. Terrorists are relentless and patient, as evidenced by their persistent targeting of the World Trade Center towers over the years. Terrorists are also opportunistic and flexible. They learn from experience and modify their tactics and targets to exploit perceived vulnerabilities and avoid observed strengths. As security increases around more predictable targets, they shift their focus to less protected assets. Enhancing countermeasures for any one terrorist tactic or target, therefore, makes it more likely that terrorists will favor another.

The Nature of Possible Attacks

Terrorists' pursuit of their long-term strategic objectives includes attacks on critical infrastructures and key assets. Terrorists target critical infrastructures to achieve three general types of effects:

- *Direct infrastructure effects:* Cascading disruption or arrest of the functions of critical infrastructures or key assets through direct attacks on a critical node, system, or function.
- *Indirect infrastructure effects:* Cascading disruption and financial consequences for government, society, and economy through public- and private-sector reactions to an attack.
- *Exploitation of infrastructure:* Exploitation of elements of a particular infrastructure to disrupt or destroy another target.

National Policy and Guiding Principles

This *Strategy* reaffirms our longstanding national policy regarding critical infrastructure and key asset protection. It also delineates a set of guiding principles that will underpin our domestic protection strategy.

Statement of National Policy

As a Nation we remain committed to protecting our critical infrastructures and key assets from acts of terrorism that would:

- Impair the federal government's ability to perform essential national and homeland security missions and ensure the general public's health and safety;
- Undermine state and local government capacities to maintain order and to deliver minimum essential public services;
- Damage the private sector's capability to ensure the orderly functioning of the economy and the delivery of essential services; and
- Undermine the public's morale and confidence in our national economic and political institutions.

We must work collaboratively to employ the tools necessary to implement such protection.

Guiding Principles

Eight guiding principles underpin this *Strategy*:

- Assure public safety, public confidence, and services;
- Establish responsibility and accountability;
- Encourage and facilitate partnering among all levels of government and between government and industry;
- Encourage market solutions wherever possible and compensate for market failure with focused government intervention;
- Facilitate meaningful information sharing;
- Foster international cooperation;
- Develop technologies and expertise to combat terrorist threats; and
- Safeguard privacy and constitutional freedoms.

Organizing And Partnering for Critical Infrastructure and Key Asset Protection

Implementing this *Strategy* requires a unifying organization, a clear purpose, a common understanding of roles and responsibilities, accountability, and a set of well understood coordinating processes. A solid organizational scheme sets the stage for effective engagement and interaction between the public and private sectors at all levels. Without it, the tasks of coordinating and integrating domestic protection policy, planning, resource allocation, performance measurement, and enabling initiatives across federal, state, and local governments and the private sector are virtually impossible to accomplish. Our strategy for action must provide the foundation these entities can use to achieve common objectives, applying their core capabilities, expertise, and experience as necessary to meet the threat at hand.

Federal Government Responsibilities

The federal government has the capacity to organize, convene, and coordinate broadly across governmental jurisdictions and the private sector. It has the responsibility to develop coherent national policies, strategies, and programs for implementation. In the context of homeland security, the federal government will coordinate the complementary efforts and capabilities of government and private institutions to raise our level of protection over the long term as appropriate for each of our critical infrastructures and key assets.

Every terrorist event has a potential national impact. The federal government will, therefore, take the lead to ensure that the three principal objectives detailed in the *Introduction* of this *Strategy* are met. This leadership role involves:

- Taking stock of our most critical facilities, systems, and functions and monitoring their preparedness across economic sectors and governmental jurisdictions;
- Assuring that federal, state, local, and private entities work together to protect critical facilities, systems, and functions that face an imminent threat and/or whose loss could have significant national consequences;
- Providing and coordinating national-level threat information, assessments, and warnings that are timely, actionable, and relevant to state, local, and private sector partners;
- Creating and implementing comprehensive, multi-tiered protection policies and programs;
- Exploring potential options for enablers and incentives to encourage stakeholders to devise solutions to their unique protection impediments;
- Developing cross-sector and cross-jurisdictional protection standards, guidelines, criteria, and protocols;
- Facilitating the sharing of critical infrastructure and key asset protection best practices and processes and vulnerability assessment methodologies;
- Conducting demonstration projects and pilot programs;
- Seeding the development and transfer of advanced technologies while taking advantage of private-sector expertise and competencies;
- Promoting national-level critical infrastructure and key asset protection education and awareness; and
- Improving the federal government's ability to work with state and local responders and service providers.

Federal Lead Departments and Agencies

The *National Strategy for Homeland Security* provides a sector-based organizational scheme for protecting critical infrastructure and key assets. It identifies the federal lead departments and agencies responsible for coordinating protection activities and developing and maintaining collaborative relationships with their state and local government and industry counterparts in the critical sectors.

In addition to securing federally owned and operated infrastructures and assets, the role of the federal lead departments and agencies is to assist state and local governments and private-sector partners in their efforts to:

- Organize and conduct protection and continuity of government and operations planning, and elevate awareness and understanding of threats and vulnerabilities to their critical facilities, systems, and functions;
- Identify and promote effective sector-specific protection practices and methodologies; and
- Expand voluntary security-related information sharing among private entities within the sector, as well as between government and private entities.

Department of Homeland Security

The Department of Homeland Security (DHS) will provide overall cross-sector coordination in this new organizational scheme, serving as the primary liaison and facilitator for cooperation among federal agencies, state and local governments, and the private sector. As the cross-sector coordinator, DHS will also be responsible for the detailed refinement and implementation of the core elements of this *Strategy*.

Other Federal Departments and Agencies

Besides the designated federal lead departments and agencies, the federal government will rely on the unique expertise of other departments and agencies to enhance the physical protection dimension of homeland security. Additionally, overall sector initiatives will often include an international component or requirement, require the development of a coordinated relationship with other governments or agencies, and entail information sharing with foreign governments. Accordingly, the Department of State (DoS) will support the development and implementation of sector protection initiatives by laying the groundwork for bilateral and multilateral infrastructure protective agreements with our international allies.

State and Local Government Responsibilities

The 50 states, 4 territories, and 87,000 local jurisdictions that comprise this Nation have an important and unique role to play in the protection of our critical infrastructures and key assets. State and local governments, like the federal government, should identify and secure the critical infrastructures and key assets they own and operate within their jurisdictions.

States should also engender coordination of protective and emergency response activities and resource support among local jurisdictions and regions in close collaboration with designated federal lead departments and agencies. States should further facilitate coordinated planning and preparedness for critical infrastructure and key asset protection, applying unified criteria for determining criticality, prioritizing protection investments, and exercising preparedness within their jurisdictions. States should also act as conduits for requests for federal assistance when the threat at hand exceeds the capabilities of local jurisdictions and private entities within those jurisdictions. Finally, states should facilitate the exchange of relevant security information and threat alerts down to the local level.

State and local governments look to the federal government for coordination, support, and resources when national requirements exceed local capabilities. Protecting critical infrastructures and key assets will require a close and extensive cooperation among all three levels of government. DHS, in particular, is designed to provide a single point of coordination with state and local governments for homeland security issues, including the critical infrastructure and key asset protection mission area. Other federal lead departments and agencies and law enforcement organizations will provide support as needed and appropriate for specific critical infrastructure and key asset protection requirements.

Private Sector Responsibilities

The lion's share of our critical infrastructures and key assets are owned and operated by the private sector. Customarily, private sector firms prudently engage in risk management planning and invest in security as a necessary function of business operations and customer confidence. Moreover, in the present threat environment, the private sector generally remains the first line of defense for its own facilities. Consequently, private-sector owners and operators should reassess and adjust their planning, assurance, and investment programs to better accommodate the increased risk presented by deliberate acts of violence. Since the events of September 11, many businesses have increased their threshold investments and undertaken enhancements in security in an effort to meet the demands of the new threat environment.

For most enterprises, the level of investment in security reflects implicit risk-versus-consequence tradeoffs, which are based on: (1) what is known about the risk environment; and (2) what is economically justifiable and sustainable in a competitive marketplace or in an environment of limited government resources. Given the dynamic nature of the terrorist threat and the severity of the consequences associated with many potential attack scenarios, the private sector naturally looks to the government for better information to help make its crucial security investment decisions.

Similarly, the private sector looks to the government for assistance when the threat at hand exceeds an enterprise's capability to protect itself beyond a reasonable level of additional investment. In this light, the federal government will collaborate with the private sector (and state and local governments) to assure the protection of nationally critical infrastructures and assets; provide timely warning and assure the protection of infrastructures and assets that face a specific, imminent threat; and promote an environment in which the private sector can better carry out its specific protection responsibilities.

Near-term Roadmap: Cross-Sector Security Priorities

The issues and security initiatives outlined in the *Cross-Sector Security Priorities* chapter of this document represent important, near-term national priorities. They are focused on impediments to physical protection that significantly impact multiple sectors of our government, society, and economy. Potential solutions to the problems identified — such as information sharing and threat indications and warning — are high-leverage areas that, when realized, will enhance the Nation's collective ability to protect critical infrastructures and key assets across the board. Accordingly, DHS and designated federal lead departments and agencies will prepare detailed implementation plans to support the activities outlined in this chapter.

This *Strategy* identifies major cross-sector initiatives in five areas:

Planning and Resource Allocation: This *Strategy* identifies eight major initiatives in this area.

- Create collaborative mechanisms for government-industry critical infrastructure and key asset protection planning;
- Identify key protection priorities and develop appropriate supporting mechanisms for these priorities;
- Foster increased sharing of risk-management expertise between the public and private sectors;
- Identify options for incentives for private organizations that proactively implement enhanced security measures;
- Coordinate and consolidate federal and state protection plans;
- Establish a task force to review legal impediments to reconstitution and recovery in the aftermath of an attack against a critical infrastructure or key asset;
- Develop an integrated critical infrastructure and key asset geospatial database; and
- Conduct critical infrastructure protection planning with our international partners.

Information Sharing and Indications and Warnings: This *Strategy* identifies six major initiatives in this area.

- Define protection-related information sharing requirements and establish effective, efficient information sharing processes;
- Implement the statutory authorities and powers of the *Homeland Security Act of 2002* to protect security and proprietary information regarded as sensitive by the private sector;
- Promote the development and operation of critical sector Information Sharing Analysis Centers;
- Improve processes for domestic threat data collection, analysis, and dissemination to state and local government and private industry;
- Support the development of interoperable secure communications systems for state and local governments and designated private sector entities; and
- Complete implementation of the Homeland Security Advisory System.

Personnel Surety, Building Human Capital, and Awareness: This *Strategy* identifies six major initiatives in this area.

- Coordinate the development of national standards for personnel surety;
- Develop a certification program for background-screening companies;
- Explore establishment of a certification regime or model security training program for private security officers;
- Identify requirements and develop programs to protect critical personnel;
- Facilitate the sharing of public- and private-sector protection expertise; and
- Develop and implement a national awareness program for critical infrastructure and key asset protection.

Technology and Research & Development: This *Strategy* identifies four major initiatives in this area.

- Coordinate public- and private-sector security research and development activities;
- Coordinate interoperability standards to ensure compatibility of communications systems;
- Explore methods to authenticate and verify personnel identity; and
- Improve technical surveillance, monitoring, and detection capabilities.

Modeling, Simulation, and Analysis: This *Strategy* identifies seven major initiatives in this area.

- Enable the integration of modeling, simulation, and analysis into national infrastructure and asset protection planning and decision support activities;
- Develop economic models of near- and long-term effects of terrorist attacks;
- Develop critical node/chokepoint and interdependency analysis capabilities;
- Model interdependencies across sectors with respect to conflicts between sector alert and warning procedures and actions;
- Conduct integrated risk modeling of cyber and physical threats, vulnerabilities, and consequences; and
- Develop models to improve information integration.

Unique Protection Areas

In addition to the cross-sector themes addressed in this *Strategy*, the individual critical infrastructure sectors and special categories of key assets have unique issues that require action. These considerations and associated enabling initiatives are discussed in the last two chapters of this *Strategy*:

Securing Critical Infrastructures: This *Strategy* identifies major protection initiatives for the following critical infrastructure sectors:

- Agriculture and Food
- Water
- Public Health
- Emergency Services
- Defense Industrial Base
- Telecommunications
- Energy
- Transportation
- Banking and Finance
- Chemicals and Hazardous Materials
- Postal and Shipping

Protecting Key Assets: This *Strategy* identifies major protection initiatives for the following key asset categories:

- National Monuments and Icons
- Nuclear Power Plants
- Dams
- Government Facilities
- Commercial Key Assets

[1] The *National Strategy for Homeland Security* defines "State" to mean "any state of the United States, the District of Columbia, Puerto Rico, the Virgin Islands, Guam, American Samoa, the Commonwealth of the Northern Mariana Islands, or the trust territory of the Pacific Islands." The *Strategy* defines "local government" as "any county, city, village, town, district, or other political subdivision of any state, any Native American tribe or authorized tribal organization, or Alaska native village or organization, and includes any rural community or unincorporated town or village or any other public entity for which an application for assistance is made by a state or political subdivision thereof."

APPENDIX C

Computer Security Incident Handling Guide

Recommendations of the National Institute of Standards and Technology

Executive Summary

Computer security incident response has become an important component of information technology (IT) programs. Security-related threats have become not only more numerous and diverse but also more damaging and disruptive. New types of security-related incidents emerge frequently. Preventative activities based on the results of risk assessments can lower the number of incidents, but not all incidents can be prevented. An incident response capability is therefore necessary for rapidly detecting incidents, minimizing loss and destruction, mitigating the weaknesses that were exploited, and restoring computing services. To that end, this publication provides guidelines for incident handling, particularly for analyzing incident-related data and determining the appropriate response to each incident. The guidelines can be followed independently of particular hardware platforms, operating systems, protocols, or applications.

Because performing incident response effectively is a complex undertaking, establishing a successful incident response capability requires substantial planning and resources. Continually monitoring threats through intrusion detection systems (IDSs) and other mechanisms is essential. Establishing clear procedures for assessing the current and potential business impact of incidents is critical, as is implementing effective methods of collecting, analyzing, and reporting data. Building relationships and establishing suitable means of communication with other internal groups (e.g., human resources, legal) and with external groups (e.g., other incident response teams, law enforcement) are also vital.

This publication seeks to help both established and newly formed incident response teams. This document assists organizations in establishing computer security incident response capabilities and handling incidents efficiently and effectively. More specifically, this document discusses the following items:

+ Organizing a computer security incident response capability
  - Establishing incident response policies and procedures
  - Structuring an incident response team, including outsourcing considerations
  - Recognizing which additional personnel may be called on to participate in incident response.
+ Handling incidents from initial preparation through the post-incident lessons learned phase
+ Handling specific types of incidents
  - **Denial of Service (DoS)** — an attack that prevents or impairs the authorized use of networks, systems, or applications by exhausting resources
  - **Malicious Code** — a virus, worm, Trojan horse, or other code-based malicious entity that infects a host
  - **Unauthorized Access** — a person gains logical or physical access without permission to a network, system, application, data, or other resource
  - **Inappropriate Usage** — a person violates acceptable computing use policies
  - **Multiple Component** — a single incident that encompasses two or more incidents; for example, a malicious code infection leads to unauthorized access to a host, which is then used to gain unauthorized access to additional hosts.

Implementing the following requirements and recommendations should facilitate efficient and effective incident response for Federal departments and agencies.

Organizations must create, provision, and operate a formal incident response capability. Federal law requires Federal agencies to report incidents to the Federal Computer Incident Response Center (FedCIRC) office within the Department of Homeland Security.

The Federal Information Security Management Act (FISMA) of 2002 requires Federal agencies to establish incident response capabilities. Each Federal civilian agency must designate a primary and secondary point of contact (POC) with FedCIRC, report all incidents, and internally document corrective actions and their impact. Each agency is responsible for determining specific ways in which these requirements are to be fulfilled.

Establishing an incident response capability should include the following actions:

+ Creating an incident response policy
+ Developing procedures for performing incident handling and reporting, based on the incident response policy
+ Setting guidelines for communicating with outside parties regarding incidents
+ Selecting a team structure and staffing model
+ Establishing relationships between the incident response team and other groups, both internal (e.g., legal department) and external (e.g., law enforcement agencies)
+ Determining what services the incident response team should provide
+ Staffing and training the incident response team.

Organizations should reduce the frequency of incidents by effectively securing networks, systems, and applications.

Preventing problems is normally less costly and more effective than reacting to them after they occur. Thus, incident prevention is an important complement to an incident response capability. If security controls are insufficient, high volumes of incidents may occur, overwhelming the resources and capacity for response, which would result in delayed or incomplete recovery and possibly more extensive damage and longer periods of service and data unavailability. Incident handling can be performed more effectively if organizations complement their incident response capability with adequate resources to actively maintain the security of networks, systems, and applications, freeing the incident response team to focus on handling serious incidents.

Organizations should document their guidelines for interactions with other organizations regarding incidents.

During incident handling, the organization may need to communicate with outside parties, including other incident response teams, law enforcement, the media, vendors, and external victims. Because such communications often need to occur quickly, organizations should predetermine communication guidelines so that only the appropriate information is shared with the right parties. If sensitive information is released inappropriately, it can lead to greater disruption and financial loss than the incident itself. Creating and maintaining a list of internal and external POCs, along with backups for each contact, should assist in making communications among parties easier and faster.

Organizations should emphasize the importance of incident detection and analysis throughout the organization.

In an organization, thousands or millions of possible signs of incidents may occur each day, recorded mainly by logging and computer security software. Automation is needed to perform an initial analysis of the data and select events of interest for human review. Event correlation software and centralized logging can be of great value in automating the analysis process. However, the effectiveness of the process depends on the quality of the data that goes into it. Organizations should establish logging standards and procedures to ensure that adequate information is collected by logs and security software and that the data is reviewed regularly.

Organizations should create written guidelines for prioritizing incidents.

Prioritizing the handling of individual incidents is a critical decision point in the incident response process. Incidents should be prioritized based on the following:

+ Criticality of the affected resources (e.g., public Web server, user workstation)
+ Current and potential technical effect of the incident (e.g., root compromise, data destruction).

Combining the criticality of the affected resources and the current and potential technical effect of the incident determines the business impact of the incident — for example, data destruction on a user workstation might result in a minor loss of productivity, whereas root compromise of a public Web server might result in a major loss of revenue, productivity, access to services, and reputation, as well as the release of confidential data (e.g., credit card numbers, Social Security numbers).

Incident handlers may be under great stress during incidents, so it is important to make the prioritization process clear. Organizations should decide how the incident response team should react under various circumstances, and then create a Service Level Agreement (SLA) that documents the appropriate actions and maximum response times. This documentation is particularly valuable for organizations that outsource components of their incident response programs. Documenting the guidelines should facilitate faster and more consistent decision-making.

Organizations should use the lessons learned process to gain value from incidents.

After a major incident has been handled, the organization should hold a lessons learned meeting to review how effective the incident handling process was and identify necessary improvements to existing security controls and practices. Lessons learned meetings should also be held periodically for lesser incidents. The information accumulated from all lessons learned meetings should be used to identify systemic security weaknesses and deficiencies in policies and procedures. Follow-up reports generated for each resolved incident can be important not only for evidentiary purposes but also for reference in handling future incidents and in training new incident response team members. An incident database, with detailed information on each incident that occurs, can be another valuable source of information for incident handlers.

Organizations should strive to maintain situational awareness during large-scale incidents.

Organizations typically find it very challenging to maintain situational awareness for the handling of large-scale incidents because of their complexity. Many people within the organization may play a role in the incident response, and the organization may need to communicate rapidly and efficiently with various external groups. Collecting, organizing, and analyzing all the pieces of information, so that the right decisions can be made and executed, are not easy tasks. The key to maintaining situational awareness is preparing to handle large-scale incidents, which should include the following:

+ Establishing, documenting, maintaining, and exercising on-hours and off-hours contact and notification mechanisms for various individuals and groups within the organization (e.g., chief information officer [CIO], head of information security, IT support, business continuity planning) and outside the organization (e.g., incident response organizations, counterparts at other organizations).
+ Planning and documenting guidelines for the prioritization of incident response actions based on business impact.
+ Preparing one or more individuals to act as incident leads who are responsible for gathering information from the incident handlers and other parties, and distributing relevant information to the parties that need it.
+ Practicing the handling of large-scale incidents through exercises and simulations on a regular basis; such incidents happen rarely, so incident response teams often lack experience in handling them effectively.

Appendix A — Recommendations

Appendix A lists the major recommendations presented in Sections 2 through 8 of this document. The first group of recommendations applies to organizing an incident response capability. The remaining recommendations have been grouped by the phases of the incident response life cycle — preparation; detection and analysis; containment, eradication, and recovery; and post-incident activity. Each group contains general recommendations for its incident response phase and any applicable recommendations for handling particular categories of incidents (e.g., denial of service [DoS]) during the phase.

A.1 Organizing a Computer Security Incident Response Capability

+ **Establish a formal incident response capability.** Organizations should be prepared to respond quickly and effectively when computer security defenses are breached. The Federal Information Security Management Act (FISMA) requires Federal agencies to establish incident response capabilities.

A.1.1 Incident Response Policy and Procedure Creation

+ **Create an incident response policy and use it as the basis for incident response procedures.** The incident response policy is the foundation of the incident response program. It defines which events are considered incidents, establishes the organizational structure for incident response, defines roles and responsibilities, and lists the requirements for reporting incidents, among other items.

+ **Establish policies and procedures regarding incident-related information sharing.** The organization will want or be required to communicate incident details with outside parties, such as the media, law enforcement agencies, and incident reporting organizations. The incident response team should discuss this requirement at length with the organization's public affairs staff, legal advisors, and management to establish policies and procedures regarding information sharing. The team should comply with existing organization policy on interacting with the media and other outside parties.

+ **Provide pertinent information on incidents to the appropriate incident reporting organization.** Federal civilian agencies are required to report incidents to the Federal Computer Incident Response Center (FedCIRC). Reporting benefits the agencies because the incident reporting organizations use the reported data to provide information to the agencies regarding new threats and incident trends.

A.1.2   Incident Response Team Structure and Services

+ **Consider the relevant factors when selecting an appropriate incident response team model.** Organizations should carefully weigh the advantages and disadvantages of each possible team structure model and staffing model in the context of the organization's needs and available resources.

+ **Select people with appropriate skills for the incident response team.** The credibility and proficiency of the team depend largely on the technical skills of its members. Poor technical judgment can undermine the team's credibility and cause incidents to worsen. Critical technical skills include system administration, network administration, programming, technical support, and intrusion detection. Teamwork and communications skills are also needed for effective incident handling.

+ **Identify other groups within the organization that may need to participate in incident handling.** Every incident response team relies on the expertise and judgment of other teams, including management, information security, information technology (IT) support, legal, public affairs, and facilities management.

+ **Determine which services the team should offer.** Although the main focus of the team is incident response, most teams perform additional functions. Examples include distributing security advisories, performing vulnerability assessments, educating users on security, and monitoring intrusion detection sensors.

A.2   Preparation

A.2.1   Denial of Service Incidents

+ **Acquire tools and resources that may be of value during incident handling.** The team will be more efficient at handling incidents if various tools and resources are already available to them. Examples include contact lists, encryption software, network diagrams, backup devices, computer forensic software, port lists, and security patches.

+ **Prevent incidents from occurring by ensuring that networks, systems, and applications are sufficiently secure.** Preventing incidents is beneficial to the organization and reduces the workload of the incident response team. Performing periodic risk assessments and reducing the identified risks to an acceptable level are effective in reducing the number of incidents. User, IT staff, and management awareness of security policies and procedures is also very important.

+ **Configure firewall rulesets to prevent reflector attacks.** Most reflector attacks can be stopped through network-based and host-based firewall rulesets that reject suspicious combinations of source and destination ports.

+ **Configure border routers to prevent amplifier attacks.** Amplifier attacks can be blocked by configuring border routers not to forward directed broadcasts.

+ **Determine how the organization's Internet service providers (ISP) and second-tier providers can assist in handling network-based DoS attacks.** ISPs can often filter or limit certain types of traffic, slowing or halting a DoS attack. They can also provide logs of DoS traffic and may be able to assist in tracing the source of the attack. The organization should meet with the ISPs in advance to establish procedures for requesting such assistance.

+ **Configure security software to detect DoS attacks.** Intrusion detection software can detect many types of DoS activity. Establishing network and system activity baselines, and monitoring for significant deviations from those baselines, can also be useful in detecting attacks.

+ **Configure the network perimeter to deny all incoming and outgoing traffic that is not expressly permitted.** By restricting the types of traffic that can enter and leave the environment, the organization will limit the methods that attackers can use to perform DoS attacks.

A.2.2   Malicious Code Incidents

+ **Make users aware of malicious code issues.** Users should be familiar with the methods that malicious code uses to propagate and the symptoms of infections. Holding regular user education sessions helps to ensure that users are aware of the risks that malicious code poses. Teaching users how to safely handle e-mail attachments should reduce the number of infections that occur.

+ **Read antivirus bulletins.** Bulletins regarding new malicious code threats provide timely information to incident handlers.

+ **Deploy host-based intrusion detection systems, including file integrity checkers, to critical hosts.** Host-based IDS software, particularly file integrity checkers, can detect signs of malicious code incidents, such as configuration changes and modifications to executables.

+ **Use antivirus software, and keep it updated with the latest virus signatures.** Antivirus software should be deployed to all hosts and all applications that may be used to transfer malicious code. The software should be configured to detect and disinfect or quarantine malicious code infections. All antivirus software should be kept current with the latest virus signatures so the newest threats can be detected.

+ **Configure software to block suspicious files.** Files that are very likely to be malicious should be blocked from the environment, such as those with file extensions that are usually associated with malicious code and files with suspicious combinations of file extensions.

+ **Eliminate open Windows shares.** Many worms spread through unsecured shares on hosts running Windows. A single infection may rapidly spread to hundreds or thousands of hosts through unsecured shares.

A.2.3   Unauthorized Access Incidents

+ **Configure intrusion detection software to alert on attempts to gain unauthorized access.** Network and host-based intrusion detection software (including file integrity checking software) is valuable for detecting attempts to gain unauthorized access. Each type of software may detect incidents that the other types of software cannot, so the use of multiple types of computer security software is highly recommended.

+ **Configure all hosts to use centralized logging.** Incidents are easier to detect if data from all hosts across the organization is stored in a centralized, secured location.

+ **Establish procedures for having all users change their passwords.** A password compromise may force the organization to require all users of an application, system, or trust domain — or perhaps the entire organization — to change their passwords.

+ **Configure the network perimeter to deny all incoming traffic that is not expressly permitted.** By limiting the types of incoming traffic, attackers should be able to reach fewer targets and should be able to reach the targets using designated protocols only. This should reduce the number of unauthorized access incidents.

+ **Secure all remote access methods, including modems and virtual private networks (VPN).** Unsecured modems provide easily attainable unauthorized access to internal systems and networks. Remote access clients are often outside the organization's control, so granting them access to resources increases risk.

+ **Put all publicly accessible services on secured demilitarized zone (DMZ) network segments.** This action permits the organization to allow external hosts to initiate connections to hosts on the DMZ segments only, not to hosts on internal network segments. This should reduce the number of unauthorized access incidents.

+ **Disable all unneeded services on hosts and separate critical services.** Every service that is running presents another potential opportunity for compromise. Separating critical services is important because if an attacker compromises a host that is running a critical service, immediate access should be gained only to that one service.

+ **Use host-based firewall software to limit individual host's exposure to attacks.** Deploying host-based firewall software to individual hosts and configuring it to deny all activity that is not expressly permitted should further reduce the likelihood of unauthorized access incidents.

+ **Create and implement a password policy.** The password policy should require the use of complex, difficult-to-guess passwords and should ensure that authentication methods are sufficiently strong for accessing critical resources. Weak and default passwords are likely to be guessed or cracked, leading to unauthorized access.

A.2.4   Inappropriate Usage Incidents

+ **Discuss the handling of inappropriate usage incidents with the organization's human resources and legal departments.** Processes for monitoring and logging user activities should comply with the organization's policies and all applicable laws. Procedures for handling incidents that directly involve employees should incorporate discretion and confidentiality.

+ **Discuss liability issues with the organization's legal departments.** Liability issues may arise during inappropriate usage incidents, particularly for incidents that are targeted at outside parties. Incident handlers should understand when they should discuss incidents with the allegedly attacked party and what information they should reveal.

+ **Configure network-based intrusion detection software to detect certain types of inappropriate usage.** Intrusion detection software has built-in capabilities to detect certain inappropriate usage incidents, such as the use of unauthorized services, outbound reconnaissance activity and attacks, and improper mail relay usage (e.g., sending spam).

+ **Log basic information on user activities.** Basic information on user activities such as File Transfer Protocol (FTP) commands, Web requests, and e-mail headers may be valuable for investigative and evidentiary purposes.

+ **Configure all e-mail servers so they cannot be used for unauthorized mail relaying.** Mail relaying is commonly used to send spam.

+ **Implement spam filtering software on all e-mail servers.** Spam filtering software can block much of the spam sent by external parties to the organization's users and spam sent by internal users.

+ **Implement uniform resource locator (URL) filtering software.** URL filtering software prevents access to many inappropriate Web sites. Users should be required to use the software, typically by preventing access to external Web sites unless the traffic passes through a server that performs URL filtering.

A.2.5   Multiple Component Incidents

+ **Use centralized logging and event correlation software.** Incident handlers should identify an incident as having multiple components more quickly if all precursors and indications are accessible from a single point of view.

A.3   Detection and Analysis

+ **Identify precursors and indications through alerts generated by several types of computer security software.** Network and host-based intrusion detection systems, antivirus software, and file integrity checking software are valuable for detecting signs of incidents. Each type of software may detect incidents that the other types of software cannot, so the use of several types of computer security software is highly recommended. Third-party monitoring services can also be helpful.

+ **Establish mechanisms for outside parties to report incidents.** Outside parties may want to report incidents to the organization; for example, they may believe that one of the organization's users is attacking them. Organizations should publish a phone number and e-mail address that outside parties can use to report such incidents.

+ **Require a baseline level of logging and auditing on all systems, and a higher baseline level on all critical systems.** Logs from operating systems, services, and applications frequently provide value during incident analysis, particularly if auditing was enabled. The logs can provide information such as which accounts were accessed and what actions were performed.

+ **Profile networks and systems.** Profiling measures the characteristics of expected activity levels so that changes in patterns can be more easily identified. If the profiling process is automated, deviations from expected activity levels can be detected and reported to administrators quickly, leading to faster detection of incidents and operational issues.

+ **Understand the normal behaviors of networks, systems, and applications.** Team members who understand what normal behavior is should be able to recognize abnormal behavior more easily. This knowledge can best be gained by reviewing log entries and security alerts; the handlers should become familiar with the typical data and can investigate the unusual entries to gain more knowledge.

+ **Use centralized logging and create a log retention policy.** Information regarding an incident may be recorded in several places. Organizations should deploy centralized logging servers and configure devices to send duplicates of their log entries to the centralized servers.

The team benefits because it can access all log entries at once; also, changes made to logs on individual hosts will not affect the data already sent to the centralized servers. A log retention policy is important because older log entries may show previous instances of similar or related activity.

+ **Perform event correlation.** Indications of an incident may be captured in several logs. Correlating events among multiple sources can be invaluable in collecting all the available information for an incident and validating whether the incident occurred. Centralized logging makes event correlation easier and faster.

+ **Keep all host clocks synchronized.** If the devices reporting events have inconsistent clock settings, event correlation will be more difficult. Clock discrepancies may also cause issues from an evidentiary standpoint.

+ **Maintain and use a knowledge base of information.** Handlers need to reference information quickly during incident analysis; a centralized knowledge base provides a consistent, maintainable source of information. The knowledge base should include general information, such as commonly used port numbers and links to virus information, and data on precursors and indications of previous incidents.

+ **Create a diagnosis matrix for less experienced staff.** Help desk staff, system administrators, and new incident response team members may need assistance in determining what type of incident may be occurring. A diagnosis matrix that lists incident categories and the symptoms associated with each category can provide guidance as to what type of incident is occurring and how the incident can be validated.

+ **Start recording all information as soon as the team suspects that an incident has occurred.** Every step taken, from the time the incident was detected to its final resolution, should be documented and time-stamped. Information of this nature can serve as evidence in a court of law if legal prosecution is pursued. Recording the steps performed can also lead to a more efficient and systematic, and less error-prone handling of the problem.

+ **Safeguard incident data.** It often contains sensitive information regarding such elements as vulnerabilities, security breaches, and users that may have performed inappropriate actions. The team should ensure that access to incident data is restricted properly, both logically and physically.

+ **Prioritize incidents by business impact, based on the criticality of the affected resources and the technical impact of the incident.** Because of resource limitations, incidents should not be handled on a first-come, first-served basis. Instead, organizations should establish written guidelines that outline how quickly the team must respond to the incident and what actions should be performed, based on the incident's current and potential business impact. This guidance saves time for the incident handlers and provides a justification to management and system owners for their actions. Organizations should also establish an escalation process for those instances when the team does not respond to an incident within the designated time.

+ **Include provisions regarding incident reporting in the organization's incident response policy.** Organizations should specify which incidents must be reported, when they must be reported, and to whom. The parties most commonly notified are the chief information officer (CIO), head of information security, local information security officer, other incident response teams within the organization, and system owners.

A.4   Containment, Eradication, and Recovery

A.4.1   Denial of Service Incidents

+ **Establish strategies and procedures for containing incidents.** It is important to contain incidents quickly and effectively to limit their business impact. Organizations should define acceptable risks in containing incidents and develop strategies and procedures accordingly. Containment strategies should vary based on the type of incident.

+ **Follow established procedures for evidence gathering and handling.** The team should clearly document how all evidence has been preserved. Evidence should be accounted for at all times. The team should meet with legal staff and law enforcement agencies to discuss evidence handling, then develop procedures based on those discussions.

+ **Capture volatile data from systems as evidence.** This effort includes lists of network connections, processes, login sessions, open files, network interface configurations, and the contents of memory. Running carefully chosen commands from trusted media can collect the necessary information without damaging the system's evidence.

+ **Obtain system snapshots through full forensic disk images, not file system backups.** Disk images should be made to sanitized write-protectable or write-once media. This process is superior to a file system backup for investigatory and evidentiary purposes. Imaging is also valuable in that it is much safer to analyze an image than it is to perform analysis on the original system because the analysis may inadvertently alter the original.

+ **Create a containment strategy that includes several solutions in sequence.** The decision-making process for containing DoS incidents

Forensic Computer Crime Investigation

is easier if recommended solutions are predetermined. Because the effectiveness of each possible solution will vary among incidents, organizations should select several solutions and determine the sequence in which the solutions should be attempted.

A.4.2 Malicious Code Incidents

+ **Contain malicious code incidents as quickly as possible.** Because malicious code works surreptitiously and can propagate to other systems rapidly, early containment of a malicious code incident is needed to stop it from spreading and causing further damage. Infected systems should be disconnected from the network immediately. Organizations may need to block malicious code at the e-mail server level, or even temporarily suspend e-mail services to gain control over serious e-mail-borne malicious code incidents.

A.4.3 Unauthorized Access Incidents

+ **Provide change management information to the incident response team.** Indications such as system shutdowns, audit configuration changes, and executable modifications are probably caused by routine system administration, rather than attacks. When such indications are detected, the team should be able to use change management information to verify that the indications are caused by authorized activity.
+ **Select containment strategies that balance mitigating risks and maintaining services.** Incident handlers should consider moderate containment solutions that focus on mitigating the risks as much as is practical while maintaining unaffected services.
+ **Restore or reinstall systems that appear to have suffered a root compromise.** The effects of root compromises are often difficult to identify completely. The system should be restored from a known good backup, or the operating system and applications should be reinstalled from scratch. The system should then be secured properly so the incident cannot recur.

A.4.4 Multiple Component Incidents

+ **Contain the initial incident and then search for signs of other incident components.** It can take an extended period of time for a handler to authoritatively determine that an incident has only a single component; meanwhile, the initial incident has not been contained. It is generally better to contain the initial incident first.

A.5 Post-Incident Activity

A.5.1 Unauthorized Access Incidents

+ **Hold lessons learned meetings after major incidents.** Lessons learned meetings are extremely helpful in improving security measures and the incident handling process itself.

+ **Separately prioritize the handling of each incident component.** Resources are probably too limited to handle all incident components simultaneously. Components should be prioritized based on response guidelines for each component and how current each component is.

APPENDIX D

Sample Language for Search Warrants and Accompanying Affidavits to Search and Seize Computers

United States Department of Justice Computer Crime and Intellectual Property Section

This appendix provides sample language for agents and prosecutors who wish to obtain a warrant authorizing the search and seizure of computers. The discussion focuses first on the proper way to describe the property to be seized in the warrant itself, which in turn requires consideration of the role of the computer in the offense. The discussion then turns to drafting an accompanying affidavit that establishes probable cause, describes the agent's search strategy, and addresses any additional statutory or constitutional concerns.

I.   Describing the Property to Be Seized for the Warrant

The first step in drafting a warrant to search and seize computers or computer data is to describe the property to be seized for the warrant itself. This requires a particularized description of the evidence, contraband, fruits, or instrumentality of crime that the agents hope to obtain by conducting the search.

Whether the property to be seized should contain a description of information (such as computer files) or physical computer hardware depends on the role of the computer in the offense. In some cases, the computer hardware is itself contraband, evidence of crime, or a fruit or instrumentality of crime. In these situations, Federal Rules Criminal Procedure P. 41 expressly authorizes the seizure of the hardware, and the warrant will ordinarily request its seizure. In other cases, however, the computer hardware is merely a storage device for electronic files that are themselves contraband, evidence, or instrumentalities of crime. In these cases, the warrant should request authority to search for and seize the information itself, not the storage devices that the agents believe they must seize to recover the information. Although the agents may need to seize the storage devices for practical reasons, such practical considerations are best addressed in the accompanying affidavit. The property to be seized described in the warrant should fall within one or more of the categories listed in Rule 41(b):

1. "property that constitutes evidence of the commission of a criminal offense"

   This authorization is a broad one, covering any item that an investigator "reasonably could ... believe" would reveal information that would aid in a particular apprehension or conviction. *Andresen v. Maryland*, 427 U.S. 463, 483 (1976). Cf. *Warden v. Hayden*, 387 U.S. 294, 307 (1967) (noting that restrictions on what evidence may be seized result mostly from the probable cause requirement). The word *property* in Rule 41(b)(1) includes both tangible and intangible property. See *United States v. New York Tel. Co.*, 434 U.S. 159, 169 (1977) ("Rule 41 is not limited to tangible items but is sufficiently flexible to include within its scope electronic intrusions authorized upon a finding of probable cause."); *United States v. Biasucci*, 786 F.2d 504, 509-10 (2d Cir. 1986) (holding that the fruits of video surveillance are property that may be seized using a Rule 41 search warrant). Accordingly, data stored in electronic form is property that may properly be searched and seized using a Rule 41 warrant. See *United States v. Hall*, 583 F. Supp. 717, 718-19 (E.D. Va. 1984).

2. "contraband, the fruits of crime, or things otherwise criminally possessed"

   Property is contraband "when a valid exercise of the police power renders possession of the property by the accused unlawful and provides that it may be taken." *Hayden*, 387 U.S. at 302 (quoting *Gouled v. United States*, 255 U.S. 298, 309 (1921)). Common examples of items that fall within this definition include child pornography, see *United States v. Kimbrough*, 69 F.3d 723, 731 (5th Cir. 1995), pirated software and other copyrighted materials, see *United States v. Vastola*,

670 F. Supp. 1244, 1273 (D.N.J. 1987), counterfeit money, narcotics, and illegal weapons. The phrase "fruits of crime" refers to property that criminals have acquired as a result of their criminal activities. Common examples include money obtained from illegal transactions, see *United States v. Dornblut*, 261 F.2d 949, 951 (2d Cir. 1958) (cash obtained in drug transaction), and stolen goods. See *United States v. Burkeen*, 350 F.2d 261, 264 (6th Cir. 1965) (currency removed from bank during bank robbery).

3. "property designed or intended for use or which is or had been used as a means of committing a criminal offense"

Rule 41(b)(3) authorizes the search and seizure of "property designed or intended for use or which is or had been used as a means of committing a criminal offense." This language permits courts to issue warrants to search and seize instrumentalities of crime. See *United States v. Farrell*, 606 F.2d 1341, 1347 (D.C. Cir. 1979). Computers may serve as instrumentalities of crime in many ways. For example, Rule 41 authorizes the seizure of computer equipment as an instrumentality when a suspect uses a computer to view, acquire, and transmit images of child pornography. See *Davis v. Gracey*, 111 F.3d 1472, 1480 (10th Cir. 1997) (stating in an obscenity case that "the computer equipment was more than merely a 'container' for the files; it was an instrumentality of the crime."); *United States v. Lamb*, 945 F. Supp. 441, 462 (N.D.N.Y. 1996). Similarly, a hacker's computer may be used as an instrumentality of crime, and a computer used to run an illegal Internet gambling business would also be an instrumentality of the crime.

Here are examples of how to describe property to be seized when the computer hardware is merely a storage container for electronic evidence:

1. All records relating to violations of 21 U.S.C. § 841(a) (drug trafficking) and/or 21 U.S.C. § 846 (conspiracy to traffic drugs) involving [the suspect] since January 1, 1996, including lists of customers and related identifying information; types, amounts, and prices of drugs trafficked as well as dates, places, and amounts of specific transactions; any information related to sources of narcotic drugs (including names, addresses, phone numbers, or any other identifying information); any information recording [the suspect's] schedule or travel from 1995 to the present; all bank records, checks, credit card bills, account information, and other financial records.

   The terms *records* and *information* include all of the foregoing items of evidence in whatever form and by whatever means they may have been created or stored, including any electrical, electronic, or magnetic form (such as any information on an electronic or magnetic storage device, including floppy diskettes, hard disks, Zip disks, CD-ROMs, optical discs, backup tapes, printer buffers, smart cards, memory calculators, pagers, personal digital assistants such as Palm Pilot computers, as well as printouts or readouts from any magnetic storage device); any handmade form (such as writing, drawing, painting); any mechanical form (such as printing or typing); and any photographic form (such as microfilm, microfiche, prints, slides, negatives, videotapes, motion pictures, photocopies).

2. Any copy of the X Company's confidential May 17, 1998, report, in electronic or other form, including any recognizable portion or summary of the contents of that report.

3. [For a warrant to obtain records stored with an ISP pursuant to 18 U.S.C. § 2703(a)] All stored electronic mail of any kind sent to, from, and through the e-mail address [JDoe@isp.com], or associated with the user name "John Doe," account holder [suspect], or IP Address [xxx.xxx.xxx.xxx] / Domain name [x.com] between Date A at Time B and Date X at Time Y. Content and connection log files of all activity from January 1, 2000, through March 31, 2000, by the user associated with the e-mail address [JDoe@isp.com], user name "John Doe," or IP Address [xxx.xxx.xxx.xxx] / Domain name [x.x.com] between Date A at Time B and Date X at Time Y, including dates, times, methods of connecting (e.g., Telnet, FTP, HTTP), type of connection (e.g., modem, cable / DSL, T1 / LAN), ports used, telephone dial-up caller identification records, and any other connection information or traffic data. All business records, in any form kept, in the possession of [Internet Service Provider], that pertain to the subscriber(s) and account(s) associated with the e-mail address [JDoe@isp.com], user name "John Doe," or IP Address [xxx.xxx.xxx.xxx] / Domain name [x.x.com] between Date A at Time B and Date X at Time Y, including records showing the subscriber's full name, all screen names associated with that subscriber and account, all account names associated with that subscriber, methods of payment, phone numbers, all residential, business, mailing, and e-mail addresses, detailed billing records, types and lengths of service, and any other identifying information.

Here are examples of how to describe the property to be seized when the computer hardware itself is evidence, contraband, or an instrumentality of crime:

1. Any computers (including file servers, desktop computers, laptop computers, mainframe computers, and storage devices such as hard

drives, Zip disks, and floppy disks) that were or may have been used as a means to provide images of child pornography over the Internet in violation of 18 U.S.C. § 2252A that were accessible via the World Wide Web site address www.[xxxxxxxx].com.
2. IBM Thinkpad Model 760ED laptop computer with a black case.

II. Drafting Affidavits in Support of Warrants to Search and Seize Computers

An affidavit to justify the search and seizure of computer hardware and/or files should include, at a minimum, the following sections: (1) definitions of any technical terms used in the affidavit or warrant; (2) a summary of the offense, and, if known, the role that a targeted computer plays in the offense; and (3) an explanation of the agents' search strategy. In addition, warrants that raise special issues (such as sneak-and-peek warrants, or warrants that may implicate the Privacy Protection Act, 42 U.S.C. § 2000aa) require thorough discussion of those issues in the affidavit. Agents and prosecutors with questions about how to tailor an affidavit and warrant for a computer-related search may contact the Computer Crime and Intellectual Property Section at (202) 514-1026.

A. Background Technical Information

It may be helpful to include a section near the beginning of the affidavit explaining any technical terms that the affiant may use. Although many judges are computer literate, judges generally appreciate a clear, jargon-free explanation of technical terms that may help them understand the merits of the warrant application. At the same time, agents and prosecutors should resist the urge to pad affidavits with long, boilerplate descriptions of well-known technical phrases. As a rule, affidavits should only include the definitions of terms that are likely to be unknown by a generalist judge and are used in the remainder of the affidavit. Here are some sample definitions:

Addresses   Every device on the Internet has an address that allows other devices to locate and communicate with it. An Internet Protocol (IP) address is a unique number that identifies a device on the Internet. Other addresses include Uniform Resource Locator (URL) addresses, such as "http://www.usdoj.gov," which are typically used to access Web sites or other services on remote devices. Domain names, host names, and machine addresses are other types of addresses associated with Internet use.

Cookies   A cookie is a file that is generated by a Web site when a user on a remote computer accesses it. The cookie is sent to the user's computer and is placed in a directory on that computer, usually labeled "Internet" or "Temporary Internet Files." The cookie includes information such as user preferences, connection information such as time and date of use, records of user activity including files accessed or services used, or account information. The cookie is then accessed by the Web site on subsequent visits by the user, in order to better serve the user's needs.

Data Compression   A process of reducing the number of bits required to represent some information, usually to reduce the time or cost of storing or transmitting it. Some methods can be reversed to reconstruct the original data exactly; these are used for faxes, programs, and most computer data. Other methods do not exactly reproduce the original data, but this may be acceptable (e.g., for a video conference).

Denial of Service Attack (DoS Attack)   A hacker attempting a DoS attack will often use multiple IP or e-mail addresses to send a particular server or Web site hundreds or thousands of messages in a short period of time. The server or Web site will devote system resources to each transmission. Due to the limited resources of servers and Web sites, this bombardment will eventually slow the system down or crash it altogether.

Domain   A domain is a group of Internet devices that are owned or operated by a specific individual, group, or organization. Devices within a domain have IP addresses within a certain range of numbers, and are usually administered according to the same set of rules and procedures.

Domain Name   A domain name identifies a computer or group of computers on the Internet and corresponds to one or more IP addresses within a particular range. Domain names are typically strings of alphanumeric characters, with each level of the domain delimited by a period (e.g., Computer.networklevel1.networklevel2.com). A domain name can provide information about the organization, ISP, and physical location of a particular network user.

Encryption   Encryption refers to the practice of mathematically scrambling computer data as a communications security measure. The encrypted information is called *ciphertext*. *Decryption* is the process of converting the ciphertext back into the original, readable information (known as *plaintext*). The word, number, or other value used to encrypt/decrypt a message is called the *key*.

File Transfer Protocol (FTP)   FTP is a method of communication used to send and receive files such as word-processing documents, spreadsheets, pictures, songs, and video files. FTP sites are online warehouses of computer files that are available for copying by users on the Internet. Although many sites require users to supply credentials (such as a password or user name) to gain access, the IP address of the FTP site is often all that is required to access the site, and users are often identified only by their IP addresses.

Firewall   A firewall is a dedicated computer system or piece of software that monitors the connection between one computer or network and another. The firewall is the gatekeeper that certifies communications, blocks unauthorized or suspect transmissions, and filters content coming into a network. Hackers can sidestep the protections offered by firewalls by acquiring system passwords, hiding within authorized IP addresses using specialized software and routines, or placing viruses in seemingly innocuous files such as e-mail attachments.

Hacking   Hacking is the deliberate infiltration or sabotaging of a computer or network of computers. Hackers use loopholes in computer security to gain control of a system, steal passwords and sensitive data, and/or incapacitate a computer or group of computers. Hacking is usually done remotely, by sending harmful commands and programs through the Internet to a target system. When they arrive, these commands and programs instruct the target system to operate outside of the parameters specified by the administrator of the system. This often causes general system instability or the loss of data.

Instant Messaging (IM)   IM is a communications service that allows two users to send messages through the Internet to each other in real time. Users subscribe to a particular messaging service (e.g., AOL Instant Messenger, MSN Messenger) by supplying personal information and choosing a screen name to use in connection with the service. When logged in to the IM service, users can search for other users based on the information that other users have supplied, and they can send those users messages or initiate a chat session. Most IM services also allow files to be transferred between users, including music, video files, and computer software. Due to the structure of the Internet, a transmission may be routed through different states and/or countries before it arrives at its final destination, even if the communicating parties are in the same state.

Internet   The Internet is a global network of computers and other electronic devices that communicate with each other via standard telephone lines, high-speed telecommunications links (e.g., fiber-optic cable), and wireless transmissions. Due to the structure of the Internet, connections between devices on the Internet often cross state and international borders, even when the devices communicating with each other are in the same state.

Internet Relay Chat (IRC)   IRC is a popular Internet service that allows users to communicate with each other in real time. IRC is organized around the chat room or channel, in which users congregate to communicate with each other about a specific topic. A chat room typically connects users from different states and countries, and IRC messages often travel across state and national borders before reaching other users. Within a chat room or channel, every user can see the messages typed by other users. No user identification is required for IRC, allowing users to log in and participate in IRC communication with virtual anonymity, concealing their identities by using fictitious screen names.

Internet Service Providers (ISPs)   Many individuals and businesses obtain their access to the Internet through businesses known as Internet service providers (ISPs). ISPs provide their customers with access to the Internet using telephone or other telecommunications lines; provide Internet e-mail accounts that allow users to communicate with other Internet users by sending and receiving electronic messages through the ISPs' servers; remotely store electronic files on their customers' behalf; and may provide other services unique to each particular ISP.

ISPs maintain records pertaining to the individuals or companies that have subscriber accounts with it. Those records could include identifying and billing information, account access information in the form of log files, e-mail transaction information, posting information, account application information, and other information both in computer data format and in written record format. ISPs reserve and/or maintain computer disk storage space on their computer system for the use of the Internet service subscriber for both temporary and long-term storage of electronic communications with other parties and other types of electronic data and files. E-mail that has not been opened is stored temporarily by an ISP incident to the transmission of the e-mail to the intended recipient, usually within an area known as the home directory. Such temporary, incidental storage is defined by statute as *electronic storage*, and the provider of such a service is an *electronic communications service* provider. A service provider that is available to the public and provides storage facilities after an electronic communication has been transmitted and opened by the recipient, or provides other long-term storage services to the public for electronic data and files, is providing a *remote computing service.*

IP Address   The Internet protocol address (or simply IP address) is a unique numeric address used by computers on the Internet. An IP address looks like a series of four numbers, each in the range 0 to 255, separated by periods (e.g., 121.56.97.178). Every computer attached to the Internet computer must be assigned an IP address so that Internet traffic sent from and directed to that computer may be directed properly from its source to its destination. Most ISPs control a range of IP addresses.

Dynamic IP address — When an ISP or other provider uses dynamic IP addresses, the ISP randomly assigns one of the available IP addresses in the range of IP addresses controlled by the ISP each time a user dials into the ISP to connect to the Internet. The customer's computer retains that IP address for the duration of that session (i.e., until the user disconnects), and the IP address cannot be assigned to another user during that period. Once the user disconnects, however, that IP address becomes available to other customers who dial in at a later time. Thus, an individual customer's IP address normally differs each time he or she dials into the ISP.

Static IP address — A static IP address is an IP address that is assigned permanently to a given user or computer on a network. A customer of an ISP that assigns static IP addresses will have the same IP address every time.

Joint Photographic Experts Group (JPEG)   JPEG is the name of a standard for compressing digitized images that can be stored on computers. JPEG is often used to compress photographic images, including pornography. Such files are often identified by the ".jpg" extension (such that a JPEG file might have the title "picture.jpg") but can easily be renamed without the ".jpg" extension.

Log File   Log files are computer files that contain records about system events and status, the activities of users, and anomalous or unauthorized computer usage. Names for various log files include, but are not limited to, user logs, access logs, audit logs, transactional logs, and apache logs.

Moving Pictures Expert Group-3 (MP3)   MP3 is the name of a standard for compressing audio recordings (e.g., songs, albums, concert recordings) so that they can be stored on a computer, transmitted through the Internet to other computers, or listened to using a computer. Despite its small size, an MP3 delivers near CD-quality sound. Such files are often identified by the filename extension ".mp3," but can easily be renamed without the ".mp3" extension.

Packet Sniffing   On the Internet, information is usually transmitted through many different locations before it reaches its final destination. While in transit, such information is contained within *packets*. Both authorized users, such as system security experts, and unauthorized users, such as hackers, use specialized technology — packet sniffers — to "listen" to the flow of information on a network for interesting packets, such as those containing logins or passwords, sensitive or classified data, or harmful communications such as viruses. After locating such data, the packet sniffer can read, copy, redirect, or block the communication.

Peer-to-Peer (P2P) Networks   P2P networks differ from conventional networks in that each computer within the network functions as both a client (using the resources and services of other computers) and a server (providing files and services for use by *peer* computers). There is often no centralized server in such a network. Instead, a search program or database tells users where other computers are located and what files and services they have to offer. Often, P2P networks are used to share and disseminate music, movies, and computer software.

Router   A router is a device on the Internet that facilitates communication. Each Internet router maintains a table that states the next step a communication must take on its path to its proper destination. When a router receives a transmission, it checks the transmission's destination IP address with addresses in its table and directs the communication to another router or the destination computer. The log file and memory of a router often contain important information that can help reveal the source and network path of communications.

Server   A server is a centralized computer that provides services for other computers connected to it via a network. The other computers attached to a server are sometimes called *clients*. In a large company, it is common for individual employees to have client computers at their desktops. When the employees access their e-mail, or access files stored on the network itself, those files are pulled electronically from the server, where they are stored, and are sent to the client's computer via the network. Notably, server computers can be physically stored in any location: It is common for a network's server to be located hundreds (and even thousands) of miles away from the client computers. In larger networks, it is common for servers to be dedicated to a single task. For example, a server that is configured so that its sole task is to support a World Wide Web site is known simply as a *Web server*. Similarly, a server that only stores and processes e-mail is known as a *mail server*.

Tracing   Trace programs are used to determine the path that a communication takes to arrive at its destination. A trace program requires the user to specify a source and destination IP address. The program then launches a message from the source address, and at each hop on the network (signifying a device such as a router), the IP address of that device is displayed on the source user's screen or copied to a log file.

User Name or User ID   Most services offered on the Internet assign users a name or ID, which is a pseudonym that computer systems use to keep track of users. User names and IDs are typically associated with additional user information or resources, such as a user account protected by a password, personal or financial information about the user, a directory of files, or an e-mail address.

Virus   A virus is a malicious computer program designed by a hacker to (1) incapacitate a target computer system; (2) cause a target system to slow down or become unstable; (3) gain unauthorized access to system files, passwords, and other sensitive data such as financial information; and/or (4) gain control of the target system to use its resources in furtherance of the hacker's agenda. Once inside the target system, a virus may begin making copies of itself, depleting system memory and causing the system to shut down, or it may begin issuing system commands or altering crucial data within the system.

Other malicious programs used by hackers are, but are not limited to, *worms*, which spawn copies that travel over a network to other systems; *Trojan horses*, which are hidden in seemingly innocuous files such as e-mail attachments and are activated by unassuming authorized users; and *bombs*, which are programs designed to bombard a target e-mail server or individual user with messages, overloading the target or otherwise preventing the reception of legitimate communications.

B.   Background — Staleness Issue

It may be helpful and necessary to include a paragraph explaining how certain computer files can reside indefinitely in free or slack space and thus be subject to recovery with specific forensic tools:

Based on your affiant's knowledge, training, and experience, your affiant knows that computer files or remnants of such files can be recovered months or even years after they have been downloaded onto a hard drive, deleted, or viewed via the Internet. Electronic files downloaded to a hard drive can be stored for years at little or no cost. Even when such files have been deleted, they can be recovered months or years later using readily available forensics tools. When a person "deletes" a file on a home computer, the data contained in the file does not actually disappear; rather, that data remains on the hard drive until it is overwritten by new data. Therefore, deleted files, or remnants of deleted files, may reside in free space or slack space — that is, in space on the hard drive that is not allocated to an active file or that is unused after a file has been allocated to a set block of storage space — for long periods of time before they are overwritten. In addition, a computer's operating system may also keep a record of deleted data in a *swap* or *recovery* file. Similarly, files that have been viewed via the Internet are automatically downloaded into a temporary Internet directory or *cache*. The browser typically maintains a fixed amount of hard drive space devoted to these files, and the files are only overwritten as they are replaced with more recently viewed Internet pages. Thus, the ability to retrieve residue of an electronic file from a hard drive depends less on when the file was downloaded or viewed than on a particular user's operating system, storage capacity, and computer habits.

C.   Describe the Role of the Computer in the Offense

The next step is to describe the role of the computer in the offense, to the extent it is known. For example, is the computer hardware itself evidence of a crime or contraband? Is the computer hardware merely a storage device that may or may not contain electronic files that constitute evidence of a crime? To introduce this topic, it may be helpful to explain at the outset why the role of the computer is important for defining the scope of your warrant request.

Your affiant knows that computer hardware, software, and electronic files may be important to a criminal investigation in two distinct ways: (1) The objects themselves may be contraband, evidence, instrumentalities, or fruits of crime; and/or (2) the objects may be used as storage devices that contain contraband, evidence, instrumentalities, or fruits of crime in the form of electronic data. Rule 41 of the Federal Rules of Criminal Procedure permits the government to search for and seize computer hardware, software, and electronic files that are evidence of crime, contraband, instrumentalities of crime, and/or fruits of crime. In this case, the warrant application requests permission to search and seize [images of child pornography, including those that may be stored on a computer]. These [images] constitute both evidence of crime and contraband. This affidavit also requests permission to seize the computer hardware that may contain [the images of child pornography] if it becomes necessary for reasons of practicality to remove the hardware and conduct a search off-site. Your affiant believes that, in this case, the computer hardware is a container for evidence, a container for contraband, and also itself an instrumentality of the crime under investigation.

1.   *When the Computer Hardware Is Itself Contraband, Evidence, and/or an Instrumentality or Fruit of Crime*

If applicable, the affidavit should explain why probable cause exists to believe that the tangible computer items are themselves contraband, evidence, instrumentalities, or fruits of the crime, independent of the information they may hold.

a. Computer Used to Obtain Unauthorized Access to a Computer (Hacking).   Your affiant knows that when an individual uses a computer to obtain unauthorized access to a victim computer over the Internet, the individual's computer will generally serve both as an instrumentality for committing the crime and as a storage device for evidence of the crime. The computer is an instrumentality of the crime because it is "used as a means of committing [the] criminal offense" according to Rule 41(b)(3). In particular, the individual's computer is the primary means for accessing the Internet, communicating with the victim computer, and ultimately obtaining the unauthorized access that is prohibited by 18 U.S.C. § 1030. The computer is also likely to be a storage device for evidence of crime because computer hackers generally maintain records and evidence relating to their crimes on their computers. Those records and evidence may include files that recorded the unauthorized access, stolen passwords and other information downloaded from the victim computer, the individual's notes as to how the access was achieved, records of Internet chat discussions about the crime, and other records that indicate the scope of the individual's unauthorized access.

b. Computers Used to Produce Child Pornography.   It is common for child pornographers to use personal computers to produce both still and moving images. For example, a computer can be connected to a video camera, VCR, or DVD player by using a device called a video capture board: The device turns the video output into a form that is usable by computer programs. Alternatively, the pornographer can use a digital camera to take photographs or videos and load them directly onto the computer. The output of the camera can be stored, transferred, or printed out directly from the computer. The producers of child pornography can also use a device known as a scanner to transfer photographs into a computer-readable format. All of these devices, as well as the computer, constitute instrumentalities of the crime.

2. *When the Computer Is Merely a Storage Device for Contraband, Evidence, and/or an Instrumentality or Fruit of Crime*

When the computer is merely a storage device for electronic evidence, the affidavit should explain this clearly. The affidavit should explain why there is probable cause to believe that evidence of a crime may be found in the location to be searched. This does not require the affidavit to establish probable cause that the evidence may be stored specifically within a computer. However, the affidavit should explain why the agents believe that the information may in fact be stored as an electronic file stored in a computer.

a. Child Pornography.   Your affiant knows that child pornographers generally prefer to store images of child pornography in electronic form as computer files. The computer's ability to store images in digital form makes a computer an ideal repository for pornography. A small portable disk can contain hundreds or thousands of images of child pornography, and a computer hard drive can contain tens of thousands of such images at very high resolution. The images can be easily sent to or received from other computer users over the Internet. Further, both individual files of child pornography and the disks that contain the files can be mislabeled or hidden to evade detection.

b. Illegal Business Operations.   Based on actual inspection of [spreadsheets, financial records, invoices], your affiant is aware that computer equipment was used to generate, store, and print documents used in [suspect's] [tax evasion, money laundering, drug trafficking, etc.] scheme. There is reason to believe that the computer system currently located on [suspect's] premises is the same system used to produce and store the [spreadsheets, financial records, invoices], and that both the [spreadsheets, financial records, invoices] and other records relating to [suspect's] criminal enterprise will be stored on [suspect's computer].

D.   The Search Strategy

The affidavit should also contain a careful explanation of the agents' search strategy, as well as a discussion of any practical or legal concerns that govern how the search will be executed. Such an explanation is particularly important when practical considerations may require that agents seize computer hardware and search it off-site when that hardware is only a storage device for evidence of crime. Similarly, searches for computer evidence in sensitive environments (such as functioning businesses) may require that the agents adopt an incremental approach designed to minimize the intrusiveness of the search. The affidavit should explain the agents' approach in sufficient detail that the explanation provides a useful guide for the search team and any reviewing court. It is a good practice to include a copy of the search strategy as an attachment to the warrant, especially when the affidavit is placed under seal. The following subsections contain sample language that can apply recurring situations.

1.   *Sample Language to Justify Seizing Hardware and Conducting a Subsequent Off-Site Search*

Based upon your affiant's knowledge, training and experience, your affiant knows that searching and seizing information from computers often requires agents to seize most or all electronic storage devices (along with related peripherals) to be searched later by a qualified computer expert in a laboratory or other controlled environment. This is true because of the following:

1. *The volume of evidence.* Computer storage devices (e.g., hard disks, diskettes, tapes, laser disks) can store the equivalent of millions of information. Additionally, a suspect may try to conceal criminal

evidence; he or she might store it in random order with deceptive file names. This may require searching authorities to examine all the stored data to determine which particular files are evidence or instrumentalities of crime. This sorting process can take weeks or months, depending on the volume of data stored, and it would be impractical and invasive to attempt this kind of data search on-site.

2. *Technical requirements.* Searching computer systems for criminal evidence is a highly technical process requiring expert skill and a properly controlled environment. The vast array of computer hardware and software available requires even computer experts to specialize in some systems and applications, so it is difficult to know before a search which expert is qualified to analyze the system and its data. In any event, however, data search protocols are exacting scientific procedures designed to protect the integrity of the evidence and to recover even hidden, erased, compressed, password-protected, or encrypted files. Because computer evidence is vulnerable to inadvertent or intentional modification or destruction (both from external sources or from destructive code imbedded in the system as a booby trap), a controlled environment may be necessary to complete an accurate analysis.

Further, such searches often require the seizure of most or all of a computer system's input/output peripheral devices, related software, documentation, and data security devices (including passwords) so that a qualified computer expert can accurately retrieve the system's data in a laboratory or other controlled environment.

In light of these concerns, your affiant hereby requests the Court's permission to seize the computer hardware (and associated peripherals) that are believed to contain some or all of the evidence described in the warrant, and to conduct an off-site search of the hardware for the evidence described, if, upon arriving at the scene, the agents executing the search conclude that it would be impractical to search the computer hardware on-site for this evidence.

2.   *Sample Language to Justify an Incremental Search*

Your affiant recognizes that the [Suspect] Corporation is a functioning company with approximately [number] employees, and that a seizure of the [Suspect Corporation's] computer network may have the unintended and undesired effect of limiting the company's ability to provide service to its legitimate customers who are not engaged in [the criminal activity under investigation]. In response to these concerns, the agents who execute the search will take an incremental approach to minimize the inconvenience to [Suspect Corporation's] legitimate customers and to minimize the need to seize equipment and data. This incremental approach, which will be explained to all of the agents on the search team before the search is executed, will proceed as follows:

1. Upon arriving at the [Suspect Corporation's] headquarters on the morning of the search, the agents will attempt to identify a system administrator of the network (or other knowledgeable employee) who will be willing to assist law enforcement by identifying, copying, and printing out paper [and electronic] copies of [the computer files described in the warrant]. If the agents succeed at locating such an employee and are able to obtain copies of [the computer files described in the warrant] in that way, the agents will not conduct any additional search or seizure of the [Suspect Corporation's] computers.

2. If the employees choose not to assist the agents and the agents cannot execute the warrant successfully without themselves examining the [Suspect Corporation's] computers, primary responsibility for the search will transfer from the case agent to a designated computer expert. The computer expert will attempt to locate [the computer files described in the warrant], and will attempt to make electronic copies of those files. This analysis will focus on particular programs, directories, and files that are most likely to contain the evidence and information of the violations under investigation. The computer expert will make every effort to review and copy only those programs, directories, files, and materials that are evidence of the offenses described herein, and provide only those items to the case agent. If the computer expert succeeds at locating [the computer files described in the warrant] in that way, the agents will not conduct any additional search or seizure of the [Suspect Corporation's] computers.

3. If the computer expert is not able to locate the files on-site, or an on-site search proves infeasible for technical reasons, the computer expert will attempt to create an electronic *image* of those parts of the computer that are likely to store [the computer files described in the warrant]. Generally speaking, imaging is the taking of a complete electronic picture of the computer's data, including all hidden sectors and deleted files. Imaging a computer permits the agents to obtain an exact copy of the computer's stored data without actually seizing the computer hardware. The computer expert or another technical expert will then conduct an off-site search for [the computer files described in the warrant] from the "mirror image" copy at a later date. If the computer expert successfully images the [Suspect Corporation's] computers, the agents will not conduct any additional search or seizure of the [Suspect Corporation's] computers.

4. If imaging proves impractical, or even impossible for technical reasons, then the agents will seize those components of the [Suspect
Corporation's] computer system that the computer expert believes
must be seized to permit the agents to locate [the computer files
described in the warrant] at an off-site location. The components will
be seized and taken in to the custody of the FBI. If employees of
[Suspect Corporation] so request, the computer expert will, to the
extent practicable, attempt to provide the employees with copies of
any files [not within the scope of the warrant] that may be necessary
or important to the continuing function of the [Suspect Corporation's]
legitimate business. If, after inspecting the computers, the analyst
determines that some or all of this equipment is no longer necessary
to retrieve and preserve the evidence, the government will return it
within a reasonable time.

3.   *Sample Language to Justify the Use of Comprehensive Data Analysis Techniques*

Searching [the suspect's] computer system for the evidence described in
[Attachment A] may require a range of data analysis techniques. In some
cases, it is possible for agents to conduct carefully targeted searches that can
locate evidence without requiring a time-consuming manual search through
unrelated materials that may be commingled with criminal evidence. For
example, agents may be able to execute a *keyword* search that searches through
the files stored in a computer for special words that are likely to appear only
in the materials covered by a warrant.

Similarly, agents may be able to locate the materials covered in the warrant by looking for particular directory or filenames. In other cases, however,
such techniques may not yield the evidence described in the warrant. Criminals can mislabel or hide files and directories; encode communications to
avoid using key words; attempt to delete files to evade detection; or take other
steps designed to frustrate law enforcement searches for information. These
steps may require agents to conduct more extensive searches, such as scanning
areas of the disk not allocated to listed files, or opening every file and scanning
its contents briefly to determine whether it falls within the scope of the
warrant. In light of these difficulties, your affiant requests permission to use
whatever data analysis techniques appear necessary to locate and retrieve the
evidence described in [Attachment A].

E.   Special Considerations

The affidavit should also contain discussions of any special legal considerations that may factor into the search or how it will be conducted. These

considerations are discussed at length in Chapter 1. Agents can use this checklist to determine whether a particular computer-related search raises such issues:

1. Is the search likely to result in the seizure of any drafts of publications (such as books, newsletters, Web site postings, etc.) that are unrelated to the search and are stored on the target computer? If so, the search may implicate the Privacy Protection Act, 42 U.S.C. § 2000aa.
2. Is the target of the search an ISP, or will the search result in the seizure of a mail server? If so, the search may implicate the Electronic Communications Privacy Act, 18 U.S.C. §§ 2701-12.
3. Does the target store electronic files or e-mail on a server maintained in a remote location? If so, the agents may need to obtain more than one warrant.
4. Will the search result in the seizure of privileged files, such as attorney-client communications? If so, special precautions may be in order.
5. Are the agents requesting authority to execute a "sneak-and-peek" search? If so, the proposed search must satisfy the standard defined in 18 U.S.C. § 3103a(b).
6. Are the agents requesting authority to dispense with the "knock and announce" rule? If so, has the agent demonstrated sufficient "probable cause" to justify and warrant a judicial "No Knock" warrant.

Forensic Computer Crime Investigation Text

Contributing Author Biographies

Chapter 2, The Digital Investigative Unit: Staffing, Training, and Issues — Chris Malinowski

Prior to joining the faculty at Long Island University, Mr. Malinowski commanded the NYPD's Computer Crime Squad in their Detective Bureau. His experiences in IS vary from the systems programming (IBM Mainframes) to investigations of computer crimes. As a manager, he had to deal with both the technical aspects, as well as the personnel-related aspects of maintaining technical working environments for the NYPD. Currently, he instructs both undergraduate, as well as graduate students in networking and computer security related courses. As NYPD's commanding officer of Computer Crimes, he participated in the National Cybercrime Training Partnership (DOJ sponsored). Additionally, he has lectured to states and local prosecutors for the National District Attorney's Association. Recently, he presented a paper on the training considerations of a computer forensics curriculum at ISECON 2004 in Newport, RI. Mr. Malinowski also serves as a Practitioner-in-Residence for the University of New Haven.

Chapter 3, Criminal Investigation Analysis and Behavior: Characteristics of Computer Criminals — Dr. William Tafoya

William L. Tafoya is Professor of the National Security and Public Safety Graduate Program at the University of New Haven (CT). A retired FBI Agent, he was assigned to the Behavioral Science Unit at the FBI Academy in the mid-80s – early 90s. Following the arrest of Theodore Kaczynski in 1996, Dr. Tafoya gained considerable notoriety for his 1993 profile of the infamous UNABOMber. Also in 1993, Dr. Tafoya was the first law enforcement investigator to make use of the Internet in the UNABOMber case. Dr. Tafoya received his Ph.D. in Criminology from the University of Maryland in 1986.

Chapter 4, Investigative Strategy and Utilities — Ross Mayfield

Ross Mayfield is a nationally recognized expert in information systems and the field of computer law enforcement investigations. Currently he holds the faculty position of Practitioner-in-Residence at the University of New Haven, in the field of Cybercrime and Computer Forensics, and also serves as an instructor for SEARCH, Inc. He is a sworn Deputy Sheriff in Marion County, Kansas, served as a sworn Reserve Police Officer and Computer Forensic Investigator for Torrance, California, is a State of California Certified Computer Crime Investigator, an Institute of Criminal Investigation Certified Instructor, and has testified as an expert witness on information systems and computer forensics. Mr. Mayfield served nearly four years as Adjunct Professor of Management Information Systems and lectured on Technology Management at Pepperdine University. He has been a featured lecturer on Internet security at U.S. Justice Department sponsored symposiums. He is the discoverer of Mayfield's Paradox, a fundamental principle of Information Security proven by the Mathematics Department of the University of Southern California. Mr. Mayfield is a patent holder. He was a recipient of Citicorp's highest Technical Achievement Award.

Chapter 5, Training Strategies for Computer Cops — Fred Cotton

Mr. Cotton is currently a Computer Training Specialist for SEARCH, Inc., The National Consortium for Justice Information and Statistics, where he provides technical assistance and training to local, state, and federal criminal justice agencies. He instructs a variety of technology crimes courses for SEARCH at its National Criminal Justice Computer Laboratory and Training Center in Sacramento, California, and at other sites nationwide. From 1986 until 2004, Mr. Cotton was the Director of Training Services, and oversaw the development of the National Criminal Justice Computer Laboratory and Training Center from its inception until his semi-retirement in 2004. Mr. Cotton has helped shape law enforcement training in the field of Computer Crime Investigation and Digital Evidence Recovery training thousands of investigators and other Criminal Justice Practitioners across the nation. He has also taught Advanced Officer courses and officer safety subjects in the Basic Police Academy, and was an invited guest of Norway's National Bureau of Criminal Investigation where he provided training on computer investigations. Mr. Cotton has 28 years of law enforcement service as a Field Supervisor with experience in operations, investigations, records, training and data processing. In addition to his duties at SEARCH, he has served as a Reserve Police Officer with the Yuba City, California, Police Department where he is assigned to the Sacramento Valley High-Tech Crimes Task Force, and a Specialist Reserve Officer with the Los Angeles Police Department where he is assigned to the Organized Crime and Vice Division.

Chapter 6, Internet Crimes Against Children — Monique Ferraro & Joseph Sudol

Monique Mattei Ferraro is an Assistant Professor of Criminal Justice at Post University in Connecticut. She is a Certified Information Systems Security Professional who has written and lectured extensively on Internet safety and child exploitation. She has worked in several different capacities within the Connecticut Department of Public Safety for eighteen years. She is a former chairperson of the Connecticut Bar Association's Computer Law Section. She is the 2003 recipient of the Connecticut Law Tribune's New Leaders of the Law "Inspiration" Award. Her book, *Investigating Child Exploitation: the Internet, Law and Forensic Science*, co-authored with Eoghan Casey, was published in 2004. She holds a Master's Degree from Northeastern University and a Law Degree from the University of Connecticut School of Law.

Joe Sudol is a Senior State police officer experienced in computer crime, arson and insurance fraud, criminal investigations, and law enforcement administration. He has twenty-six years of law enforcement experience; fourteen years in a supervisory position. As a guest lecturer at international law enforcement conferences, universities, and training seminars, he's been the subject of numerous television and print media interviews on computer crimes involving online fraud, child pornography and misuse of computer systems. Mr. Sudol has conducted high-profile homicide investigations and sensitive internal investigations. He's completed training for certification as a State Fire Marshal. He's served as Executive Officer for the Division of Scientific Services, encompassing the computer crime and electronic evidence unit, forensics lab, and toxicology laboratory. He's responsible for administrative oversight of all three divisions, and charged with managing over one million dollars in state and federal grants. Mr. Sudol is accountable for daily computer crime investigation, forensic examinations of electronic evidence, and training of both law enforcement agencies and the public.

Chapter 7, Digital Forensic Evidence and Legal Issue — Dr. Fred Cohen

Dr. Fred Cohen is best known as the inventor of computer virus defense techniques, the principal investigator whose team defined the information assurance problem as it relates to critical infrastructure protection today, as a seminal researcher in the use of deception for information protection, and as a top flight information protection consultant. But his work on information protection extends far beyond these areas. In the 1970s, he designed network protocols for secure digital networks carrying voice, video, and data; and he helped develop and prototype the electronic cash watch for implementing personal digital money systems. In the 1980s, he developed integrity mechanisms for secure operating systems, consulted for many major corporations, taught short courses in information protection to over 10,000 students worldwide, and in 1989, he won the prestigious international Information Technology Award for his work on integrity protection. In the 1990s, he developed protection testing and audit techniques and systems, secure Internet servers and systems, defensive information warfare techniques and systems, early systems using deception for information protection, and bootable CDs designed for forensics and secure server applications. All told, the protection techniques he pioneered now help to defend more than three quarters of all the computers in the world. Dr. Cohen has authored almost 200 invited, refereed, and other scientific and management research articles. He received his M.S. Information Science from the University of Pittsburgh in 1980 and his Ph.D. in Electrical Engineering from the University of Southern California in 1986.

Chapter 8, International Hacking Crimes — Dario Forte, CISM, CFE

Dario Forte, CFE, CISM, a 36-year-old former police detective, is the DFlabs Founder. He has been a top-profile operator in the area of Information security since 1992. Member of the Computer Security Institute, USENIX and Sage, Mr. Forte has been requested to send his subject-area-related articles for publication all over the world and was a contributor and/or panelist at numerous international conferences on Information Warfare, such as RSA Conference, DFRWS, Computer Security Institute, U.S. Department of Defense Cybercrime Conference, and US Department of Homeland Security (NYECTF). He was also the keynote speaker at Black hat conference in Las Vegas, NE. As an Info Security Analyst, Dario worked both in the Government and Corporate sectors, and is a member of the IS International project, under NdA. Mr. Forte teaches classes and presents lectures on Information Security Management at universities and other accredited institutions worldwide.

Over the last 10 years, Dario, who is present in the International Editorial Board of "Network Security" and "The International Journal of Digital Investigations" (Elsevier Science Group) has been working on a global scenario with a number of government agencies, such as NASA, US Army/Navy, providing his services to aid resolving incident-response matters, setting up forensics procedures, and successfully finalizing many important hacking-related investigations. Currently, Dario is Adjunct Faculty Professor at the University of Milan, Italy, and President of the European Chapter of HTCIA (High Tech Crime Investigation Association). He started IRItaly Project and is Project Leader of the Italian Honeynet Project. Finally, he provides security consulting and Incident Response/Forensics services to the Italian Government, law enforcement agencies, and the corporate world.

Index